£5.00

CW00551765

The Mountains of England & Wales

Vol. 2: ENGLAND

Wastwater (Chapter 3)

The Mountains of
England and Wales

Vol. 2: England

by

John and Anne Nuttall

_____

Maps and Drawings
by John Nuttall

CICERONE PRESS
MILNTHORPE, CUMBRIA

ISBN 1 85284 037 4

Acknowledgements

We are grateful for the help given by the staff of the Ordnance
Survey who answered our many queries and especially to
Peter Opie-Smith for his advice which enabled us to survey
accurately the marginal summits.

Thanks also to our sons Jeremy and Joe for their tolerance
of our time consuming obsession and to Joe for his self
sufficiency during our holidays and at weekends and for
programming the computer to produce the alphabetical
index and lists of maps for checking.

Front cover: The Langdale Pikes
Back Cover: Cross Fell from Meg's Cairn

CONTENTS

Primroses

INTRODUCTION

It was late afternoon and although it was windy and cold with snow still lying in drifts as we trudged up the Pennine Way towards Cross Fell the cloud was off the tops. Cross Fell however was not our objective but Long Man Hill, an insignificant and undistinguished mound to the north. This was our third and hopefully final attempt to determine precisely whether it met the criteria for inclusion. Twice the matter had been left in doubt with mist, low cloud and rain swirling in at the last moment frustratingly to blot out the view. Carefully we took the measurements. From above the broad flat peaty col Long Man Hill rose 53ft. It was in! The total was at last complete; 432 summits in England and Wales.

Completing the ascent of all the mountains of England and Wales has been for a long time an ambition to which we looked forward, but it was not an objective with which we set out. It came rather as the goal of a task already partly achieved after many years in the hills. First it was all the two thousanders in Wainwright, then all the rest of his 214 Lake District tops and then more and more of the hills as we sought out fresh summits and explored new areas. But gradually it became apparent that the list from which we were working was sadly out of date. Not only were we finding unlisted summits, but others, often reached after long approaches through bog and heather turned out to rise only negligible amounts above their surroundings. A new list was certainly needed and after many hours spent in Manchester Central Reference Library poring over large scale maps we set out once again to visit all the tops. Wales was our first objective, one to which we returned eagerly each weekend and it was almost reluctantly that we descended from the last Welsh top and looked towards England. But if we missed Wales, the English mountains were old friends which we were glad to see again and among them was the added excitement of several new discoveries.

For us our last top was also a first; our first ascent of Pillar Rock. Just as Sir Hugh Munro's tables of the 3000ft mountains of Scotland include but one summit requiring climbing skills, so it is fitting that the mountains of England and Wales should have one too. Pillar Rock, a magnificent tower of rock above Ennerdale in the Lake District, is a rock climb, one which we had left until last, not because it was difficult, but because it was the last summit in England to be attained by man, so too it would be ours.

While the year in which we began proved to be the wettest this century, the year that followed set records for the driest. Week after week the sun shone till the rivers and streams dwindled and vanished and wild camping on the hills was only possible after careful searching for the few tiny springs still flowing. Then almost within sight of completion there were yet more records with gales and storms that kept us frustrated in the valleys and on the penultimate top the map was torn from our hands by the wind and hurled across the moor into

7

the distance.

Wind and rain, hail, snow and storm, the cold clear air of winter and the hazy heat of summer, have given us magnificent days and one collects memories as a store to be enjoyed at leisure: a calm December evening watching a glorious sunset on Dollywagon Pike, the sky streaked with red and gold and the sun setting in a blaze of fire behind Pillar; another day the sun breaking through the grey mist on the tops to show us the shimmering colours of our Glories on the clouds beneath; camping in an April blizzard on Crinkle Crags followed by a brilliantly clear day of sun, blue sky and and snow covered tops; submerging to our necks in a stream on the Coniston fells to escape the burning sun of the summer heatwave, and lastly a leisurely dinner with a bottle of wine on the summit of Ingleborough as we celebrated the final night of a backpack round all the mountains of Yorkshire.

There are dozens of hills that didn't make it into our list simply because they lacked a few feet in height. It would be tempting to go below 2000ft, or perhaps to ignore height completely and just pick the 'best' mountains. But what is best? There are days when there is more enjoyment on the lowly fells than on the grandest of peaks and weather and seasons so colour one's view that the best is never the same.

If it was not an objective with which we started, neither is it something which is ever finished. There are too many mountains ever to tire of repeating them, there are too many seasons ever to tire of the weather and there are too many wild and beautiful places ever to tire of exploration.

NOTES

There are two hundred and fifty one mountain summits in England which reach the height of 2000ft. This book describes how to ascend them all in a series of fifty eight walks. By completing all the walks the reader will ascend all the English two thousanders.

SELECTION OF THE TOPS

Over the years several lists have been compiled of the English and Welsh mountains. Various criteria for selection have been adopted, but although there seems to be common agreement about the height, 2000ft being universaliy accepted as the height of a mountain, there has been little consistency about anything else.

Some fanatics have determined to visit every separate ring contour of 2000ft. While relatively easy in the high hills, it must be a boring task among the undulating moors of north-east England and the heather clad Berwyn Hills where the multiplicity of such separate rings makes nonsense of their claim to be tops. One recent list selected only tops with two or more concentric contours, but this has the anomaly that some tops are omitted which actually rise above their surroundings by a greater amount than others which are included.

During the 1970s the Ordnance Survey undertook a complete re-survey of Great Britain using a process of photogrammetry from aerial photographs. The contour interval chosen for this new survey was 10 metres. The publication of the new maps, known as the second series, is now complete. The most commonly available maps are the 1:50 000 scale (Landranger) and 1:25 000 (Pathfinder). In addition most, but not all, of the mountain areas in England and Wales are covered by the Outdoor Leisure series at a scale of 1:25 000 which are excellent value, covering an area of several Pathfinder maps at considerably lower cost.

The impact of this new survey has been quite dramatic on the old lists. Many official heights have changed, several tops have proved to lack the necessary rise to merit inclusion, while other brand new tops have been discovered. The collector of single ring contours will find the greatest change in undulating terrain where a few feet more or less creates and deletes tops with gay abandon.

After careful consideration the definition of a mountain adopted for this book is any summit of 2000 ft or more which rises above its surroundings on all sides by at least 50ft. Using metric maps this has been refined to 610m and 15m. This choice was based on three factors. Firstly an earlier list, now dethroned by the new survey, used these criteria, secondly to choose more than 15m eliminated too many tops generally considered as separate mountains, and thirdly to choose less than 15m meant including an excessive number of un-named minor bumps which were unworthy of elevation to mountain status.

No attempt has been made to differentiate between mountains and subsidiary tops. The word 'top' has however also been used to denote a summit which has no accepted name on the OS maps. Rather than referring to them as nameless summits, they have been named by reference to a nearby summit or other feature; eg High Spy North Top. (NB Chapel Fell Top, Randy Gill Top and Bram Rigg Top are OS names).

The vast majority of the 251 tops listed in this book can easily be seen to merit inclusion. The rest can mostly be proved from the contours and spot heights of the new survey, but in a few instances, where no absolute data is available, the case has been decided by personal on the spot surveying using a technique recommended to us by the Ordnance Survey.

It is interesting to note that the spot heights given on the present 1:50 000 maps are derived from the old survey rather than the new, although the contour information itself is the latest. As a result there is sometimes a discrepancy between spot heights given on the 1:50 000 and 1:25 000 maps. In such cases the spot heights from the 1:25 000 and/or the base map at 1:10 000 scale have been used. At the end of the book will be found a list of deleted tops which may be of interest to people already hooked on the game. Game it certainly is, but any game worth playing has rules and we have done our best to provide the reader with as definitive a list as possible.

MAPS

The maps in this book are drawn at a scale of 1:50 000. They are to enable the reader to locate the walk on the relevant OS map and should be used to supplement the OS maps, not replace them.

The best maps for walkers are the 1:25 000 Pathfinder series and the Outdoor Leisure. The latter series covers all the mountains of the Lake District with the exception of Back o' Skiddaw, while Yorkshire is well served with maps covering most of the Yorkshire Dales. Teesdale too has an Outdoor Leisure map as have the Peak District and Dartmoor, but The Cheviot and the extreme northern and eastern parts of the Pennines are still ignored. While it is possible to manage with the 1:50 000 Landranger maps for all the walks in this book, the larger scale, which shows walls, fences and in general much more detail, is highly recommended.

The spelling of place names has been taken throughout from the latest OS maps. Note however that not all names referred to in the text will necessarily be found on the 1:50 000 series. The meaning of the name is given in brackets after each heading.

The start of each walk is marked 'S' on the map and while every effort has been made to keep north at the top, which is how most people like it, in a few cases this rule has had to be broken. For clarity the route has been marked with a dashed line, but this does not always indicate the presence of a footpath, merely the suggested way.

ACCESS

We have endeavoured wherever possible to use public rights of way, concession paths and routes which are in general use by hillwalkers.

The fact remains however that there is no universal right of access to all the mountains described in this book. Some areas have specific restrictions e.g during the grouse shooting season. These are mentioned in the relevant walks. A few areas are exceptionally sensitive, where walkers are at best tolerated. Fortunately in most places there is no objection to walkers on the hills and we have completed all the walks described without problems, nevertheless if in doubt ask permission of the landowner.

Scaley Beck, Blencathra

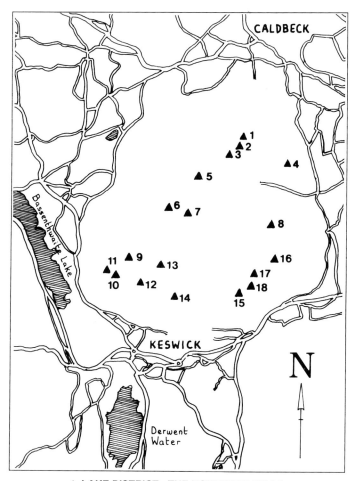

1. LAKE DISTRICT - THE NORTHERN FELLS

CHAPTER 1 LAKE DISTRICT - THE NORTHERN FELLS

TOP	NAME	HEIGHT	GRID REF	WALK No.
1	High Pike	658m	90-319350 NY	1.3
2	Hare Stones	627m	90-315344 NY	1.3
3	Great Lingy Hill	616m	90-310340 NY	1.3
4	Carrock Fell	660m	90-342336 NY	1.3
5	Knott	710m	90-296330 NY	1.3
6	Little Calva	642m	90-282315 NY	1.3
7	Great Calva	690m	90-291312 NY	1.3
8	Bowscale Fell	702m	90-333305 NY	1.1
9	Skiddaw	931m	90-260291 NY	1.2
10	Carl Side	746m	90-255281 NY	1.2
11	Long Side	734m	90-249284 NY	1.2
12	Skiddaw Little Man	865m	90-267278 NY	1.2
13	Sale How	666m	90-276286 NY	1.2
14	Lonscale Fell	715m	90-285271 NY	1.2
15	Gategill Fell Top	851m	90-318274 NY	1.1
16	Bannerdale Crags	683m	90-335290 NY	1.1
17	Atkinson Pike	845m	90-324283 NY	1.1
18	Blencathra	868m	90-323277 NY	1.1

WALK 1.1 BLENCATHRA

SUMMITS		
	Blencathra	2848 ft (868m)
	Gategill Fell Top	2792 ft (851m)
	Atkinson Pike	2772 ft (845m)
	Bowscale Fell	2303 ft (702m)
	Bannerdale Crags	2241 ft (683m)
DISTANCE	8¹/₂ miles	
ASCENT	2700 feet	
MAPS	OS Landranger sheet 90	
	Outdoor Leisure - The English Lakes,	
	North Eastern area (partial cover only)	
STARTING POINT		
	(90-340268) Scales, 6 miles east of Keswick on the A66.	
	Several lay bys on the main road at the start of the walk.	

Approaching through pastoral scenery from Penrith the scene changes almost in a moment from green fields to towering buttresses of heather and rock and suddenly one has arrived in the Lake District. Unlike many of the fells whose finest aspects are concealed from casual aquaintance, Blencathra's best is on view to all from the race track of the A66 which passes its foot. Not one, but five fells rise to a long common summit ridge and the many buttresses and gullies present probably the greatest variety of routes to the summit of any fell. There must be few people who have tried every one of the ways up.

Sharp Edge, prized as one of the finest and also the most difficult of all the ridges rising to Blencathra's summit, is concealed from view at the north-eastern end above the gloomy crags which encircle Scales Tarn. However Narrow Edge, described by Wainwright as positively the finest way to any mountain top in the district, has the added distinction that it leads directly to Hallsfell Top, the summit of the whole mountain.

Gate Gill is the site of probably the oldest lead mine in the district. In production long before gunpowder was introduced for blasting, it used the ancient 'stope and feather' method in which two strips of iron inserted in the rock were driven apart by a wedge and so split the rock. At its peak between 1880 and 1900 it produced over 10,000 tons of lead ore and 13,400 tons of zinc. The once Celtic hamlet of Threlkeld became a mining village with about a hundred men working in the local mines and refining sheds though by 1910 the last mine had closed. Now bypassed by the main road, which opened in 1965, there is a church, a cluster of cottages, a fair number of houses and two inns. In one of the latter we contrived to spend most of a very wet morning on a backpacking trip, not as it happened imbibing ale, but lingering over

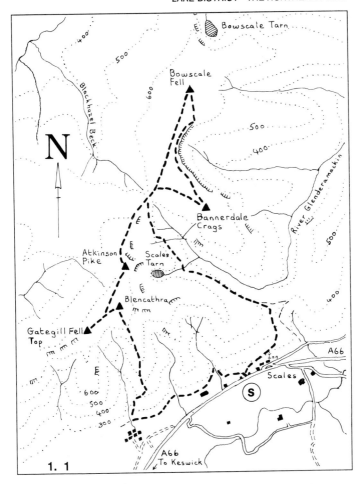

1. 1

coffee and warm scones with jam and cream. The blue-grey granite quarry on the other side of the main road, was used for roadstone and was the major local employer until it closed in 1980.

In 1976 the old sanatorium below Blease Fell, which was opened in 1904 to treat tuberculosis, was purchased by the Lake District Special Planning Board. It is now the Blencathra Centre, offering self catering accommodation for groups in either cottages or hostels and provides information, teaching facilities and a reference library.

ROUTE DESCRIPTION

BLENCATHRA *(Chair Top)*
Between the two buildings, 300 yards west of the White Horse Inn, take the track up to a gate and turn left on the path which runs along the bottom of the fellside. It is a good mile to the foot of Hall's Fell, crossing first Scaley Beck and then Doddick Gill. You will probably hear the famous Blencathra foxhounds barking in the distance as they are kennelled nearby. The third beck reached is Gate Gill which has a ruined mine building by the stream. From here a delightful little path twists its way up Hall's Fell, climbing first through heather and then along the narrow crest of the ridge to emerge at the very highest point of Blencathra, which is marked Hallsfell Top on the OS map. This popular spot has only a tiny cairn, but none is needed as this magnificent viewpoint is obviously the highest point. To the south-east lie the Eastern fells and to the south-west and beyond Borrowdale the Southern and Central fells offer a challenge to the identifier of mountain skylines.

GATEGILL FELL TOP *(Goats Gill Fell)*
After following the escarpment round to the left for about a third of a mile, an ascent of 56 ft leads to Blencathra's second top. A small cairn stands on a rock outcrop, the highest point of the south-west ridge, which then continues westwards dropping gradually before rising once again to Blease Fell, but this final high point, with an ascent of only 47ft fails to qualify as a separate summit.

ATKINSON PIKE
In mist navigation is made simpler by returning nearly to Hallsfell Top and then following the Sharp Edge path north to the col above Scales Tarn. In fine weather this top can be bypassed and a beeline made directly for Atkinson Pike. To the north of the col is a large cross made of white quartz piled on the ground. This was built as a memorial to a walker who died near here and was enlarged to its present size by Harold Robbins of Threlkeld. A detour to the right gives spectacular views of Sharp Edge and Scales Tarn. Continuing northwards Blencathra's third top is soon reached. The northernmost of the two cairns is the highest point and gives grand views towards the north and looking down upon the flat pancake of Wainwright's Mungrisdale Common, a fell with no redeeming features at all and surely included in his Northern Fells as a joke or as a penance!

BOWSCALE FELL *(Bow shaped mountain with hut)*
A yard or two to the north a small cairn marks the start of the little path which descends round the top of Foule Crag to the col dividing Blackhazel Beck from the Glenderamackin River. To the right tiny figures are silhouetted on the top of Sharp Edge. From the col head north-east on a small path straight for the

summit of Bowscale Fell about a mile away. The central portion is a bit boggy, but the path soon climbs to higher ground and the windshelter on the summit. A slightly lower cairn a few yards further on is the better viewpoint for High Pike and its surrounding fells, but even from here you can't see the famous Bowscale Tarn which nestles under crags to the north-east. Much visited by the Victorians, it has two legendary immortal fish and is the subject of one of Wordsworth's poems.

BANNERDALE CRAGS *(Holly Tree Valley Crags)*

Heading south over the pathless moor the next objective about a mile away is fringed by a dramatic row of cliffs. After several visits in mist when the top appeared flat and featureless, the first sight of this edge on a clear day was very impressive. Joining a path round the top of the crags, follow the edge and climb to a cairn in a commanding position. The highest point on the flat grassy top is about 100 yards to the west of this cairn and marked by a flattened heap of grey stones. Blencathra dominates the view and it is easy to see how it got its alternative name of Saddleback. William Gilpin used this mountain as an example of 'disagreeable lines' when he toured the Lake District in 1772. He invented 'Picturesque Beauty' and a theory of correct and incorrect mountains based on whether or not they were pleasing to the eye. However more people remember Blencathra than are ever likely to remember him or his theory.

Returning west to the col at the head of the Glenderamackin River, follow the narrow path on the far side of the infant river to the head of Mousthwaite Comb where you fork right. A narrow little alpine path curves round the flanks of Scales Fell high above Mousthwaite Comb and then zigzags down to the intake wall continuing to descend gently above the White Horse Inn back to the start of the walk.

Atkinson Pike, Blencathra

WALK 1.2 SKIDDAW

SUMMITS		
	Long Side	2408 ft (734m)
	Carl Side	2447 ft (746m)
	Skiddaw	3054 ft (931m)
	Skiddaw Little Man	2838 ft (865m)
	Lonscale Fell	2346 ft (715m)
	Sale How	2185 ft (666m)
DISTANCE	13 miles	
ASCENT	4550 feet	
MAPS	OS Landranger sheet 89 or 90	
	Outdoor Leisure - The English Lakes,	
	North Western area (partial cover only)	
STARTING		
POINT	(90-235296) 5 miles north of Keswick on the A591,	
	there is a lay by just south of the Ravenstone Hotel.	

Though not the highest of the Lakeland fells, Skiddaw is the elder statesman, far older than the Borrowdale volcanics, its crumbling slaty rocks are more ancient than reason can comprehend. Up there is a wild barren landscape where the wind roars unimpeded over the broad rounded summit of grey rock and stones. Below is Keswick, busy with the preoccupations of a town, but always concious of its mountain, where eyes look up to Skiddaw sensing a change in the weather as the cloud settles lower on its flanks or more expectantly as the mists disperse and the sun breaks through.

As we emerged onto the summit ridge, the wind which had been roughly jostling us all morning rose to storm force. There was no standing against it and as it threatened to lift us from the ground we doubled low over the ridge to escape down the highway of the tourist path. This was the only summit on which we had been turned back by the weather in the two years we spent revisiting all the two thousand foot tops. Usually Skiddaw is a much friendlier place. Here we sat and watched the sun slip down into the sea in the company of three men just completing a long day round the Lakeland Threes and here, to the amazement of the woolly hatted anorak brigade drinking tea from their thermos flasks, a young woman strode briskly past clad only in walking boots and bikini.

In the woods at the foot of Dodd, which crouches under Skiddaw, is an old sawmill built about 1880, now a café, where there is a small exhibition of photographs and forestry tools. Opposite, a footpath leads to the parish church of St Bega on the edge of Bassenthwaite Lake. Snowdrops were in

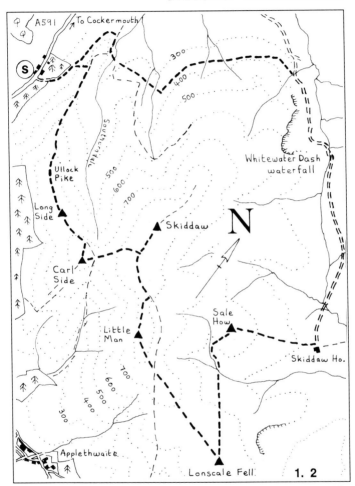

bloom as we climbed over the stile into the churchyard and on the lake white horses were breaking as a storm approached, but inside the church was peace. Originally built during the Norman period and restored in 1874, the exterior of the church was completely renovated in the Gothic style, but the lovely Norman features of the interior were carefully preserved. The church is set within a circular churchyard a few yards from the shore of Bassenthwaite

Lake, where Alfred Lord Tennyson sat in 1836 when he wrote the Excalibur story in his poem 'Morte d'Arthur', *'I heard the water lapping on the crag and the long ripple washing in the reeds'.* He was staying in the nearby Georgian manor house, Mirehouse, which dates from 1666 and is now open to the public. In 1794 William Wordsworth stayed at Armathwaite Hall with his old school friend John Spedding and behind the church to the east is *'Distant Skiddaw's lofty height'.* The church is considerably older than Bassenthwaite village which, standing back from the lakeside, comprises a cluster of cottages and farms, a village green and pub, a school and a ruined mill. Access to St Bega's church was originally by boat and in 1878 the new church of St John was built nearer the village.

East of Skiddaw steep slopes of grass and heather descend to the headwaters of the river Caldew in an area of quiet and deserted hills with more affinity for the Pennines than the Lakeland fells. There is one dwelling only here and that is Skiddaw House, a row of shepherd's cottages which sits sheltered among pine trees at the foot of the little visited top of Sale How. The last shepherd retired in 1969 and it was then used as an Outdoor Pursuit Centre by a local school, with part of the building being available as a bothy. It has since been much renovated and converted into a Youth Hostel. It was empty on our last visit and the owner was somewhat belatedly applying for planning permission. Surprisingly the locals were in favour of this scheme. "Somewhere to get a cup of tea when you're gathering the sheep" said a farmer when we were admiring his flock of Rough Fell. He was dismissive of the less intelligent Swaledales which his dog was busily chasing away as he

Skiddaw from Derwentwater

distributed feed for his own flock. "If one of these was lying in the road on the white line, it wouldn't move, you'd have to go round, a Swaledale would jump up and you'd probably run over it". He had been farming here for ten years having brought his flock with him from Tebay and it took five years for them to settle in their new home.

ROUTE DESCRIPTION

LONG SIDE *(Long Hill Slope)*
Take the very steep path to the south of the Ravenstone Hotel up to a forest road and a gate just beyond. Continue on the path beside Thornthwaite Forest almost to the corner and turn right to join the ridge. Heading now southwards the path climbs over Ullock Pike which fails by only 3 ft to make separate mountain status. Below can be seen the isolated church of St Bega in the fields beside Bassenthwaite Lake, the only 'Lake' in the Lake District. The ridge continues easily to Long Side where the small cairn is just past the highest point. Skiddaw rises hugely to the left with Little Man straight ahead and in the distance on the far shore of Bassenthwaite Lake are the North Western fells. On the lower slopes of Lord's Seat the Bishop of Barf shines whitely, but poor Dodd, recently felled, cowers miserably by the lake like a half-shorn sheep.

CARL SIDE *(Karl's Hill Slope)*
The ridge now broadens, but follow the path high above Southerndale before turning south-east over pathless ground for the summit cairn, which vanishes from sight as you approach. A few paces towards Derwent Water on the flat grassy stone-sprinkled top, reveals an aerial view of Keswick with Borrowdale beyond.

SKIDDAW *(Archer's Hill)*
A gentle stroll north-east, past the puddle grandly named Carlside Tarn, rejoins the path which climbs steadily across the grey slates of Skiddaw's western flank. Here one cold, clammy, misty August day we were stopped by a man wearing a raincoat and town shoes. "What mountain is this?" he wanted to know. On arriving on the summit there is no doubt as to where you are, no other mountain is quite like Skiddaw with its long stony ridge at over 3000 ft. Turn left to the OS trig point, topograph and windshelter which mark the highest spot on the undulating ridge a quarter of a mile away. On a day of good visibility to the west and north Scotland is in view beyond the Solway Firth, but the rest of the compass is filled with the hills of Lakeland.

SKIDDAW LITTLE MAN *(Little Hill with a Cairn)*
Return to the southern end of the ridge and descend south-east on a broad highway to where a fence crosses the path. Following the fence up on the right side, it leads nearly to the top of Little Man's shapely cone, one of the best viewpoints in the Lakes. A small cairn overlooks Derwent Water, Keswick and Borrowdale.

LONSCALE FELL

Descending south-east to a lower cairn the path returns to the broad track and the fence which then acts as a handrail for the mile to the next summit, a grassy mound with all the interest in its craggy eastern slopes. A small cairn stands on the highest point 100 yards beyond the fence corner with wide views of the empty Northern fells, while a few steps to the south-west are rewarded by views of Borrowdale.

SALE HOW *(Hill Spur of the Sallows)*

Return to the fence corner and descend north-west over easy slopes aiming just to the left of the pudding shaped mound that constitutes the next top. After passing Jackson's Fold climb beside Stile Gill with its little falls, Sale How's best feature, then turn right to trudge up grassy slopes to the cairn on the undistinguished summit.

The broad grassy track eastwards leads down to the isolated Skiddaw House and bothy, then turn left along the landrover track for a good 2 miles, past Whitewater Dash, which is spectacular after heavy rain, and under Dead Crags. Leave the track when it goes through the wall and keeping above the intake wall follow it round for another couple of miles to Southerndale. Cross the beck at a bridge and continue following the wall back to the corner of Thornthwaite Forest from which it is steeply downhill, reversing the outward route, for a scant ten minutes to the main road.

Skiddaw House

1.3 BACK O'SKIDDAW

SUMMITS	Carrock Fel	2165 ft (660m)
	High Pike	2159 ft (658m)
	Hare Stones	2057 ft (627m)
	Great Lingy Hill	2021 ft (616m)
	Knott	2329 ft (710m)
	Little Calva	2106 ft (642m)
	Great Calva	2264 ft (690m)

DISTANCE	10½ miles
ASCENT	2550 feet
MAPS	OS Landranger sheet 90
STARTING POINT	(90-328327) At the end of the surfaced road leading to Carrock Mine from the hamlet of Mosedale, 11 miles west of Penrith.

Back o'Skiddaw is not a name you will find on the map, but it is the name by which the hills to the north, or back, of Skiddaw and Blencathra are known to walkers and locals alike. These are deserted hills, grassy and heathery with very little rock, where another walker in view is something of an event and the miles pass easily. There is rock of course and for geologists Carrock Fell is a Mecca where the Skiddaw slates give way to a mixture of volcanic rocks in which veins of many minerals have been found. The mines, all marked disused on the map, some worked since the sixteenth century, are scattered over these Caldbeck fells and while lead and copper mines predominate, many other minerals such as zinc, manganese and silver occur, there is even a china clay mine. The only road to penetrate any distance runs from the hamlet of Mosedale beside the river Caldew to terminate at Carrock Mine where the rare metal tungsten was found in the mid nineteenth century. The mine was re-opened during both world wars to obtain the precious metal and was working again when we visited it only a few years ago, but now it is once more silent. It is all lovely country and, since the closure of the mines, quite empty. We have camped there on several occasions, once in the shelter of a sheepfold where we had to cut the rushes to make a flat space for the tent while the rain poured down. Such wilderness camps, a tiny refuge from the storm and in the morning the great hills about us with the cloud swirling around their summits, are memories that last forever.

Caldbeck fells are linked with the huntsman John Peel, immortalised in the song by his friend John Woodcock Graves. Peel, who it is recorded was a hard hunter and a hard drinker, usually hunted on a fell pony, and was easily

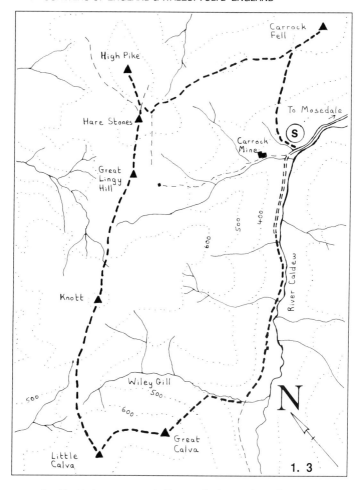

recognised by his long grey coat. Frequently the word grey is sung as 'gay' in the mistaken belief that all huntsmen wear red. Fell huntsmen usually go on foot, and keeping down the foxes, while undeniably a sport, is also of vital concern to the farmers whose new born lambs fall easy prey to the predators.

ROUTE DESCRIPTION

CARROCK FELL *(Rock Fell)*
Poddy Gill tumbles down to join the River Caldew just before the road end and the slopes above are grassy providing an easy ascent. Trending right as height is gained, join the ridge to the east of Round Knott and a short walk soon brings you to the summit of Carrock Fell, where there is a cairn with a circular wind shelter below. The summit is enclosed by the ruins of an Iron Age hill fort similar to that on Ingleborough, so in addition to the geologists, fellwalkers have to share the summit with antiquarians. There was no-one about however on our last visit and we cowered behind the windshelter adding extra clothing while a hailstorm roared past. In clear weather there are good views over to the east towards the Pennines.

HIGH PIKE *(High Peak)*
Eventually emerging to face the stinging onslaught of wind driven hail, we staggered off westwards along the ridge, thankful for the clear path to follow as it was quite impossible to face the storm. After just a mile and a half of easy going with good views of the mine workings ahead, fork right and after crossing a stony track, follow the path up to High Pike. The summit has a cairn and a trig point linked by a shelter wall of stones and a little beyond there is another cairn and the ruins of a shepherd's hut, but also very unusually there is a seat made of hewn slate. In the roaring gale we could barely stand and the seat facing westwards over the Uldale fells was exposed to the full blast, but by scraping away some of the snow the inscriptions could just be read beneath the ice. '*In memory of Mick Lewis who loved all these fells*'. He died on the 8th May 1944 aged sixteen years and a small addition is in memory of his mother Millicent Mary Lewis who died on the 10th November 1970. This is the most northerly top of the Lake District two thousanders and consequently gives good views of the Solway Firth and over to Scotland.

HARE STONES
Returning down the path to join the main track, turn right to the crest of the rise which is Hare Stones. The flat moor top is just off the track to the right and is marked with a few big stones.

GREAT LINGY HILL *(Great Heathery Hill)*
The track is little help now as it slides off left missing the next top and it is better to make a bee-line south-west across the scraggy heather. At the lowest point a solid plank bridges a small stream in the peat groughs. Perhaps it was placed for shooting parties, but it looks quite new, though the heather has deteriorated and is now of little use to grouse either as food or as cover. There is a mere 59 ft of ascent to reach the top and its small cairn.

KNOTT *(Hill)*
The next section is without a path and the way lies first west to pass round the

The summit of Knott

head of Miller Moss which is drained by Grainsgill Beck, and then to the left of the minor top above the Roughten Gill mines. Once in the two thousanders list, it has been excluded by the latest survey which records it at 609 metres. Crossing the headwaters of Roughten Gill the final ascent of Knott begins. Progress is rather slow heading south-west up these pathless slopes, but soon the extensive flat grassy top is reached with its central cairn.

That freezing Easter for a few fleeting minutes the clouds parted to reveal a blue sky with towering white clouds. The hills shone in the brilliant sunlight and we braced ourselves against the wind to take in the sudden view. There was Carrock Fell away to the east, while to the south were the giants of Blencathra and Skiddaw with Great Calva as a foreground, but the cloud quickly closed in again and another hail shower chased us down.

LITTLE CALVA *(Little Hill where Calves were kept)*
Follow the left side of the broad ridge from Knott south-westwards down to the col on a faint path. This saddle in the hills where Hause Gill flows west and Wiley Gill flows east is a difficult place to find in mist requiring concentration on the compass. It is probably easier from this side, but coming the other way down the broad flank of Little Calva on a backpacking trip with our children there was less than 50 yards visibility and we found ourselves dropping down to Hause Gill before realising our error.

A good path appears after the col, but as it is going to Great Calva it must be soon abandoned and the heathery slopes tackled direct to reach the ruined wire fence on the summit. The highest point is marked with a pile of stones and is close by the fence just south-west of a handful of small tarns. A dissenting hand has built a small cairn a little way to the west on an alternative rise.

GREAT CALVA *(Great Hill where Calves were kept)*

Following the fence round over boggy moorland the path is rejoined leading easily to the summit of Great Calva. The northern end of the summit ridge is the true top where there is a windshelter and a cairn adorned with fence posts. From 100 yards south at two lower cairns and another shelter there is a good view of Skiddaw House tucked into its sheltering trees with Lonscale Fell forming a backdrop and in the far distance the gleam of Thirlmere.

A ruined fence leads east down the heathery slopes and this gives the easiest line, a path following it to reach Wiley Gill. South now and the Cumbria Way is joined where a useful footbridge crosses the beck. Two miles of easy walking beside the River Caldew remain, all on a path which soon becomes a track. As we made our way down, the snow started to fall steadily and soon we and the fells were covered in a soft mantle of white driven along by the final gusts of the subsiding storm.

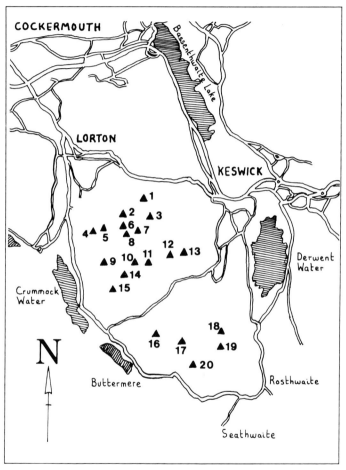

2. LAKE DISTRICT - THE NORTH WESTERN FELLS

CHAPTER 2 LAKE DISTRICT - THE NORTH WESTERN FELLS

TOP	NAME	HEIGHT	GRID REF	WALK No.
1	Hobcarton End	634m	90-195235 NY	2.3
2	Ladyside Pike	703m	89-185228 NY	2.2
3	Grisedale Pike	791m	90-198225 NY	2.3
4.	Whiteside	707m	89-170219 NY	2.2
5	Whiteside East Top	719m	89-175221 NY	2.2
6	Hopegill Head	770m	89-186221 NY	2.2
7	Hobcarton Crag	739m	90-194220 NY	2.3
8	Sand Hill	756m	89-187219 NY	2.2
9	Grasmoor	852m	89-175203 NY	2.2
10	Crag Hill	839m	90-193204 NY	2.3
11	Sail	773m	90-198203 NY	2.3
12	Scar Crags	672m	90-208206 NY	2.3
13	Causey Pike	637m	90-219208 NY	2.3
14	Wandope	772m	89-188197 NY	2.2
15	Whiteless Pike	660m	89-180190 NY	2.2
16	Robinson	737m	89-202169 NY	2.1
17	Hindscarth	727m	89-216165 NY	2.1
18	High Spy North Top	634m	89-236171 NY	2.1
19	High Spy	653m	89-234162 NY	2.1
20	Dale Head	753m	89-223153 NY	2.1

Robinson from Little Town

WALK 2.1 ROBINSON AND HINDSCARTH

SUMMITS		
	Robinson	2418 ft (737m)
	Hindscarth	2385 ft (727m)
	Dale Head	2470 ft (753m)
	High Spy	2142 ft (653m)
	High Spy North Top	2080 ft (634m)

DISTANCE   9½ miles

ASCENT   3500 feet

MAPS   OS Landranger sheet 89 or 90
Outdoor Leisure - The English Lakes, North Western area

STARTING
POINT   (89-232194) Just west of Little Town in the Newlands valley, 3 miles south of Braithwaite.
Limited parking by the side of the road.

Robinson and Hindscarth, or Hindscarth and Robinson, whichever way you put it these two fells go together like inseparable twins. Does anyone climb one without the other? It would seem like desertion to leave one of them out. Linked by Littledale Edge which overlooks Buttermere,these are grassy fells for the most part with rock asserting its presence in outcrops and mine workings on the flanks of the hills. Each has a long ridge descending gradually northwards towards Little Town, the home of Mrs Tiggy Winkle. The cottage illustrated by Beatrix Potter is still there, the village looking very much the same as when in 1905 she wrote '*Once upon a time there was a little girl called Lucy, who lived at a farm called Little Town*'.

These summits form a perfect horseshoe and an easy day, but having made the ascent very little extra effort is needed to include Dale Head. A little more energy is required for the continuation to High Spy, dipping first to Dalehead Tarn, but this is succeeded by a stroll along a grassy ridge with a gentle easy descent and on either hand the perfection of the Lake District fells.

Dale Head is not always gained so easily. We stood by the cairn one summer's day to watch the runners in the Borrowdale fell race. The leaders looked incredibly fresh, chatting easily with the officials, but the ascent from Honister Pass is the last climb on one of the toughest races in the calendar and many of the runners were down to a walk as they came up to the cairn. However pride, and the onlookers, drove them to a final effort and they broke into a run towards Dalehead Tarn and the finish in Borrowdale. 17 miles and 6500 ft of ascent with the leaders home in under 3 hours makes even the tail enders something aproaching supermen.

31

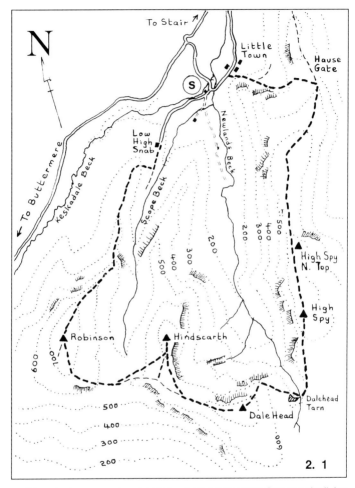

2.1

It is not only men, and women too, who run these fells. One grey April day on the High Spy ridge there came on the breeze the strong sweet smell of aniseed. No sooner had we linked this with hound trails, than the dogs were upon us. Oblivious of people, looking neither to right nor left, scattering the sheep and completely ignoring everything except the job in hand, they raced past at a furious pace. As a trail of some ten miles, made by dragging a rag soaked in paraffin and aniseed over the fells, takes the dogs a mere half hour to complete, their speed is indeed tremendous. Hound trailing is very popular, not only with the locals and visitors, but also with people from the towns some distance away. The sport is controlled by a ruling body, established in 1906 to end the cheating which used to take place, for the chief appeal to humans seems to be the betting. Seeing the dogs on the fells it is difficult to believe that all they care about is their dinner, despite the eagerness with which they gulp it down at the end of the race. As they hurtled past us on High Spy it was obvious - they were in a race, they knew it and they loved it.

At Goldscope mine on Scope End lead, copper, silver and possibly even gold was obtained from as early as the thirteenth century. The Society for the Mines Royal was founded in 1561 when German miners were imported by Elizabeth I to work the mines. At first they were not trusted and they had to live in isolation on Derwent Island, but later, when accepted by the community, they married local girls. Although a smelter was built at Brigham near Keswick and for a time the mines were very profitable, they closed in less than a hundred years. Reopened for a period by the Dutch in 1690 and again between 1847 and 1866, a final short period of activity came to a close in 1920, leaving Scope End with over a mile of tunnels.

ROUTE DESCRIPTION

ROBINSON *(named after Richard Robinson in the sixteenth century)*
Take the road to Newlands Church and after the church fork right on the tarmac road beside Keskadale Beck with the day's objective clearly in view ahead. At Low High Snab the road ends and a rough track leads to open countryside. To the left are the mine workings of the Goldscope mine on Scope End. At the end of the intake wall, turn right up the path that climbs very steeply over the short grass of High Snab Bank. On reaching the ridge Causey Pike appears ahead and Derwent Water can be glimpsed to the right. Turn left on the broad undulating grassy ridge high above Scope Beck with its deep pool of the old mine reservoir. Where High Snab Bank joins the mountain's north-east ridge there is a rocky scramble. It is a steep pull up on a good path to the cairn at the end of the extensive summit area, and an easy walk over grass to the top, which especially in mist seems a long way beyond. There are several cairns dotted about, but there is no difficulty in spotting the highest which is on the right-most of two small rocky ribs. Honister Pass with its miniature cars looks a long way below and there is an extensive panorama of the surrounding fells, but with Scafell Pike hidden behind Great Gable.

HINDSCARTH *(Deer's Gap)*
On our last visit the cloud was right down and there was little to detain us on the summit. We set off briskly remarking that we knew these fells so well it was

hardly necessary to check the route. After several minutes steady progress downhill second thoughts made us get out the compass. This confirmed that we were by now quite a long way down the wrong side of the mountain! In clear weather it's obvious enough and an easy stroll south along the flattish top joins the main path leading south-east. A steep stony descent beside a fence leads to the lowest point on Littledale Edge. Here a stile is opposite the start of a faint path which cuts the corner, setting off more directly towards Hindscarth. When the path ends in a boggy patch, climb steeply uphill over short grass to join the ridge. Turn left to the cairn which marks the highest point and there is a large shelter cairn a few yards away on a lower point.

DALE HEAD *(Valley Summit)*
About half way back along the ridge, take a small path that contours round to Hindscarth Edge. To the left is the deep ravine of Far Tongue Gill and from the col you can look down over the steep shattered cliffs to Honister Pass and Buttermere. This is also a good vantage point from which to appreciate the continuously steep north-west ridge of Fleetwith Pike above Gatesgarth. The broad main path then climbs quite steeply to the flat summit of Dale Head. The highest point is just to the west of the once fine stone column which has been recently truncated. To the south the view is filled by Great Gable, Pillar and the Buttermere Fells.

HIGH SPY *(High Look-out)*
It is a long and steep descent to Dalehead Tarn, but there is a clear path to be followed down the broad north-east ridge with a steep drop to the left. As the path becomes less distinct aim for the north end of the tarn passing a welcome source of drinking water. The environs of Dalehead Tarn are rather boggy. Walk between it and the sheepfold, which offers shelter in bad weather, then round to the left to cross Newlands Beck, an ideal paddling spot for hot tired feet. The path now climbs northwards towards High Spy with the steep drop over crags close on the left. Down below is the ruined Dale Head Copper Mine and the old zigzag mine track. Like the mine at Scope End, this was mined by the Society for the Mines Royal in the sixteenth century. German workers were employed here too, and later a smelter was built. The summit of High Spy is the southern end of an almost level ridge about one and a half miles long with the almost imperceptible rise of Maiden Moor at the far end. The grassy top is dotted with a few rocks and has a large cairn.

HIGH SPY NORTH TOP
The easy grassy ridge of High Spy has a minor rise about half a mile north of the main top, where a cairn stands on the top of a rocky knoll to the right of the main path giving a good view of Derwent Water.

The path continues over Maiden Moor and then descends to Hause Gate. Below to the right is Brackenburn, the home of the author Hugh Walpole from 1924 to his death in 1941. Keep straight on to include Cat Bells, but a left turn continues the descent through the old mine workings of the Yewthwaite lead mine on a very rough path. Contour round to the left to see an old level, while below there are extensive spoil heaps and a fenced shaft. Though all is peaceful now, at one time this must have been a busy and noisy place. Cross Yewthwaite Gill to join the main track down to Little Town.

WALK 2.2 THE CRUMMOCK HORSESHOE

SUMMITS		
	Whiteside	2320 ft (707m)
	Whiteside East Top	2359 ft (719m)
	Hopegill Head	2526 ft (770m)
	Ladyside Pike	2306 ft (703m)
	Sand Hill	2480 ft (756m)
	Grasmoor	2795 ft (852m)
	Wandope	2533 ft (772m)
	Whiteless Pike	2165 ft (660m)
DISTANCE	10 miles	
ASCENT	3800 feet	
MAPS	OS Landranger sheet 89	
	Outdoor Leisure - The English Lakes, North Western area	
STARTING POINT	(89-158207) Lanthwaite Green, at the north end of Crummock Water, car park.	

The North Western Fells provide many miles of easy high level ridge walking over popular, but seldom crowded hills. Good paths and springy turf lie underfoot and the miles seem much shorter than in the more rugged fells further south. Of all these fells Grasmoor is the most obviously impressive with a vast unbroken slope of pink scree falling to Crummock Water over two thousand feet below, but the full frontal assault is not to be preferred to the ridges of Whiteless Pike and Whiteside on either hand. Wordsworth was the first to point out how the Lake District fells radiate from a centre like the spokes of a wheel and here is a miniature version with ridges centred upon Coledale Hause whose fenced open shafts mark the remains of old copper mines.

The radial pattern is of course ideally suited to horseshoe walks, but longer trips inevitably result in out and back visits to pick up other tops. Recently in a fit of enthusiasm we spent a day visiting all the 2000 ft tops between Newlands and Whinlatter. It is a challenging, but not too strenuous walk best saved for a long summer day when there is plenty of time to enjoy the views and no need to hurry. In the cool of the evening we came down to Braithwaite and it was only afterwards that we discovered Hobcarton End should have been included too!

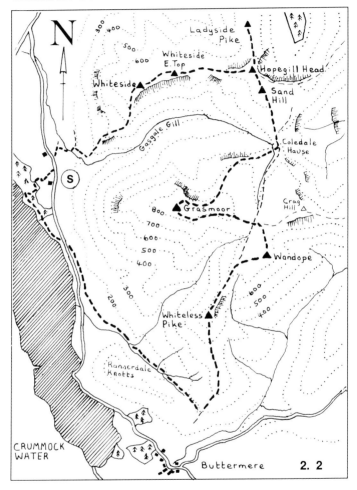

ROUTE DESCRIPTION

WHITESIDE *(White Hill Slope)*
From the open common at Lanthwaite Green which is the site of an old
settlement, head towards Whiteside to cross the footbridge over Liza Beck

and join the ridge on a steep path which is climbed to Whin Ben. From here it is easy going to a rocky knoll, and then the path again becomes steep, climbing above Gasgale Crags where the ribs of rock running down from the ridge, in certain lighting conditions, are outlined like a series of miniature Striding Edges. The path ascends over heather, juniper and crowberry to arrive at the grassy top of Whiteside whose first unmarked rocky bump is the highest point. The views to the north are extensive over the Solway Firth to Scotland and the summit looks and feels very much on the edge of the Lake District.

WHITESIDE EAST TOP
About a quarter of a mile to the east, an easy walk along the ridge path, is the second and higher top of Whiteside. It is at the far end of the obvious highest part and overtops Whiteside by 12 metres. This is a brand new summit revealed by the Ordnance Survey on their latest map. As is fitting for a new summit it has a new cairn, a bit on the small side at the moment, but no doubt it will grow as it gets older.

HOPEGILL HEAD *(Source of Hopegill)*
The ridge continues to Hopegill Head whose ascent looks daunting, a narrow

Hopegill Head from Whiteside

37

rocky ridge climbing perilously to the top, but it is an illusion and there is no difficulty at all. The pointed stony summit has a tiny cairn and the ground drops steeply over the awesome Hobcarton Crag.

LADYSIDE PIKE *(Lady's Upland Pasture Peak)*

Once known as Lady's Seat, an out and back expedition is the solution for this summit. The ridge is delightful, and though the descent over steep rocks is a little awkward, the re-ascent is a pleasant scramble. A small path from the summit cairn on Hopegill Head descends north by the edge of the crags to the rocky slopes and rounds a rocky knoll to gain the grassy ridge. It is then an easy walk beside a ruined wall to the highest point at the end of the ridge, situated mid-way between two cairns.

SAND HILL

Returning by the same route to Hopegill Head it is then an easy walk south-east to this rather uninteresting grassy mound of a summit which has a small cairn on the top, but it is a good point from which to survey the Grisedale Horseshoe walk.

GRASMOOR *(Wild Boar Moor)*

An initially steep and stony descent to the south leads to Coledale Hause, a flat grassy expanse looking rather out of place among these craggy hills. Join lovely Gasgale Gill and cross it by the waterfalls. The ascent westwards on an improving path following the ridge first steeply and then more gradually, keeping to the edge for the best views, is very quiet. One Bank Holiday, when even Ladyside Pike was busy, we had this part of Grasmoor to ourselves although the top was popular enough. Where the ridge turns west again, a series of spectacular gullies run down to the gill. The last gully, before the edge turns north, has an interesting pinnacle. From here it is only a short stroll south-west over stony moss to the summit cairn. Constructed as a windshelter, with numerous bays on all sides, you are assured of a non windy spot for a late lunch or early tea, and by taking a few paces to the south Crummock Water and Buttermere appear with the high fells of Pillar and Gable behind.

WANDOPE *(Willow Valley)*

A good path on the southern edge of the Grasmoor plateau leads east to the crossroads on Wandope Moss. Go across to look down the tremendous drop to Addacomb Hole and then follow the edge south to the grassy summit which has a small cairn and is dwarfed by Grasmoor.

WHITELESS PIKE *(unknown)*

Walk west gently downhill to join the Whiteless Edge path. A delightful rocky ridge runs down to Saddle Gate and then up to the summit of Whiteless Pike, a grassy and rocky top marked with a little cairn.

It is an easy descent on a good path down the broad ridge to the end of the Rannerdale Knotts ridge. Turn right taking the green path north-west beside

Squat Beck towards Rannerdale where once there was a fourteenth century chapel. After a mile a ladderstile, then a footbridge, lead to an old grassy track which continues in the same direction to the road. The bluebells here growing in the open are a lovely splash of colour in the spring and some new trees have been planted to augment the few that remain. After crossing the road a ladder stile on the other side, signposted Scale Hill, leads to Fletcher Fields which is National Trust land. A path then hugs the lakeside making a lovely end to the walk, the open fields giving way to a newly felled area. In the mature woodland which follows, turn sharp right on a little path after a boathouse, and follow the edge of the wood round to join the right of way to Lanthwaite Green Farm. The path crosses the fields and joins the road to the left of the farm.

Grasmoor from Crummock Water

WALK 2.3 THE GRISEDALE PIKE HORSESHOE

SUMMITS	Hobcarton End	2080 ft (634m)
	Grisedale Pike	2595 ft (791m)
	Hobcarton Crag	2425 ft (739m
	Crag Hill	2753 ft (839m)
	Sail	2536 ft (773m)
	Scar Crags	2205 ft (672m)
	Causey Pike	2090 ft (637m)
DISTANCE	11 miles	
ASCENT	4000 feet	
MAPS	OS Landranger sheet 89 or 90	
	Outdoor Leisure - The English Lakes, North Western area	
STARTING POINT	(90-226248) Thornthwaite, just north of Braithwaite, on the minor road which runs parallel to the A66. Parking by the lane to Hallgarth farm in lay by.	

From Grisedale Pike with its roots buried in the Thornthwaite Forest, to Causey Pike whose distinctive bump of a summit is recognisable from afar, the high level circuit of the Coledale Fells is an excellent walk on easy paths. Causey Pike seems to have grown since Wainwright's day having gained over fifty feet in height, but while Crag Hill, commonly known as Eel Crag, is the highest in the group, Grisedale Pike, steep on all sides with four fine ridges rising to its top, is the chief. Starting and finishing at the village of Braithwaite, Grisedale Pike is usually climbed via its east ridge, but the inclusion of Hobcarton End then requires a demoralising out and back visit early in the day. However by starting from the village of Thornthwaite the approach through the forest where deer may still be seen is an attractive alternative.

Thornthwaite Forest is not only the plantations which flank the Whinlatter Pass, but also refers to the woods on Dodd, the small hill below Skiddaw where Thomas Storey of Mirehouse began planting trees in 1790 to restore natural woodland felled for mining. The Forestry Commission started planting after the first world war to replace timber felled during the war and while early work was strictly utilitarian with unnatural lines and massed conifers, much more attention is now given to landscaping using a mixture of trees and avoiding harsh contrasts. Nevertheless Thornthwaite Forest, like all working forests, is in the continual process of flux and as newly planted areas grow rapidly and skylines change, others suddenly vanish under the onslaught of chain saws. It is a guidebook writer's nightmare to keep up to date. Fortunately visitors are encouraged to visit the forest which has a Visitor Centre full

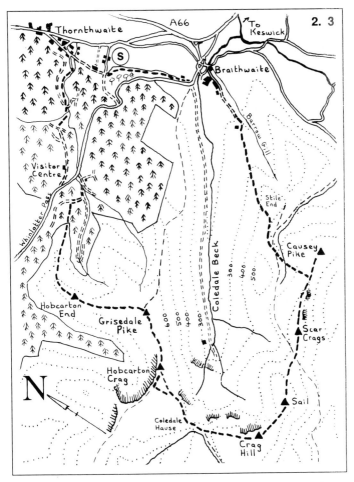

of information with displays, leaflets and film shows. Waymarked trails are provided, while the popular sport of orienteering is well catered for. There is a guide map to the forest and an orienteering map on sale at the centre. Opened in 1977, the centre is staffed by Rangers and has the amazing number of 100,000 visitors a year.

The village of Braithwaite, meaning broad clearing, is now a pleasant residential area. With two pubs, a campsite and a timeshare development as well as a tea room and second hand bookshop, it is quite busy in the season. In 1868 it was the home of the Cumberland Pencil Company, but after the factory was burned down manufacture moved to Keswick in 1898. Thornthwaite, the thornbush clearing, is just over a mile up the road. Little more than a hamlet on the edge of Thornthwaite Forest, it has a seventeenth century hotel and a picture gallery.

ROUTE DESCRIPTION

HOBCARTON END *(End of Kjartan's Valley)*
The lane which leads to Hallgarth farm is a mass of daffodils every spring and a lovely approach at this time of year. Passing the farm, the road becomes unsurfaced and starts to climb. In about 200 yards turn right towards Thornthwaite at the track junction, passing the rear of the Ladstock Hotel. On reaching Thornthwaite, turn left and walk up the tarmac road to the right of Comb Beck to the end house where a path along a rocky shelf leads uphill to enter the wood.

The path climbs beside the stream through woodland with a mixture of different trees, passes an old mine level and crosses a forest road. Continue up the path until a small stream is reached. Now walk up the left bank of the stream and shortly the path joins a forest road. Turn left on the road and then in 50 yards fork right uphill, then straight on to the Visitor Centre. To the left you can see Lakeland View, originally a fever hospital, hence the name Hospital Plantation for the forest opposite. Planted in 1919, this was the first Forestry Commission planting in the Lake District.

From the Visitor Centre turn left down the Whinlatter Pass, then right at Comb Bridge onto a forest road. Keep right, downhill and over a bridge with Grisedale Pike straight ahead. Take the next road on the right at junction 41 then after 100 yards fork left up a track and then left again in 50 yards at the junction. This rough tractor track leads up the north-east ridge to join the narrow path which climbs above Black Crag, high above the Whinlatter Pass to the summit. A fence crosses the ridge just before the highest point which is a heathery mound topped by a small cairn.

GRISEDALE PIKE *(Pig Valley Peak)*
Walk south along the broad grassy ridge, then up over a slaty section to join the ruined wall which climbs to the summit of Grisedale Pike. It is an ascent of about 500ft to the rocky top which is a magnificent viewpoint crowned by a small cairn, whose stones are frequently rearranged by visitors. You can see all the summits of the walk from here, also Ladyside Pike, Grasmoor and Whiteside.

HOBCARTON CRAG *(Kjarton's Valley Crag)*
A path descends south-west beside the ruined wall, with steep slopes on the

left falling to Coledale Beck and then continues over the highest point of Hobcarton Crag, which is marked with a cairn.

CRAG HILL
A path from Hobcarton Crag's rocky summit descends directly to Coledale Hause, but by continuing straight on, make a small deviation from the direct route in order to admire the fearsome drop over the crags at the col. From here head south down a grassy gully to rejoin the path above the fenced in chasms of old mine workings, and this leads to the flat green expanse of Coledale Hause. The pretty falls of Gasgale Gill are on the far side of the hause.

The north-east ridge of Crag Hill appears steep and uninviting, but is much easier than it looks with first an easy scramble which zigzags up over rocky scree, to be followed by a pleasant walk over a subsidiary top to the flat orange coloured summit which has an OS trig point.

At the end of the Coledale valley you can see the Force Crag Mine which was reopened around 1970 to work barytes and below Long Crag there is an old cobalt mine. The scramble up the edge can be avoided by heading south from Coledale Hause until the rough ground is passed and then climbing to the summit over easy slopes. Although Crag Hill is the official name of this mountain as given by the Ordnance Survey, it has been known to generations of walkers as Eel Crag.

SAIL *(Swampy Hill)*
The ridge over the next three tops culminating in Causey Pike is a succession of ups and downs, with every descent followed by a lesser ascent; much the best way for the end of the day. A stony path down the ridge to the col is followed by a short easy ascent leading to the cairned, flat grassy top of Sail, a rather disappointing summit, dominated by the bulk of Crag Hill.

SCAR CRAGS *(Notched Crags)*
Descend eastwards on the broad orange stony path to the crossroads at the next col and a short but steep ascent brings you to the rather muddy black top. The highest point is at the far end of the grassy ridge at the start of the rocky section and is marked by a little cairn.

CAUSEY PIKE *(Paved Way Peak)*
A delightful rocky ridge runs to the col where there is a flat grassy section. A short steep ascent then leads to the final four bumps of the ridge, the last of which is the highest. The rocky summit has a small cairn and beyond there is a very steep way down to Rowling End and the village of Stair.

In order to return to Braithwaite however, the ridge of Barrow and Outerside must be crossed. Retrace your steps to the cairn at the east end of the col and then aim north, down over easy grassy slopes, to meet a small path which runs from Stonycroft Gill towards Stile End. At the bottom of the gill to the right above Stonycroft is the site of a lead mine. This was first worked in the sixteenth century and in the seventeenth century a large lead smelter

Causey Pike from Derwent Water

was built here. Cross the stream and walk up towards Stile End, crossing the main track. Where the path becomes indistinct above a sheepfold, fork left to pass between Outerside and Stile End. From here a good grassy path descends, passing the ruined High Coledale farm buildings, to join a track which leads beside Barrow Gill down to Braithwaite.

Keep left to the Coledale Inn then go round the back of the cottages to cross Coledale Beck at a footbridge. Turn downstream and then left onto the Whinlatter Pass road. Go through the small gate by the Hope Memorial Camp and a track then leads by the edge of the wood back to the lane at Hallgarth Farm.

Wast Water

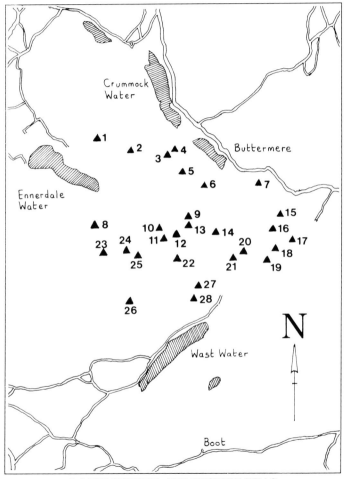

3. LAKE DISTRICT - THE WESTERN FELLS

CHAPTER 3 LAKE DISTRICT - THE WESTERN FELLS

TOP	NAME	HEIGHT	GRID REF	WALK No
1	Great Borne	616m	89-124164 NY	3.6
2.	Starling Dodd	633m	89-142158 NY	3.6
3	Red Pike	755m	89-160155 NY	3.5
4	Dodd	641m	89-164158 NY	3.5
5	High Stile	807m	89-170148 NY	3.5
6	High Crag	744m	89-180140 NY	3.5
7	Fleetwith Pike	648m	89-206142 NY	3.1
8	Iron Crag	640m	89-123119 NY	3.4
9	Pillar Rock	780m	89-174124 NY	3.3
10	Steeple	819m	89-157117 NY	3.2
11	Scoat Fell	841m	89-160114 NY	3.2
12	Black Crag	828m	89-166116 NY	3.2
13	Pillar	892m	89-171121 NY	3.2
14	Looking Stead	627m	89-186118 NY	3.2
15	Grey Knotts	697m	89-217126 NY	3.1
16	Brandreth	715m	89-215119 NY	3.1
17	Base Brown	646m	89-225115 NY	3.1
18	Green Gable	801m	89-215107 NY	3.1
19	Great Gable	899m	89-211103 NY	3.1
20	Kirk Fell East Top	787m	89-199107 NY	3.1
21	Kirk Fell	802m	89-195105 NY	3.1
22	Red Pike	826m	89-165106 NY	3.2
23	Caw Fell	690m	89-132109 NY	3.4
24	Little Gowder Crag	733m	89-140110 NY	3.4
25	Haycock	797m	89-145107 NY	3.4
26	Seatallan	693m	89-140084 NY	3.4
27	Yewbarrow North Top	616m	89-176092 NY	3.2
28	Yewbarrow	628m	89-173085 NY	3.2

WALK 3.1 GREAT GABLE

SUMMITS		
	Grey Knotts	2287 ft (697m)
	Brandreth	2346 ft (715m)
	Base Brown	2119 ft (646m)
	Green Gable	2628 ft (801m)
	Great Gable	2949 ft (899m)
	Kirk Fell East Top	2582 ft (787m)
	Kirk Fell	2631 ft (802m)
	Fleetwith Pike	2126 ft (648m)
DISTANCE	10 miles	
ASCENT	4800 feet	
MAPS	OS Landranger sheet 89 or 90	
	Outdoor Leisure - The English Lakes, North Western area	
STARTING POINT	(89-225136) The Youth Hostel at the summit of the Honister Pass, 7 miles south of Keswick. Large car park.	

Wainwright devotes twenty eight pages to Great Gable and with good reason. Of all the peaks in the Lake District this is among the very best and when seen from Wast Water, flanked by Yewbarrow and Sca Fell with the peaks mirrored in the lake catching the evening sunlight, Great Gable is the centre of one of the finest mountain views anywhere.

Despite its nearness to the Scafells, Great Gable is not overpowered by its neighbours, being set apart by steep almost unbroken slopes on all sides, with a drop to Sty Head of over 1300 feet. The characteristic outline against the sky is often a reference point from which the rest of the distant hills are identified, but the mountain which was known to Wordsworth as Great Gavel and affectionately nowadays often referred to simply as Gable is, according to experts, named simply and prosaically from its resemblance to the gable end of a house.

As Great Gable presents its most spectacular face to Wasdale, an ascent from Honister might be thought cheating, coming from the rear on the unguarded side, but there aren't really any routes which trivialise the mountain and the approach over Brandreth and Grey Knotts is a fitting apéritif to the main course.

The modern road over Honister from Seatoller, which provides a high level start to the walk, has only been built since the last war and before that a crossing by car was considered a sporting challenge. In thick fog at night, or

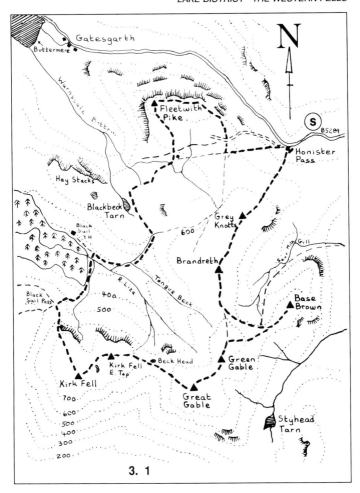

3. 1

in the middle of winter, it still is! The original route over the pass was a toll road, but when this was to be bought and modernised the owner demanded a price of £2000. As this was considered far too much, a new road was built, the old toll road remaining now as a pleasant track on the Borrowdale side well away from the traffic.

On the slopes of Fleetwith Pike and Dale Head opposite, the Honister slate quarries were worked from tunnels or caves excavated in the fells and more recently by opencast methods. These quarries with their attractive green slate have been worked continuously since 1643 and until 1870, when tramways were built, the slate was brought down from the face on sledges. As many as eight trips a day were made with loads of around a quarter of a ton, the quarryman running in front to steer the sledge. Each trip, with the momentum of the enormous load behind, must have been a hazardous undertaking, a controlled fall with no way of stopping once started. Loads of peat had from early times been brought down from the fells on sledges in this way. The lines of the old tramways can be very clearly seen on the slopes of Dale Head and on the southern side of the pass. The route of a tramway now serves as a path to the ruined drum house, which housed the winding gear. More recently lorries crawled up and down the new zigzag quarry road with huge blocks of stone for the cutting sheds, but now these are shuttered, the lorries gone and the quarry closed.

ROUTE DESCRIPTION

GREY KNOTTS *(Grey Rocky Hill)*
Behind the old slate trimming sheds of the Honister quarry a fence sets off steeply uphill towards Grey Knotts and this can be followed to within a few yards of the summit. It is a very steep climb and a bit rough, but is a quick way up onto the tops and the interest rapidly increases. Stay on the left of the fence until, after about 1000 ft of climbing, it turns left and starts to go downhill. Cross at the stile, carrying on for a few yards in the same direction and then a line of old iron fence posts leads rightwards up to a rocky tor on whose top is a cairn. The map shows the spot height on a tor 100 yards to the west, which has the better views. This has a smaller cairn and the Buttermere fells are well seen from here.

BRANDRETH *(Trivet)*
Return to the line of old fence posts and they lead easily in half a mile to the summit cairn of Brandreth which lies astride the path on the flat stony top.

BASE BROWN *(Bruna's Cowshed)*
Still following the fence posts descend to the little tarns south of Brandreth where although the fence has long since disappeared, a gate still remains. The view ahead is dominated by Great Gable, whose cliffs look formidable with Moses Trod traversing high on the mountain. This was reputedly named after a quarryman who distilled illicit whisky at his hut on Fleetwith Pike and took it this way to Wasdale hidden under loads of slate. At first sight it would appear necessary to ascend Green Gable, detour to Base Brown and then do the ascent of Green Gable all over again, but in fact an easy traverse of the north-eastern slopes of Green Gable is possible. Starting shortly after the col, pass above the first outcrop and then a gradually descending line should be

followed to cross the screes on a faint path passing below the buttress on the far side, to reach the col where the Sourmilk Gill path comes up. From here Base Brown is an easy ascent on grass. Having reached what appears to be the highest point, the true summit and its cairn is about 100 yards further across a dip, on a slight rise dotted with boulders.

GREEN GABLE
Returning to the col, join the parties from Seathwaite on a well trodden path. A stiff climb of 600 ft leads to the stony top whose cairn and wind shelter are overshadowed by Great Gable ahead.

GREAT GABLE
The descent southwards to Windy Gap is dominated by the bright red colour of the rather slippery screes. The climb which follows usually seems much less than the 500 ft it actually is because of the interest of the ascent on a rough but clear path which, despite the usual crowds, is most enjoyable. The summit in anything like good weather is usually full of people eating lunch, photographing each other, admiring the view or just resting. Despite its height and popularity Great Gable hasn't got an impressive cairn, just a few stones on the highest rocks of the bare stony top where a bronze plaque set into the rock is the Fell and Rock Climbing Club memorial where every year on Remembrance Sunday, members of the club hold a service. In the distance Skiddaw, Helvellyn and the Scafells are all in view while closer to hand is Kirk Fell with Pillar beyond. But the favourite and most cherished view is of Wast Water from the Westmorland Cairn, 150 yards to the south-west of the summit above Westmorland Crags and built by two brothers of that name in 1876.

KIRK FELL EAST TOP
A line of cairns on Gable summit heads north-west for Ennerdale and these give the route for the descent, scrambling down over boulders to the grassy col at Beck Head with its two shallow tarns. Pausing to rest during the ascent of Kirk Fell and looking back at Great Gable, it seems, although you have just come down that way, an impossibly steep ascent. After a steady climb of about 500 ft on a good path, the angle relents and an easy walk over grass, following the line of the old fenceposts, leads to the first top which is a rocky knoll with a small cairn.

KIRK FELL *(Church Fell)*
About a quarter of a mile to the south-west, across a grassy dip with two small tarns, is the true summit, the second and higher top, where the cairn has been fashioned into a wall shelter. South-west is Wast Water while westwards are the enticing peaks of the Mosedale Horseshoe.

FLEETWITH PIKE *(Wooded Stream Peak)*
Heading just west of north the descent to Black Sail Pass after an easy start is a bit intimidating, but not too difficult, although the path picks its way down

Fleetwith Pike

some very steep ground. At the pass turn right into the head of Ennerdale and follow the path beside Sail Beck down to cross the footbridge over the River Liza above the Black Sail Youth Hostel which was once a shepherd's hut. Turn right on a path which after a quarter of a mile crosses and then recrosses Tongue Beck to climb beside Loft Beck. The ascent is concentrated, but short and beside a pleasant stream. At the top, cross the obvious col with Hay Stacks, Wainwright's favourite mountain, in view ahead. Heather and grass slopes lead down to Blackbeck Tarn. Keep high above the tarn on its right and join a major path which meanders across the fell, heading north-east. In less than half a mile Warnscale Beck is reached below the climbing club hut in Dubs Quarry.

Fording the beck is usually easy, but some years ago it was so swollen by heavy rain that a crossing was only possible after our group had built an island of rocks. From the hut, an ascent trending left will bring you to an unmapped and recent path which leads up the south slopes of the ridge direct to the tall cairn on Fleetwith Pike. This is in a commanding position on the end of the rocky ridge with a steep drop to Buttermere. Looking back there is a panoramic view of nearly all the tops passed on the walk, only Base Brown being concealed from view.

A clear path follows the crest above Honister Pass with tiny toy-like cars over 1500 ft below. In half a mile the cairned path turns away from the edge and descends, crossing the new quarry road to join the Drum House path and so down to the Youth Hostel.

WALK 3.2 THE MOSEDALE HORSESHOE

SUMMITS	Looking Stead	2057 ft (627m)
	Pillar	2926 ft (892m)
	Black Crag	2717 ft (828m)
	Scoat Fell	2759 ft (841m)
	Steeple	2687 ft (819m)
	Red Pike	2710 ft (826m)
	Yewbarrow North Top	2021 ft (616m)
	Yewbarrow	2060 ft (628m)

DISTANCE	11 miles

ASCENT	4100 feet

MAPS   OS Landranger sheet 89
Outdoor Leisure - The English Lakes, South Western area
& The English Lakes, North Western area

STARTING
POINT   (89-187087) Wasdale Head. Car parking on open land
just before the hotel. Toilets.

As the reddening sun cast long shadows across Wast Water lighting The Screes with an orange glow, we came down the southern ridge of Yewbarrow. Climbing up was a man and a dog. The dog ran beside its master whose long easy strides belied the speed of his ascent and as the runner greeted us cheerily we recognised Joss Naylor whose long fellrunning exploits have spread his fame far beyond these Lakeland hills. Joss, for 13 years, held the record for the Lake District Round with 72 peaks over 2000 ft in 24 hours, covering 108 miles and climbing 40,000 ft, an incredible achievement. His dog appeared considerably more out of breath than him.

Although the Lake District has five Mosedales, the Mosedale Horseshoe is unique. Encircling the quiet valley of Mosedale Beck beyond Wasdale Head, mountain links to mountain in a succession of rough rugged summits with Pillar, Scoat Fell, the lovely summit of Steeple, Red Pike and Yewbarrow making one of the classic walks we never tire of repeating.

Wordsworth's Guide to the Lake District describes an aerial view of the valley *'Look down into, and along the deep valley of Wastdale, with its little chapel and half a dozen neat dwellings scattered upon a plain of meadow and corn-ground intersected with stone walls apparently innumerable, like a large piece of lawless patch-work.'* The tiny network of fields at Wasdale Head has been laboriously cleared of stones, so many that even after building the massive stone walls that separate the fields the remainder have been

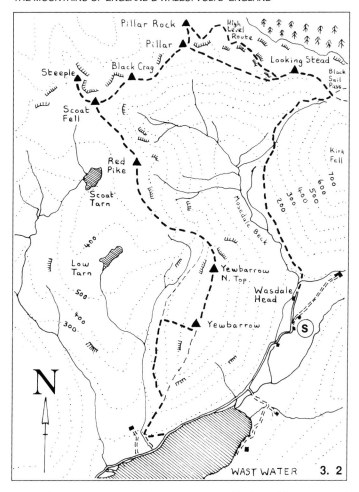

3. 2

gathered into great mounds. The clearance started in the twelfth century and concluded with the Enclosure Act in 1808.

ROUTE DESCRIPTION

LOOKING STEAD *(Looking Place)*

Walk up to the Wasdale Head Hotel and go between it and the small climbing shop (useful if you've just discovered you've left the map at home or forgotton your waterproofs). Row Head Bridge, on the line of the old road up the valley, crosses Mosedale Beck, but stay on the right side to follow the main stony path upstream to the foot of Kirk Fell and then up Mosedale. It is an attractive approach with the steep slopes of Yewbarrow on the left and the high mountains which ring the head of Mosedale drawing you on. The path climbs steadily swinging right to cross Gatherstone Beck at a ford which usually causes problems for the nervous and hesitant, gaining height in a not too exhausting way until Black Sail Pass summit is reached. Far below is the primitive Black Sail Youth Hostel at the head of conifer clad Ennerdale.

Turning left a clear path undulates along the grassy rim of Ennerdale. The first top of the day is no more than a quarter of a mile from the head of the pass and it is only a few minutes detour up grassy slopes to the cairn which surrounds an old iron fence post. Across the valley is the ridge of High Crag, High Stile and Red Pike, with Grasmoor and the North Western fells beyond, while on the flanks of Pillar Robinson's Cairn marks the High Level Route.

PILLAR

A steady climb on a clear rocky path makes the ensuing ascent of Pillar a rapid matter, very much quicker than the High Level Route, though not quite as attractive or entertaining. The summit is a large flat area with a stone trig point and a wind shelter at its centre. The distant views are extensive indeed. Northward Grasmoor is seen beyond the High Crag, Red Pike ridge, Robinson, Hindscarth and Dale Head are a foreground to distant Skiddaw and Blencathra, while Great Gable and the Scafells dominate the south-eastern horizon. Before leaving the summit however, walk across to the cairn on the edge of the northern slopes to look down on Pillar Rock rising massively above Ennerdale Forest.

BLACK CRAG

A line of cairns points the way to the stony path descending steeply south-west to Wind Gap and a short ascent leads to Black Crag. The summit is the first cairn reached, but the large cairn just beyond provides a good seat from which to take in the westward view of Scoat Fell and the impressive cone of Steeple with Ennerdale Water beyond.

SCOAT FELL *(Rocky Projection Fell)*

Descending gradually on grassy slopes with Mirk Cove to the north and Black Comb to the south, Scoat Fell is reached after a short ascent over boulders. The cairn, at least the one traditionally regarded as the top, sits on top of the wall, while a more recent addition stands beside it.

Pillar from High Crag

STEEPLE

Continue west along the wall for 200 yards to its corner where a cairned path leads out to the superbly situated peak of Steeple. A narrow ridge connects Steeple to the mass of Scoat Fell and although not at all difficult it sets Steeple apart as one of the very special mountains of the Lake District. There is a small cairn on the top which is quite superfluous there being no mistaking the summit which is small and surrounded on all sides by sheer drops. There are grand views of Ennerdale Water and back to Pillar.

RED PIKE *(Red Peak)*

Return along the arête and, passing to the right of Scoat Fell summit, head south-east down gentle slopes of grass and stones to the col where there is a useful spring. The ascent of Red Pike takes little effort, the rise being at most 250 ft, but stay near the edge as the path inexplicably bypasses the highest point, the second rocky top, where the cairn is poised on the very brink of the precipice into Mosedale.

YEWBARROW NORTH TOP

Mighty Yewbarrow, that splendid fell which so perfectly completes the ring of mountains at the head of Wast Water, is humbled from this vantage point and one expects to complete its ascent with barely a pause, but it is an illusion. Rejoining the path the descent to Dore Head seems to go on for a long time and with every downward step the stature of Yewbarrow increases until finally on arrival at the col the mountain has regained its eminence. For some walkers it is too much and, braving the vertiginous scree shoot, they descend into Mosedale omitting Yewbarrow entirely. The ascent however should not be missed. Apart from there being two summits still to attain, the climb itself is entertaining with a scramble up steep rocks to the summit. Several cairns on a handful of knolls vie for supremacy, but the true northern top of Yewbarrow is virtually unmarked, a knoll to the right of the path about 200 yards after the summit ridge is reached.

YEWBARROW *(Ewe Mountain)*
A pleasant stroll south along the grassy ridge brings you in half a mile to the southern and higher summit of Yewbarrow, a rocky knoll crowned with a cairn cum windshelter. Far below is Wast Water with that infamous pile of stones simply called The Screes which plunge into the lake from Whin Rigg and Ilgill Head.

The usual way off Yewbarrow is from the southern end of the ridge where a steep and badly eroded path descends westwards from Great Door. For a more pleasant route, walk south along the ridge for about 200 yards to the first dip where a mossy bilberry covered rake slants right through the crags to the hillside above Over Beck. A path is joined which leads to the wall stile below Bell Rib and then back to the road beside Wast Water, where you turn left to Wasdale Head.

WALK 3.3 PILLAR ROCK

SUMMITS	Pillar Rock	2560 ft (780m)
CAUTION	The ascent of Pillar Rock is a rock climb and although its grade is 'Moderate' it must only be tackled by experienced climbers or under their supervision.	
DISTANCE	8 miles	
ASCENT	2800 feet	
MAPS	OS Landranger sheet 89 Outdoor Leisure - The English Lakes, North Western area	
STARTING POINT	(89-187087) Wasdale Head. Car parking on open land just before the hotel. Toilets. N.B. The map for this route is the same as for walk 3.2.	

On the northern flank of Pillar overlooking the dense packed conifers of Ennerdale is a massive, magnificent tower of rock, rising some five hundred

Pillar Rock

feet from the hillside on its northern edge and cut off from Pillar by a vertical sided chasm above which the summit of the rock is tantalisingly out of reach.

The first ascent of all other mountains in both England and Wales goes back to pre-history, often with ancient cairns to long forgotton chieftains crowning their summits. Not so Pillar Rock. The simple fact is that even the easiest way up is a rock climb and until the nineteenth century no-one had done it.

We approached from Black Sail Pass along the High Level Route which undulates along the northern slopes of Pillar, after an exhausting ascent in scorching hot weather from Wasdale. Beside the narrow path grew Alpine

Lady's Mantle, Starry Saxifrage, Yellow Saxifrage, Roseroot and Golden Rod, but on this occasion we barely paused to look at the alpine flora; our eyes were seeking Robinson's Cairn and Pillar Rock beyond. The cairn, marking one of the best viewpoints in the Lakes, was built in memory of John Wilson Robinson, who discovered the High Level Route and it is a good spot to pause and consider the details of the giant rockface across the combe. The buttress nearest the mountain is Pisgah which is separated from High Man, the highest part of Pillar Rock, by Jordan Gap, the vertical slot in the skyline. The Rock then slopes down to the lower peak of Low Man before taking the final plunge to the valley. On the far side and out of sight is the Old West Route by which John Atkinson, an Ennerdale shepherd, on July 9th 1826 first gained the summit. In 1870, a woman, Miss A Barker, made the ascent and soon the rock was yielding routes to the tigers of the day.

We scrambled down the scree to below Jordan Gap, dumped our rucksacs and unpacked the rope. Anne looked up at the rock rising vertically overhead. "Isn't there an easier way?" she asked

again. It was a rhetorical question; the guide-book was quite clear on the point. '*Slab and Notch is one of the easiest routes*' it said. Wainwright was equally clear and emphatic - '*Pillar Rock is positively out of bounds*'. We roped up.

The ascent went easily enough although as Anne said we did spend most of the time tying ourselves on to bits of rock. "Beautiful isn't it?" a young man with a rucksac remarked as he scrambled past unroped. He was right. Poised between earth and sky, surrounded by steep clean rock, the sun beating down from a blue sky; it was a thoroughly magnificent way to spend a morning. Finally Anne led through to unrope on the grassy top. We had arrived. There was the cairn, the man with the rucksac and a couple festooned with dozens of multi-coloured slings

Anne on the ascent of Pillar Rock

and ropes. They too were pleased. They had just come up the west face, one of the hard climbs.

Descent proved easier than expected. Gravity is there to assist and surprisingly one remembers where the holds are. Down the staircase, round the corner. Down the next staircase to the notch. The slab and final crack and it's all over. Pillar Rock had been climbed. We had ticked off our last summit. Rope packed away we stopped to look back. A sudden thought. "Let's do the New West next time, it starts down at the bottom so we'd have done it properly". "No. I've had enough. I'm not a rock climber". For the moment it is enough to look, the rock has not changed, but somehow this is a beginning not an end.

ROUTE DESCRIPTION

PILLAR ROCK

While climbers may well choose to add this ascent to walk 3.2, for most walkers Pillar Rock itself will be enough for one day. In any event the route as far as the top of Black Sail Pass is the same, but instead of ascending Pillar the approach to Pillar Rock is via the High Level Route. This lovely path turns off at a cairn just after the col beyond Looking Steads and then winds its way across the northern side of Pillar mountain to Robinson's Cairn.

Continue on the path across the Shamrock Traverse which crosses a rock slab high above Pillar Cove, to reach Pillar Rock where it adjoins the mountainside. The start of the climb is beyond Jordan Gap, about level with this point, but a little way out on the Rock and it is necessary to descend a little and scramble across. The point to aim for is a ledge about 8ft below a sloping slab. Above the slab is a vertical crack which leads up to a notch.

SLAB AND NOTCH CLIMB 125ft MODERATE

1. Climb the 8 ft wall and cross the sloping slab to belay at the foot of the vertical crack.
2. Climb the vertical crack and belay on a ledge at its top (the Notch).
3. Go right along a ledge and up a staircase of good holds to another ledge. Belay.
4. Go right, round the corner, up more good holds and into a gully above the Great Chimney which leads easily to the top of the Rock where the summit cairn is to the left.

The grassy summit, which seems quite spacious with little sense of exposure, gives long views down Ennerdale.

Return the same way or abseil down the short side of the Rock. The walk can be extended to the top of Pillar by climbing south-west up a good path from Pisgah. This gives ample opportunity for retrospective views of the climb and nicely rounds off the day with a descent by the east ridge to Black Sail Pass.

WALK 3.4 SEATALLAN & CAW FELL

SUMMITS	Seatallan	2274 ft (693m)
	Haycock	2615 ft (797m)
	Little Gowder Crag	2405 ft (733m)
	Caw Fell	2264 ft (690m)
	Iron Crag	2100 ft (640m)

DISTANCE   11½ miles

ASCENT   3800 feet

MAPS   OS Landranger sheet 89
Outdoor Leisure - The English Lakes, South Western area
& The English Lakes, North Western area

STARTING
POINT   (89-144056) Greendale, 1 mile north of the southern end
of Wast Water. Parking on the grass verge.

Beyond Pillar, Scoat Fell and Steeple the fells continue westwards, still rough and rugged, but gradually petering out in deserted grassy hills where the sheep look up nervously, unaccustomed to human figures in the landscape. On a spur overlooking Ennerdale and a little separated from the rest of the fells is Iron Crag which when it does see anyone, is crossed by walkers bound for Haycock rather than visited for itself. Seatallan is the real solitary though. There are few Lakeland fells devoid of paths, but Seatallan still remains unmarked despite the delightful approach up Greendale Gill where the valley is loud with the sounds of water as becks tumble down in narrow ravines to join the gill.

To the west of Seatallan the River Bleng meanders slowly down towards the forest, gathering its waters in the swamps of the long, remote and deserted valley of Blengdale. Although once a drove road followed this valley, there is very little sign of it now, only a cleared passage through the scree marks where the herds passed and there are no signs that man was ever other than a transitory visitor. Yet on Stockdale Moor which rises just a thousand feet above the Blengdale Forest there is more evidence of the ancient past than practically anywhere else in the Lake District. On this lonely moor are hundreds of cairns and the remains of Bronze Age settlements in walled enclosures, hut circles and the traces of extensive field systems. Sampson's Bratfull is a prehistoric, probably neolithic, burial mound 96ft long and 6ft high, whose stones, so the legend says, fell from the devil's apron (brat means apron in Old Welsh). The once wooded slopes were probably cleared by prehistoric man and although the Forestry Commision have put a few trees

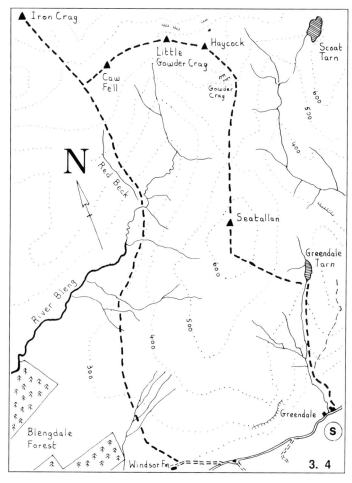

back they are the ubiquitous conifers. The whole area lies within the medieval Copeland Forest, meaning the bought land; a deer preserve, a vast area which stretched from the Irish Sea to Eskdale and Ennerdale. Gradual encroachment during the sixteenth century established the small farms and while hunting the red deer continued in Ennerdale, the statesmen farmers concentrated on the sheep.

ROUTE DESCRIPTION

SEATALLAN *(Aleyn's Upland Pasture)*
Take the grassy path that climbs through the bracken to the east of Greendale Gill past the splendid falls in the ravines of Tongues Gills. Ignoring the right fork to Middle Fell, stay beside the stream all the way to Greendale Tarn which is not as Wainwright says *'unattractive'* and even on a dank, misty day, managed to look most picturesque. Crossing the gill by the tarn outflow at some convenient stepping stones head north-west up the boulder strewn pathless slopes, avoiding the rocky outcrops, to gain the grassy ridge where the angle eases for the final half mile. The flattish summit has a huge hollowed out ancient cairn beside the OS stone trig point, but the small cairn to the north-east is 3ft higher. However we must agree with AW when he says that *'As a viewpoint Seatallan does not rank highly.'* as on all our visits the top has been shrouded in mist and the visibility down to a few feet.

HAYCOCK *(High Hillock)*
Descend north-east down a grassy rib, then if you can see Haycock make straight for it. A faint path crosses the col to lose itself in the rocks of Gowder Crag which can easily be climbed on its eastern side to a prominent cairn. From here it is a short stroll over grass to the wall which crosses the highest point with a cairn on either side. The one to the north forms a windshelter, but the cairn to the south is marginally higher. On a good clear day the Scafells can be seen to the south-east, Helvellyn to the east and Skiddaw to the north-east.

LITTLE GOWDER CRAG *(Little Echoing Crag)*
Follow the wall westwards to cross the next top. At first it is rather stony underfoot, but after descending for barely a quarter of a mile there is a short climb of only 55ft to the unmarked summit. On our last visit the mist suddenly lifted for a moment and we were treated to silvery views of the Irish Sea at the end of Blengdale with the less welcome silhouette of the towers and turrets of Sellafield.

CAW FELL *(Calf Fell)*
Continue beside the guiding wall which descends a rocky staircase before setting off to the rounded grassy slopes of Caw Fell. A fine pink cairn to the north of the wall marks the highest point from which there are extensive views across Ennerdale to the High Stile ridge and beyond to the Grasmoor Fells.

IRON CRAG
The wall marches on, first westwards then after a right-angled bend, north to dip and then climb again to the long ridge of Iron Crag. The cairn, another pink one, is to the east of the wall.

Returning to the right-angled wall corner west of Caw Fell summit, continue in the same direction descending south over grassy slopes to Red

Beck. Keep to the left of the beck on a grassy strip down into Blengdale, a forgotten, empty and extremely boggy valley. After choosing a swamp free spot and fording the shallow river, join the old bridleway of which only faint traces remain. Sheep having a good race memory continue to tread the path of their ancestors and following their trods the route climbs gradually, veering away from the river and keeping well above the bogs. A cleared section through the screes confirms the route which finally descends equally gradually to the left of Blengdale Forest. Keep above the wall then follow it down to join the path which slants down to join the track to Windsor Farm, which was once a Youth Hostel. It is then only a short way down to the road for the last mile back to Greendale.

Wasdale farmhouse

WALK 3.5 RED PIKE, BUTTERMERE

SUMMITS		
	High Crag	2441 ft (744m)
	High Stile	2648 ft (807m)
	Red Pike	2477 ft (755m)
	Dodd	2103 ft (641m)
DISTANCE	7 miles	
ASCENT	2650 feet	
MAPS	OS Landranger sheet 89	
	Outdoor Leisure - The English Lakes, North Western area	
STARTING POINT	(89-196150) Gatesgarth farm at the south-east end of Buttermere. Plentiful car parking.	

Between Buttermere and the head of Ennerdale is the short but rocky ridge of High Crag, High Stile and Red Pike. The southern mainly grassy slopes of the ridge fall steeply to the Ennerdale Forest and provide little incentive to overcome their difficulties, but to the north is the best side where an almost continuous wall of crags drops towards Buttermere. Ascending via Scarth Gap, the first section of the ridge is rough and craggy, composed of the Borrowdale Volcanics, but at Red Pike, whose rocks are pink granophyre, the character changes to more rounded shapes leading to the grassy unfrequented tops above the Floutern Pass.

The ridge itself is only a little over a mile and a half in length, but to hurry would be to miss some of the best; better to linger over lunch and take in the views, especially of the steep crags around the head of Burtness Comb tucked between High Crag and High Stile, the highest summit of the ridge. The comb has been known to generations of rock climbers as Birkness Comb, and the variation in pronunciation and spelling has stuck despite the best efforts of the Ordnance Survey to correct everyone. To the north across Buttermere lie Robinson, Hindscarth and Dale Head, but not seen at their best from this angle as they tend to merge to form an undulating and rather undistinguished skyline, while to the south and east the view is of more challenging summits, the Scafells, Gable and Pillar. Unlike many ridge walks where the return is problematical, the descent from Red Pike is followed by a delightful stroll beside the wooded shores of the lake and perhaps if the weather is warm enough a final swim to end the day.

The picturesque village of Buttermere is very small, composed of little more than two pubs, a Youth Hostel and a church built in 1840. Here at one of the pubs lived Mary Robinson, the 'Beauty of Buttermere'. Immortalised by

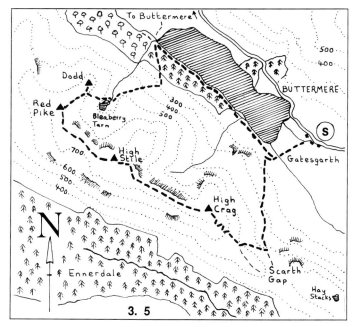

3. 5

the Lake poets who were fascinated by the story, De Quincy, Wordsworth, Coleridge and Southey all wrote about her as more recently did Melvyn Bragg in 'The Maid of Buttermere'. In 1802 Mary was courted and married by a bigamist who called himself the 'Honourable Augustus Hope'. This was not his only crime however and the following year he was arrested for Post Office forgeries, tried and sent to the gallows in Carlisle. Happily Mary later married a farmer at Caldbeck and had a large family.

ROUTE DESCRIPTION

HIGH CRAG

The fields behind Gatesgarth farm, which featured in the BBC programme 'One man and his dog', are crossed by a public bridleway signed 'Buttermere and Ennerdale'. Go straight across the fields to another signpost and take the left fork signed 'Ennerdale via Scarth Gap'. This recently repaired path climbs steeply, turning left to join another path coming up from the lake. At one time this area was badly eroded, but much excellent footpath restoration work has been done and trees have been planted to hide the scars. The path climbs very steeply and the angle then eases to pass High Wax Knott. To avoid the screes on Seat, leave the bridleway to follow the wall which crosses the path steeply uphill. When the wall turns sharp right, follow the ruined wall up to the col by Gamlin End, where Pillar and Gable appear ahead. Turn right and, keeping to the left side of the ridge, follow the fair path which zigzags up the screes to the top, a magnificent viewpoint. The summit is a flat grassy top with two cairns about 10 yards apart. Ornamented with fence posts they are of equal height.

HIGH STILE *(High Steep Ridge Path)*
An easy walk along a broad ridge beside a line of old fence posts, with to the right precipitous views of Buttermere far below, leads to the next top. Leave the fence near the summit and head over right on the flat stony top to point 807m, the second cairn out on the promontory. This is, according to the Ordnance Survey, one metre higher than the more westerly cairn which is about 250 yards away, though the latter is the better viewpoint and also is recognised by most people as the summit.

RED PIKE *(Red Peak)*
Descend now to the left for an easy walk on grass, or trend more to the right for a scramble down, taking care not to get too close to the cliffs. The fence again acts as a guide over the broad grassy col with Bleaberry Tarn far below in the glacial combe. The fence continues nearly to the summit which really is red, with a large red cairn on the highest point which has recently been refashioned to form a windshelter. From here you can admire the full length of Crummock Water and much of Buttermere.

Red Pike from High Stile

DODD *(Bare Round Hill)*
The initial part of the descent towards Bleaberry Tarn is on a badly eroded scree path, but soon it can be left for the grass slopes leading to the col with an easy climb of only 65 ft to the summit of Dodd. The top is covered with short grass and reddish-pink boulders with a matching cairn. It is very quiet here after the three popular ridge tops, with no signs of erosion, or those horrid bits of litter that people stuff into cairns. It is a pleasant place to spend some time before finishing the walk and has good views back to Chapel Crags.

Return towards the col, then cut down over short grass and heather for an easy descent to join the main path to Bleaberry Tarn. The tarn is a quiet spot, as it is a long haul up from Buttermere to here. Follow Sourmilk Gill down from the tarn till the path turns right and descends gradually to the east. Suddenly, where the path turns north steeply downhill, you meet a brand new repaired way, a masterpiece of crazy paving and stone walling. For some inexplicable reason walking down this is very hard work. It seems a long, long way down and when the shore of Buttermere is finally reached it is gained with some relief. In preference to the right of way through Burtness Wood, take the delightful permissive path beside the lake, first through newly replanted woodland and then over the open fellside to the Gatesgarth fields.

WALK 3.6 GREAT BORNE AND STARLING DODD

SUMMITS	Great Borne	2021 ft (616m)
	Starling Dodd	2077 ft (633m)
DISTANCE	7 miles	
ASCENT	2050 feet	
MAPS	OS Landranger sheet 89	
	Outdoor Leisure - The English Lakes, North Western area	
STARTING POINT	(89-110154) Bowness Knott on the north shore of Ennerdale Water. Large free Forestry Commission car park, toilets.	

Starling Dodd and Great Borne lie beyond Red Pike at the western end of the long high ridge which divides Buttermere from Ennerdale, but while the eastern summits of the ridge are probably the most popular mountain walk from Buttermere, these two tops are usually ignored and quite deserted. The approach from Buttermere is long, and as much of the way is through bogs defending the Floutern Pass, there is little enough reason to visit them, with

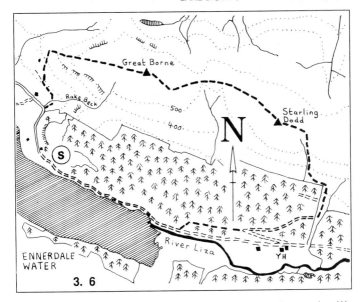

3. 6

Scale Force, reputedly the highest in the Lake District, the only attraction. We came this way once on a backpacking expedition, finally abandoning our seemingly never ending soggy trudge to Floutern Tarn by climbing out of the pass up the steep slopes to gain the ridge. Despite the boggy ground it was a very dry summer and the little spring on the slopes of Starling Dodd was the only source of fresh water on this scorching day until we reached Scarth Gap.

Conditions were very different the Easter we were writing this book. After several frustrating days of bad weather and determined to get at least one walk done we set out to climb Great Borne from the Ennerdale side. This is by far the best approach and the theory was that it would be sheltered. It was windy, misty and drizzling, but the ground underfoot was firm and dry, the weather didn't seem too bad and had it been clear the views indeed would have been magnificent along the ridge. As we neared the summit of Great Borne the strength of the wind became apparent, but wanting to press on before the weather worsened we staggered along the ridge into the teeth of a gale. The final few feet to the cairn on Starling Dodd were finally reached on hands and knees and the descent to Dodsgill Beck required a great effort simply to walk downhill, yet soon we were again relatively sheltered and it was hard to believe how bad the conditions were on the tops.

The lower slopes of Ennerdale for over five miles are covered in dense conifers which defend the ridges from both tourists and walkers and there are very few ways through. However the road stops half way down the lake and cars are barred from the forest track beyond, so the dale is secluded and little visited when compared with more popular beauty spots in the Lake District. A proposition in 1884 to build a railway through the valley was defeated and more recently attempts have been made to extend the lake by both the North West Water Authority and British Nuclear Fuels, but fortunately the proposals were turned down in 1980, though in anticipation of success the famous Angler's Hotel at the foot of the lake was demolished and rebuilt on higher ground. There are two Youth Hostels in Ennerdale and a Field Centre and much of the unplanted land is let to the National Trust.

Tree planting began in Ennerdale in 1926 and was gradually extended until 1950 since when no further encroachment on the fellside has been allowed. It is of course a working forest and is constantly changing. The first felling took place in 1979 and the hard edges to the plantations have recently been softened in an attempt to landscape the dale which hopefully will be successful. Visitors are now encouraged and several trails and walks have been laid out; there are picnic areas and a car park. The Nine Becks Walk, some 10 miles of waymarked paths through the woods, makes a pleasant alternative to the high fells on a windy or wet day. The River Liza is reputed to be exceptionally pure and clean and the two and a half mile lake, which supplies Whitehaven with water and is popular with fishermen, has brown trout, salmon and char.

ROUTE DESCRIPTION

GREAT BORNE *(Great Stream)*

From the car park walk back down the road for 500 yards, skirting Bowness Knott which, unlike the main ridge whose rocks are pink granophyre, is composed of Skiddaw Slate. Just after the corner of the wood, climb a hurdle on the right beside the National Trust sign and follow the path up Rake Beck for a short way. Fording the beck follow the wall up to join a broad grassy track which climbs north-west gently through the bracken. Almost immediately turn right up a narrower grassy path and climb steeply until it meets a fence and the end of the ridge. Here the path turns right and heads uphill soon becoming indistinct. Continue to climb up the steep moss covered hillside until the ground suddenly eases at a cairn. The path over the tussocky moor beyond is unclear but aim east for the summit of Great Borne, joining a fence which passes between its twin summits. The bouldery top to the north of the fence sports a fine cairn, but the highest point is to the south and is marked by a stone OS trig column. There is a good windshelter on this rough and stony summit with extensive views of the North Western fells and over the Ennerdale valley.

STARLING DODD *(Aleyn's Steep Path Round Hill)*

Following the south side of the fence, navigation to the next top is simple as a clear path, at first following the fence, leads east for 1½ miles directly to the summit cairn. A spring is passed on the final slopes after which the path steepens to climb the grassy cone. The cairn is liberally decorated with the remnants of the old fence posts which once marched along this ridge. Red Pike stands just over a mile away to the east while to the west is a fine view of Ennerdale Water.

Continue east along the ridge to the col before Little Dodd. At the lowest point turn south and follow a bit of a path down Dodsgill Beck to the gentle bracken covered slopes above the Ennerdale Forest. Trending left along sheep trods to the wide break in the trees by Gillflinter Beck the right of way from Red Pike is joined. After crossing a stile turn right over another stile into the forest and follow the waymarked Nine Becks Walk for 2 miles, first high above the River Liza on a forest road and then down through an old oakwood to the shore of Ennerdale Water and back to Bowness Knott.

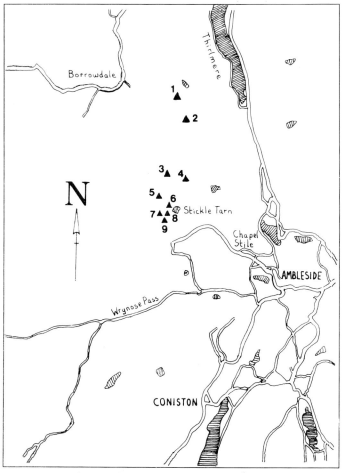

4 LAKE DISTRICT - THE CENTRAL FELLS

CHAPTER 4 LAKE DISTRICT - THE CENTRAL FELLS

TOP	NAME	HEIGHT	GRID REF	WALK No.
1	Low Saddle	656m	89-288133 NY	4.2
2	Ullscarf	726m	89-292122 NY	4.2
3	High Raise	762m	89-281095 NY	4.1
4	Codale Head	730m	89-289091 NY	4.1
5	Thunacar Knott	723m	89-279080 NY	4.1
6	Pavey Ark	700m	89-285079 NY	4.1
7	Pike of Stickle	709m	89-274074 NY	4.1
8	Harrison Stickle	736m	89-282074 NY	4.1
9	Loft Crag	670m	89-277071 NY	4.1

The Langdale Pikes from Elterwater

WALK 4.1 THE LANGDALE PIKES

SUMMITS		
	Codale Head	2395 ft (730m)
	High Raise	2500 ft (762m)
	Thunacar Knott	2372 ft (723m)
	Pavey Ark	2297 ft (700m)
	Harrison Stickle	2415 ft (736m)
	Pike of Stickle	2362 ft (709m)
	Loft Crag	2198 ft (670m)

DISTANCE	7 miles
ASCENT	3020 feet
MAPS	OS Landranger sheet 89 or 90 Outdoor Leisure - The English Lakes, South Western area
STARTING POINT	(89-294063) New Dungeon Ghyll Hotel, Great Langdale, 5 miles west of Ambleside. Free car park, toilets.

The outline of the Langdale Pikes must be the best known and certainly the most easily identified mountain skyline in Britain. That view, when seen from afar, is like the signature of the Lake District on the skyline, the instantly recognised familiar scrawl of an old friend. Great Langdale is probably the most popular of the Lakeland valleys, but thank God (or the Planning Board!) it has not been 'improved', the road is as narrow as ever, twisting and turning its way up the valley between uncompromisingly solid stone walls and the National Trust, in whose care much of the valley rests, have kept faith with the spirit of the hills. The Langdale Timeshare built on the derelict site of the old gunpowder works is one of the better such developments and fits discretely into the valley. The gunpowder factory was started in 1824 and Stickle Tarn, below Pavey Ark was enlarged to provide water power; the dam still remains, repaired by the National Park in 1959, even though the works closed about 1918.

Until recently the ascent beside Stickle Ghyll to Stickle Tarn was a weary toil over rivers of scree produced by tens of thousands of tramping feet, but the newly laid stone path is already beginning to blend in and now the waterfalls can be enjoyed while gaining height without having to watch every step. We first climbed this path while on honeymoon, then 25 years later, almost to the day found us toiling up again, this time laden with backpacking gear for a weekend surveying the minor humps and bumps of the Langdale Pikes and the Scafell range. Older but fitter than on our first visit we remembered holidays spent at the Old Dungeon Ghyll Hotel in the days of Sid

The Langdale Pikes from Blea Tarn

Cross. Full board in 1968 was 14 guineas a week, and our walking day was always cut short in order to get back in time for a sumptuous afternoon tea.

ROUTE DESCRIPTION

CODALE HEAD

A gate from the car park beside the hotel signed 'Stickle Ghyll' leads to the main highway to the Langdale Pikes. The path crosses the gill at a stout footbridge and then climbs steadily to Stickle Tarn. Turn right along the eastern shore and then follow Bright Beck for a short way before leaving it to head north up a tributary stream beside which a faint cairned path makes directly towards the cone of Sergeant Man. This path stops abruptly on reaching a narrow trod which contours the slope, but a short ascent right-wards brings you to the clear main path coming up from Grasmere which leads to Sergeant Man. This prominent top does not qualify as a separate summit despite its striking appearance as there is much less than 50ft of ascent to it from High Raise, but surprisingly only a short distance east there

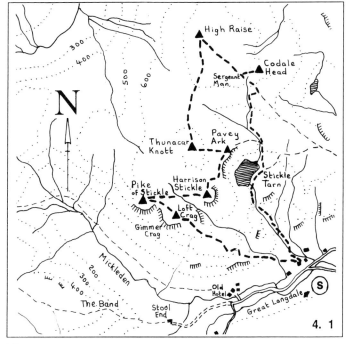

is one which does. Just before the path dips to Sergeant Man and across a mossy hollow to the right with some tiny tarns, rises Codale Head, an ascent of 53ft. On the summit of grass and rocks there is a jumbled cairn from which there is a good panorama in all directions except to the north-west where High Raise blocks the view.

HIGH RAISE *(High Cairn)*
Disappointment at missing Sergeant Man is short lived as the simplest route to High Raise is to return to the main path which passes almost over its top. There is a clear path which climbs gently north-west to reach the trig point in under a mile of easy going. There is also a cairn cum wind shelter on the summit which is also known as High White Stones. There are good prospects in all directions too with Skiddaw in view away to the north, the Scafells to the south-west and Helvellyn in the north-east. A pleasant few minutes can be spent on a clear day identifying all the other summits in sight. Being able to name them all, better still having climbed them all, is very satisfying.

THUNACAR KNOTT
A mile to the south of High Raise and centred between the shapely and prominent summits of Harrison Stickle and Pike of Stickle on the skyline, Thunacar Knott is, even on a clear day, easily overlooked. There is a good path leading to it which is usually left just before the summit is reached in order to visit a prominent cairn. From this point the true summit and its smaller cairn will be seen a hundred yards or so beyond the pretender on the far side of a small tarn.

PAVEY ARK *(Pavia's Mountain Hut)*
Only a quarter of a mile east across a dip, rises the rocky summit of Pavey Ark, just scraping mountain status. It is a shame really to approach from the rear, far better to ascend by way of Jack's Rake when the full glory of the east face is up against one's nose. No cairn adorns the rocky summit and you can sit almost on the edge with the precipice beneath your feet and enjoy the downward view to Stickle Tarn.

HARRISON STICKLE *(Harrison's Steep Place)*
A rough path skirts the edge and leads round to Harrison Stickle, the highest of the Langdale Pikes. The summit is a platform of bare rock with several small cairns, while to the east and south steep, though broken, rocky cliffs fall towards Langdale.

PIKE OF STICKLE *(Steep Peak)*
This cone shaped rocky mountain gives the Langdale Pikes its unique and easily identifiable outline. Descend a rocky staircase from Harrison Stickle and cross the grassy Harrison Combe to pick one of several lines which give an enjoyable scramble to this shapely summit. Though the top can never be in doubt, a large cairn has been built. In 1947 the site of a Neolithic stone axe

factory was discovered nearby. The greenish grey hard volcanic rock was shaped like flints into axe heads, sent to Ravenglass and exported. These axe heads have been found as far away as Poland.

LOFT CRAG *(High Crag)*

This summit is well seen from Pike of Stickle. After scrambling down, follow the rocky ridge south-east to the highest of the bumps overlooking Langdale where a cairn of a few stones marks the top. This final Langdale Pike, although given a separate name, is in fact the summit of Gimmer Crag, Langdale's most famous climbing cliff.

Descend the path turning left to the foot of the rocks and from a cairn the descent into Langdale continues south-east at first over loose scree, but the path soon improves and leads gently down with excellent views into the valley. Dungeon Ghyll lies to the left and lower down the path approaches the ravines within which lie spectacular waterfalls. Dungeon Ghyll Force will be seen at its best by scrambling down a few steps into the bed of the stream a little below the fall. Shortly the main valley path is reached, turn left and the New Dungeon Ghyll Hotel is only a little further.

Middle Fell Farm

WALK 4.2 ULLSCARF

SUMMITS	Ullscarf	2382 ft (726m)
	Low Saddle	2152 ft (656m)
DISTANCE	7½ miles	
ASCENT	1650 feet	
MAPS	OS Landranger sheet 89 or 90	
	Outdoor Leisure - The English Lakes, North Western area	
STARTING POINT	(89-276164) The hamlet of Watendlath in Borrowdale 5 miles south of Keswick. Free Car Park	

The most central fell in the Lake District, yet one of the least well known, Ullscarf was one of our last major summits. Rather put off by Wainwright's description *'featureless and inexpressibly dreary'* and the top *'the dullest imaginable',* we left it unvisited for many years. However our first ascent, on a stormy day from Thirlmere through the pine forest to gain the ridge, turned out to be far from dreary and a most enjoyable easy expedition. One sunny Easter we were rewarded with an enchanting half hour spent watching a large herd of deer, descendants of the Martindale herd, just north of Ullscarf, while our last visit, to check Low Saddle in the grey half light of a winter afternoon with the snow falling, showed the mountain again in a new way. Perhaps Wainwright chose a bad day!

The beautiful hamlet of Watendlath (meaning head of the lake) from which this walk begins is the setting for 'Judith Parish' by Hugh Walpole.

'Watendlath was an exceedingly remote little valley lying among the higher hills above Borrowdale. It could indeed be scarcely named a valley: rather it was a narrow strip of meadow and stream lying between the wooded hills, Armboth on the Grasmere side and King's How and Brund Fell on the other. It was utterly remote, with some twenty dwellings, a dark tarn and Watendlath Beck that ran down the strath until it tumbled over the hill at Lodore.'

Fold Head Farm was the fictional home of Judith Paris in the second novel of the four volume Herries family saga which spans the eighteenth century to the 1930's. Walpole settled in the Lake District which he loved and made his home beside Derwent Water on the slopes of Cat Bells. At one time the Watendlath cottages were liberally sprinkled with notices proclaiming 'The Home of Judith Paris', 'Rogue Herries Tea Room' etc. One suspects the hand of the National Trust behind their removal.

It must be said that despite its attractions the fell is very boggy and the

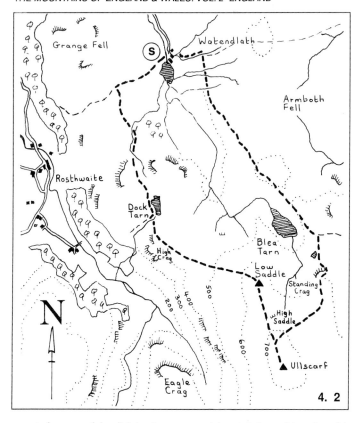

4. 2

secret of a succesful walk is to choose a good dry spell, if possible a drought, and then wet feet won't detract from your appreciation. We make no apologies for the return by Dock Tarn as it is purely a sentimental self indulgence. This was one of our favourite spots when we had young children and it took all day to walk from Stonethwaite to Watendlath. Recently the paths seem to be getting more eroded and a fire has done damage it will take time to repair, but Dock Tarn is still one of Lakeland's most attractive tarns, especially when the heather is in bloom.

ROUTE DESCRIPTION

ULLSCARF *(Wolf Pass)*
Take the newly restored old packhorse way signed 'Wythburn' that zigzags east uphill above the hamlet of Watendlath. At the top of the steep slope cross a small stream and turn right above the wall signed 'Wythburn and Blea Tarn'. The path, which is at first well cairned, heads south-east, away from the wall, climbing gradually for about a mile to a major cairn overlooking Blea Tarn. In wet weather the path is boggy and the next section is worse. Carry on in the same direction, passing an old guide post, to find the driest line somewhere between the tarn and the edge of the new fence which runs along the top. Aiming for the col to the left of Standing Crag, cross the fence at a kissing gate, then follow it south, climbing round Standing Crag to the left. Regaining the fence above the crag, it runs south-west for about half a mile, climbing gently over grass and rocks to a high point where it bends sharp right and sets off downhill. From here it is a short stroll south following the line of an old fence to the summit cairn which is decorated with a few fence posts. This is a grassy top with a few small rocky outcrops and wide views in all directions of the higher surrounding fells.

LOW SADDLE
Retrace your steps to the fence corner, cross a stile and follow the fence north. When it bends away, continue north over grassy Coldbarrow Fell, passing the neat top of High Saddle before descending to the col and then climbing up to the summit of Low Saddle. The reason for the names Low and High Saddle is very apparent when the fell is viewed from Glaramara, when it will be seen that these two high points are separated by a saddle shaped depression. The craggy little hill, worthy of a grander name, with steep rocks on its northern side, is crowned with a cairn and you look across to Eagle Crag with High Raise behind. Further west is Glaramara, eastwards lies the Helvellyn Range, while to the north is Watendlath with Derwent Water and Bassenthwaite Lake beyond.

For the quickest return to Watendlath, descend to the north end of Blea Tarn and retrace your steps. A more interesting route is to return by Dock Tarn which can be glimpsed to the north-west. To avoid scrambling over crags, leave Low Saddle by the back door heading back towards the col and then descend easily to the west of the summit, over grass and between rough boulders to the boggy plateau. Cross this, aiming for the little grassy pass to the right of High Crag which abuts the wall, and then descend to join the main path on the west side of Dock Tarn. Follow the path north past the tarn and descend to a kissing gate. Taking the left fainter but slightly drier path, cross another boggy section with the sweet smell of bog myrtle to a second kissing gate, then contour along a welcome dry grassy stretch to join the Rosthwaite path at its highest point. From here it is a short descent to Watendlath with the classic view of the hamlet spread out picturesquely below.

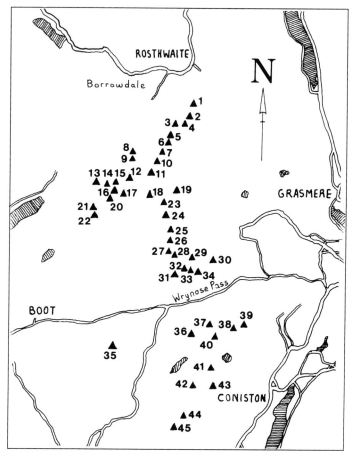

5 LAKE DISTRICT - THE SOUTHERN FELLS

CHAPTER 5 LAKE DISTRICT - THE SOUTHERN FELLS

TOP	NAME	HEIGHT	GRID REF	WALK No.
1	Rosthwaite Fell	612m	89-256118 NY	5.4
2	Dovenest Top	632m	89-256114 NY	5.4
3	Combe Head	735m	89-250109 NY	5.4
4	Combe Door Top	676m	89-253109 NY	5.4
5	Glaramara	783m	89-246105 NY	5.4
6	Looking Steads	775m	89-246102 NY	5.4
7	Red Beck Top	721m	89-243097 NY	5.4
8	Seathwaite Fell	632m	89-227097 NY	5.4
9	Seathwaite Fell South Top	631m	89-228094 NY	5.4
10	High House Tarn Top	684m	89-240092 NY	5.4
11	Allen Crags	785m	89-237085 NY	5.4
12	Great End	910m	89-227084 NY	5.1
13	Lingmell	800m	89-209082 NY	5.1
14	Middleboot Knotts	703m	89-214081 NY	5.1
15	Round How	741m	89-219081 NY	5.1
16	Broad Crag	934m	89-219075 NY	5.1
17	Ill Crag	935m	89-223073 NY	5.1
18	Esk Pike	885m	89-237075 NY	5.2
19	Rossett Pike	651m	89-249076 NY	5:2
20	Scafell Pike	978m	89-215072 NY	5.1
21	Symonds Knott	959m	89-208068 NY	5.1
22	Sca Fell	964m	89-207065 NY	5.1
23	Bowfell North Top	866m	89-245070 NY	5.2
24	Bowfell	902m	89-245064 NY	5.2
25	Shelter Crags North Top	775m	89-249057 NY	5.3
26	Shelter Crags	815m	89-250053 NY	5.3
27	Crinkle Crags	859m	89-249049 NY	5.3
28	Crinkle Crags South Top	834m	89-250046 NY	5.3
29	Great Knott	696m	89-260043 NY	5.3
30	Pike of Blisco	705m	89-271042 NY	5.3

TOP	NAME	HEIGHT	GRID REF	WALK No.
31	Little Stand	740m	89-250034 NY	5.3
32	Cold Pike Far West Top	670m	89-256037 NY	5.3
33	Cold Pike West Top	683m	89-259036 NY	5.3
34	Cold Pike	701m	89-263036 NY	5.3
35	Harter Fell	653m	96-219997 SD	5.6
36	Grey Friar	770m	89-260004 NY	5.5
37	Great Carrs	785m	89-270009 NY	5.5
38	Black Sails	745m	89-283008 NY	5.5
39	Wetherlam	763m	89-288011 NY	5.5
40	Swirl How	802m	89-273005 NY	5.5
41	Brim Fell	796m	96-271985 SD	5.5
42	Dow Crag	778m	96-262978 SD	5.5
43	The Old Man of Coniston	803m	96-272978 SD	5.5
44	Walna Scar	621m	96-258963 SD	5.5
45	White Maiden	610m	96-254957 SD	5.5

Sca Fell from Lingmell

WALK 5.1 THE SCAFELLS

SUMMITS		
	Lingmell	2625 ft (800m)
	Middleboot Knotts	2306 ft (703m)
	Round How	2431 ft (741m)
	Great End	2986 ft (910m)
	Ill Crag	3068 ft (935m)
	Broad Crag	3064 ft (934m)
	Scafell Pike	3209 ft (978m)
	Sca Fell	3163 ft (964m)
	Symonds Knott	3146 ft (959m)
DISTANCE	9 miles	
ASCENT	4650 feet	
MAPS	OS Landranger sheet 89 or 90	
	Outdoor Leisure - The English Lakes, South Western area	
STARTING POINT	(89-182075) The north end of Wast Water. There is a free National Trust car park next to the campsite.	

On October 7th 1818, a still cloudless day, Dorothy Wordsworth in the company of William and a shepherd-guide climbed to the summit of Scafell Pike.

> *'Round the top of Scawfell Pike not a blade of grass is to be seen. Cushions or tufts of moss, parched and brown, appear between the huge blocks and stones that lie in heaps on all sides to a great distance, like skeletons or bones of the earth not needed at the creation, and there left to be covered with never-dying lichens, which the clouds and dews nourish; and adorn with colours of vivid and exquisite beauty.'*

Dorothy's account was included in the 1823 edition of Wordsworth's 'Guide to the Lakes'and her enthusiasm was not even dampened by a storm on the way down when they saw two rainbows over the Langdale Pikes.

Scafell Pike, the highest point in England, attracts constant attendance even from those who may never climb another mountain in their lives, and to have the summit to oneself is certainly unusual. We rose early and were away by 7am one October morning from our tent at Sprinkling Tarn. Passing two men descending, both warmly dressed, each with a balaclava surmounted by a torch, they admitted their attempt to see the dawn had failed. We climbed on into a silent grey world. The huge cairn around which we once counted a hundred multi-coloured walkers was deserted and we paused only briefly before hastening on down to Mickledore. Sca Fell too was a place of grey sky

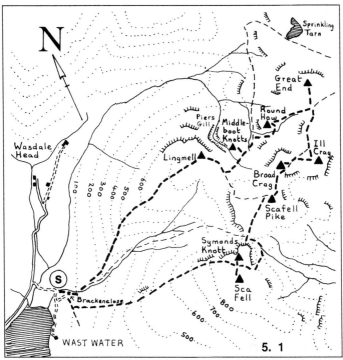

5. 1

and stones which we gained and left by way of Foxes Tarn. Coleridge was made of sterner stuff. Taking the direct route via Broad Stand he writes,

> '*So I began to suspect that I ought not to go on; but then unfortunately tho I could with care drop down a smooth rock of 7 feet high, I could not climb it, so go on I must, and on I went ..... To return was impossible .... my limbs were all in a tremble*'.

Superlatives describe the tiny hamlet of Wasdale Head, famed for the highest mountain, deepest lake, smallest church and biggest liar in England. The Screes plunging straight into Wast Water continue at the same angle to the bottom of the lake which is 258 ft deep with the bed 58 ft below sea level. The church, whose timber is reputed to have come from a shipwreck, is dedicated to St Olaf and among the yews are the graves of climbers who died on these hills. Its churchyard was not consecrated until 1889, so before this date coffins were carried over the Old Corpse Road to Boot.

Will Ritson, self proclaimed the greatest liar, was a farmer and huntsman

Mickledore

born at Row Foot in 1818 who turned guide to the new fashion of climbing the fells. Licensing his farmhouse at Row Foot he named it the Huntsman Inn and here this great raconteur and teller of tall stories lived until his death in 1890. Ritson's Force, the waterfall at the foot of Mosedale, was so named as a memorial to him and the climber's bar at the inn which was rebuilt in 1880 and renamed 'The Wastwater Hotel', is now Ritson's Bar, and usefully serves refreshments all day.

ROUTE DESCRIPTION

LINGMELL *(Heathery Bare Hill)*
Go down the lane towards the lake and take the Public Bridleway signed 'Eskdale, Scafell route', to the left of Brackenclose. Cross the footbridge and after passing through a field take the path up the west ridge of Lingmell for an ascent of some 2300 ft. The path climbs steeply at first to a cairn with aerial views of the Wasdale Head Hotel and its toy cars, then more gradually, as the ridge broadens and the angle eases, to Goat Crags. After crossing a ruined wall the final section is pathless over short grass. The rocky top has the remains of a once splendid cairn perched high above the chasm of Piers Gill. It is a superb viewpoint, the face of Great Gable looking quite unassailable from this side and the route over to the Scafells can be followed with the eye.

MIDDLEBOOT KNOTTS *(Middle River Bend Rocky Hill)*
Descend south-east to Lingmell Col and follow the ruined wall east for a short way. Middleboot Knotts can be seen ahead on the other side of Piers Gill. Passing to the right of a small knoll, join the Corridor Route briefly to cross the head of the gill where the stream plunges over into the ravine and then immediately fork left to follow a minor path to the east of the gill. After 100 yards climb the rocky knoll from which you can look down into Piers Gill with Lingmell towering above. A small cairn stands beside the topmost rock which just lifts this to the status of a separate top. Adjacent knolls surveyed assiduously on a March backpacking trip all failed the test.

ROUND HOW *(Round Knoll)*
Less than half a mile to the east and on the western flank of Great End above the Corridor Route lies another unfrequented little craggy top. The north and west slopes of Round How are steep and rocky but to the south-east the mountain presents a sloping grassy flank. To be sure of finding the summit in mist, return from Middleboot Knotts to the Corridor Route. After a main path from Scafell Pike has entered from the right there is a short descent to Greta Gill. Follow the gill upstream for a quarter of a mile and then climb the easy slopes on the left to the small summit cairn.

GREAT END
Descend the gentle grassy slopes of Round How then climb beside Greta Gill on a faint path to the col above Calf Cove. Just beyond is the main path to Scafell Pike from Esk Hause, but first, to visit Great End turn left and head north on a good path to the summit which has three widely separated cairns. The eastern one, chosen by the Ordnance Survey for their spot height, has a cairn on top of the highest boulder. The top is wide and flat and the north face which looks so impressive from Sprinkling Tarn is unsuspected without a visit to the cliffs beyond.

Scafell Pike from Foxes Tarn

ILL CRAG *(Steep Crag)*
Return south to the col and then follow the main highway to Scafell Pike for a quarter of a mile to the highest point on the path. A short walk to the south leads to the huge heap of piled boulders on the summit of Ill Crag. The rocky mound is mossy and rather slippery and from the twin tops of naked rock, which are of equal height, there is a dramatic view down into the upper Eskdale valley.

BROAD CRAG
Rejoin the main path and after the col scramble west over awkward boulders to gain the summit which has a small cairn on the highest of them. Although only a matter of yards from the path the difficulty of approach ensures that Broad Crag is seldom visited. This massive pile of jumbled boulders must be the roughest summit in the Lake District.

SCAFELL PIKE *(Bare Summit Fell Peak)*
After a slow and awkward descent to the south-west over trackless boulders, rejoin the main path and the stream of people heading for the top of the highest mountain in England. From the Broad Crag col it is only a short ascent on a good path to the bleak and stony summit. The large flat cairn, built in 1921 and recently restored, has a flight of steps on one side. There is also the standard OS trig point and a multitude of assorted windshelters. The summit of Scafell Pike was given to the nation in 1919 and this is commemorated by a plaque

'*In perpetual memory of the men of the Lake District who fell for God and King, for freedom peace and right in the Great War 1914-1918*'. If you are fortunate enough to have a clear day, the views from here are very fine with the panorama stretching from Blencathra in the north to Black Combe in the south and from Yoke in the east to the Irish Sea in the west.

SCA FELL *(Bare Summit Fell)*
After the descent on a good path south-west to Mickledore, the way straight ahead via Broad Stand is for climbers and mad poets only. From the stretcher box descend left about 300 ft on a slanting path which crosses the screes to follow the cliffs down to the Foxes Tarn path. The start of this is always further down than you expect, but the stony gully has an obvious path leading into it. A rather damp scramble up the boulders, as there is usually a fair bit of water coming down, and the tarn, really little more than a large puddle, is soon reached. Loose eroded screes now lead up to a grassy col where a line of cairns goes left to the summit. The highest point is marked by a small cairn on a large rock at the northern end of the ridge and there is a windshelter close by. Conditions permitting, there is a superb view across to Scafell Pike where the tiny figures on the summit cairn stand silhouetted against the sky, while westward there is the sea and no more mountains till you reach the Isle of Man.

SYMONDS KNOTT *(Named after Rev H H Symonds founder of 'The Friends of the Lake District')*
A short walk north leads to the grassy area below Symonds Knott, but before scrambling up over the boulders peer down into Deep Gill and admire the sheer rock face of the Pinnacle. This is the best place in the Lake District from which to enjoy the exposure of a rock climb without actually having to do it. The large heap of rocks which constitutes Symonds Knott has a small cairn on the top, a magnificent viewpoint set high above the gully.

For the easiest descent return to the col and join the main path which descends west above Scafell Crag passing the top of Lord's Rake. After an initial stony section it is easy going over grass with good views towards Lingmell. When the path plunges suicidally over the edge by Rakehead Crag continue along the ridge, still on a path, then descend over grassy slopes between two streams to a stile at the fence. Follow the stream down over open ground, no longer wooded as shown on the OS map, to another stile and then join the track which passes to the left of Brackenclose where the walk began.

WALK 5.2 BOWFELL

SUMMITS	Bowfell	2959 ft (902m)
	Bowfell North Top	2841 ft (866m)
	Esk Pike	2904 ft (885m)
	Rossett Pike	2136 ft (651m)
DISTANCE	9 miles	
ASCENT	3400 feet	
MAPS	OS Landranger sheet 89 or 90	
	Outdoor Leisure - The English Lakes,South Western area	
STARTING POINT	(89-286061) The head of Great Langdale, 7 miles west of Ambleside. Car park by the Old Dungeon Ghyll Hotel.	

If Bowfell were a few feet higher it would be a three thousander, but then like Great Gable it has no need of feet or metres to give it status, it is a magnificent mountain, one of the finest in the Lake District. Massive buttresses face east at the head of the Langdale valley, to the south Bowfell Links presents an impregnable face, while to the north a rugged line of rocks descends to Hanging Knotts overlooking Angle Tarn. Above these ramparts is the summit, a tangled mass of boulders through which tiny figures wind their way to their goal, the cairn at the very top.

As the sky darkened to a thunderous black, large white snowflakes began to fall. Soon the path had vanished and with it the patches of ice that now lay hidden awaiting the first careless step. The wind rose and the snow whirled along in gusts, piling up on the rocks and freezing our gloves into blocks of ice. We turned and fled; slowly, carefully, probing each downward step until we were safely descending The Band. Many years later and again we were descending Bowfell. The sky again was black, but this time it was fast approaching night and our head torches stabbed the darkness as we picked our way slowly down The Band to the friendly warmth of the Old Dungeon Ghyll Hotel. Another time, another impression; waking on Crinkle Crags in our snow covered mountain tent to see through the doorway Bowfell brilliantly white against the clear blue sky of the early morning.

While the name Bowfell dates back to the thirteenth century and derives from a person called Bowe, Esk Pike was nameless before 1870 when it was christened by Mr JC Ward, a geologist, the author of 'The Geology Of The Northern Part Of The English Lake District' which was published in 1876. Between the two lies Ore Gap where the ground is stained red by haematite. In medieval times the iron ore was mined here by the monks from Fountains

Bowfell from Crinkle Crags

Abbey in Yorkshire and transported all the way down Langstrath to an iron smelter on Smithymire Island at the confluence of Greenup Gill and Langstrath Beck. Mining was resumed in the eighteenth century and at one time there was a proposal to construct a rack railway to mine the ore, but fortunately this was thought to be an uneconomical plan. The iron in the rocks on Bowfell is reputed to affect the compass, but although a special survey concluded that it was only noticeable if the compass was laid on a rock, to us even this effect has proved elusive and as haematite is non magnetic it seems unlikely to be true.

While the lower reaches have been re-paved, Rossett Gill itself remains unimproved and it is a rough descent to the moraines at its foot, the head of Mickleden. This way over the mountains to the sea is very old and was probably the route to the outside world for the axes from the Langdale Pikes stone axe factory. On a grassy shelf beside Rossett Gill is the Old Packwoman's grave, a cross of stones laid to mark her lonely passing.

ROUTE DESCRIPTION

BOWFELL *(Bowe's Fell)*
From the Old Dungeon Ghyll Hotel go out to the road, turn right and then through the gate signed 'Stool End'. The track leads across the fields to Stool End farm, going to the left of the farmhouse. Just beyond the gate the repaired path turns right up The Band. This is the most usual route up Bowfell and one

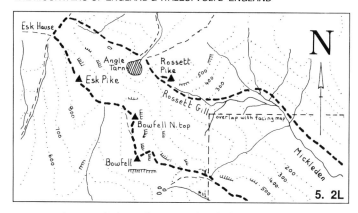

passes or is passed, depending on one's relative fitness, by many other walkers as one climbs the ridge. It usually seems further than it is with little to provide excuse for a stop. However, where the ground flattens before the final climb to Three Tarns, the crowds may be left by forking right to climb above the main path to the Climbers' Traverse. This is not as its name suggests a fearsome passage where one clings by fingertips above a vertical precipice, but a very pleasant narrow path beneath Bowfell's eastern buttresses. The path ambles along keeping beneath the cliffs for about a quarter of a mile until a spring is reached and a scree slope leading up beside the Great Slab of Flat Crags. This gigantic slab is set at such an angle that it can just be walked up, though most people stay for much of the ascent on the scree to its right. On arriving at the top, climb west over rough boulders with encourging cairns for another 300 yards. The highest point is a jumble of rocks surmounted by

a cairn and scattered with parties of fellwalkers having lunch. They are usually there whatever the weather as there are plenty of recesses in which to get out of the wind. The view has on nearly all our visits over the years been excellent. An odd foggy day and once a nasty surprise when black clouds were seen racing in to blot out the blue sky with a blizzard, but on many trips we have sat by the cairn and picked out favourite summits on the skyline: the Scafells of course, Skiddaw, Helvellyn, the Coniston fells and many more.

BOWFELL NORTH TOP

Descend over the rocks and stroll easily

north for about half a mile to the end of the northern ridge where a rise of just 50 ft distinguishes this top. Great Gable now comes into view behind Great End, almost, but not quite concealed by the nearer Esk Pike.

ESK PIKE *(Esk Peak)*
Descending west the main path is rejoined and this leads down to Ore Gap. The path now climbs easily to the summit of Esk Pike where there are two rocky rises of which the one to the south-west is higher, though the other boasts the cairn.

ROSSETT PIKE *(Horse Upland Pasture Peak)*
The path, slightly west of north, goes down over rocky ground becoming

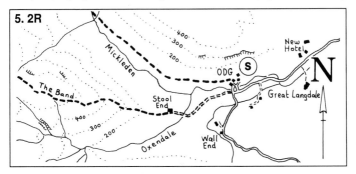

grassy as Esk Hause is approached. Cutting the corner, go down to the wall shelter about 300 yards north-west where the main highway to Langdale is joined. It would be difficult to go wrong here, but it has been done; the way required is east down to the head of Allencrags Gill followed by a slight rise before the descent continues to Angle Tarn. If it is late afternoon there will already be people setting up their tents for this must be the most popular high campsite in the Lake District. From Angle Tarn the path climbs again to reach the head of Rossett Gill with the Pike above it on the left. It is the work of only a moment to reach this last top where there is a cairn a few yards beyond the highest point and to the right a good downward view of Rossett Gill and east across to the Langdale Pikes.

Retrace your steps to the head of Rossett Gill as a direct descent from the summit is much too steep. The gill itself is loose, but not as bad as some Lakeland paths and the zigzag packhorse route which avoids the top section is not much better and also longer. From the foot of the gill the path has been neatly restored with stone blocks and in half a mile the footbridge over Stake Gill is reached. All that remains is the 2 miles back down Mickleden to the Old Dungeon Ghyll Hotel with lengthening shadows chasing your footsteps.

WALK 5.3 CRINKLE CRAGS

SUMMITS	Pike of Blisco	2313 ft (705m)
	Great Knott	2283 ft (696m)
	Cold Pike	2300 ft (701m)
	Cold Pike West Top	2241 ft (683m)
	Cold Pike Far West Top	2198 ft (670m)
	Little Stand	2428 ft (740m)
	Crinkle Crags South Top	2736 ft (834m)
	Crinkle Crags	2818 ft (859m)
	Shelter Crags	2674 ft (815m)
	Shelter Crags North Top	2543 ft (775m)
DISTANCE	9½ miles	
ASCENT	3800 feet	
MAPS	OS Landranger sheet 89 or 90	
	Outdoor Leisure - The English Lakes, South Western area	
STARTING		
POINT	(89-286061) The head of Great Langdale, 7 miles west of Ambleside. Car park by the Old Dungeon Ghyll Hotel.	

As the sun sinks and lengthening shadows stretch down Great Langdale, detail fades and the hills darken to a black silhouette with a serrated skyline of fells encircling the head of Oxendale. Whether you accept the derivation from the Norse word Kringla, a circle, or the alternative descriptive wrinkly, both describe this succession of rocky tops above steep buttresses, known simply to fell walkers as 'The Crinkles'. It is about a mile in length, but it is not a mile to hurry, nor can it be, with up followed by down, and down followed by up, until one is not quite sure where one is on the ridge. The highest of the many summits is Long Top and here descending one evening with night almost upon us and the snow falling steadily, familiarity led to carelessness. Hastily we clambered down looking for the remembered flat space for our tent. The rocks seemed steep and strangely unfamiliar. We stopped, though the path tempted us on down. Map, compass; why had we not checked before? We were ninety degrees off course and ahead lay Eskdale.

Much of the land and many of the farms in Great Langdale are owned by the National Trust who have made great, and successful, efforts to conserve the valley. Stool End and Wall End farms and the Old Dungeon Ghyll Hotel were bought by the historian George Trevelyan and given to the National Trust in 1928.

As the glaciers which had shaped Great Langdale and its steep cliffs

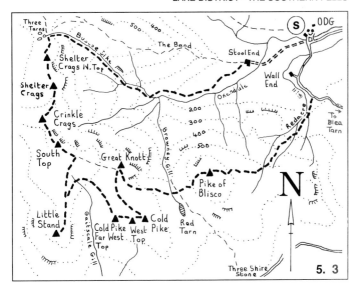

retreated up Mickleden, debris in the form of glacial drift was deposited at the head of the valley where it is seen as huge grass covered mounds at the foot of Rossett Gill. In post glacial times Elterwater had a companion lake which filled the head of the valley above the rock sill at Chapel Stile where hard rocks resisted the scouring of the ice. In heavy rain in spite of all the flood fortifications there is often a lake today.

At one time these high bare fells were covered in trees. Red Tarn, in the gap between Pike of Blisco and Cold Pike, has yielded evidence in pollen grains trapped in layers of sediments that about 5000 BC this whole area was forest. Less than a mile to the south of Red Tarn is Wrynose Pass which was the route the Romans used from their fort at Ambleside to Hardknott Fort and Ravenglass. The road which was unsurfaced before the last war was so damaged by army vehicles that it was repaired extensively with concrete. The summit of the pass is marked by the Three Shire Stone, on which is inscribed 'Lancashire WF 1816', and at this point the three counties of Lancashire, Westmorland and Cumberland met, but in 1974, with the formation of Cumbria, it became a lonely reminder of the past.

ROUTE DESCRIPTION

PIKE OF BLISCO *(unknown)*

From the Old Dungeon Ghyll Hotel follow the road to Blea Tarn past Wall End where the barn beside the road is entirely of drystone construction. A clear path soon turns off to the right to follow the left side of Redacre Gill. After climbing steadily for nearly 1000 ft, easier slopes are reached on the shoulder of Wrynose Fell and the path bears right. Heading west on the cairned path the final steep slopes are soon reached and a short section of rock scrambling brings you to the summit. Pike o'Blisco (does anyone apart from the OS say 'of Blisco'?) has two rocky tors, each with a cairn, the north-western one being slightly higher than its twin. The orange colour of some of the rocks gives the illusion on the greyest of days that the sun is about to break through. Crinkle Crags stretches away to the north-west and north across Langdale is the well known outline of the Langdale Pikes.

GREAT KNOTT *(Great Rocky Hill)*

Descending roughly west a clear path leads down to pass north of Red Tarn and then climbs steadily at a more relaxed angle towards Crinkle Crags. After about half a mile, passing the head of Browney Gill, Great Knott is a little to

The Scafells from Crinkle Crags - winter

the right with steep rocky slopes dropping into the gill. It is an easy stroll up over grass to the top with two cairns about 50 yards apart. The one nearest Crinkle Crags is the higher, though from the other there is a better view of the head of Great Langdale spread out with its jigsaw pattern of green fields.

COLD PIKE *(Cold Peak)*
Going south-west and then south across the grassy hollow, aim for the middle summit of Cold Pike until the ground begins to rise and then turn left to climb the more interesting rocky slopes of the main summit. There are several rocky tors, two with the same spot height, but the highest is on the northern side looking towards Pike of Blisco. Cold Pike is at the end of a spur running out from Crinkle Crags and beyond the ground drops increasingly steeply towards the Wrynose Pass.

COLD PIKE WEST TOP
About 400 yards west across a grassy dip is the second top of Cold Pike. There is just 65 ft of ascent to its top where the westernmost of two boulders is crowned by three stones for a cairn on the dappled yellow and green lichen covered rocks.

COLD PIKE FAR WEST TOP
The third of Cold Pike's tops is to the north-west, just 50 ft of ascent and only 200 yards away. Previous visitors have left a neat cairn on this isolated rocky pillar, though it must be one of the most unfrequented summits in the Lakes.

LITTLE STAND *(Little Stones)*
Cross the head of Gaitscale Gill and then climb west up grassy slopes to gain the ridge of Little Stand. Go south along the ridge winding your way round the little knolls and tarns to its end where there is a cairn on a rocky rib. The fell slopes fall steeply to Mosedale and Cockley Beck and this summit, which is on the route of the Duddon Fell Race, must have raised many a groan from already tired runners after their ascent of Harter Fell. To the south are the Coniston Fells, which are later crossed by the runners during their 20 mile race.

CRINKLE CRAGS SOUTH TOP
Now return north along the ridge, dropping to a col then slowly climbing, and after three quarters of a mile the path from Red Tarn is rejoined. The going is much rougher now and the stony path climbs through the rocks to a cairn on the first summit of Crinkle Crags.

CRINKLE CRAGS *(Wrinkled Crags)*
The path continues at first on the level and then descends to a col. The ascent of the rocks ahead is referred to by Wainwright as the 'Bad Step', a short but very steep wall of rock to the right of a chockstone. Harry Griffin dismisses it rather contemptuously saying that no-one would have noticed it if it wasn't

for Wainwright - though in fact it was known as the bad step long before Wainwright popularised it. On the last occasion with the holds covered in wet snow and heavy backpacking sacks, we were glad to take the easier way, which is a cairned path to the left from the col that lands one on the ridge a little way to the west of the main summit. After passing a tiny tarn the highest point of the Crinkles is reached at Long Top where there is a solid pile of stones, the northernmost of the cairns.

SHELTER CRAGS
Taking care to go north-east now, not back along Long Top, the path descends gently to a col visiting a couple of minor tops and Gunson Knott. Another col follows with a tarn a little way to the left off the ridge and then shortly a small tarn is reached astride the ridge with two rocky rises one on either side. The one to the left has been checked as the higher and the view from the cairn is remarkably extensive.

After a grey Saturday and a night spent up high in our tent with the snow falling steadily, Sunday's blue skies and sunshine were a delight. To the north-west we could see the Scafells, looking very close, while northwards Bowfell's southern scree slopes, Bowfell Links, gleamed whitely. North-east the Langdale Pikes now looked somewhat lower than they did earlier, eastwards the snow on Pike of Blisco reflected the sun and away to the south-east were the Coniston Fells while beyond the Langdale Pikes the Helvellyn range should have been in view, but a brief snow shower was sweeping in to hide it as we continued along the ridge.

SHELTER CRAGS NORTH TOP
The final top is avoided by the path which is making for Three Tarns just beyond. Descending past a little spring to the left, turn off right beyond the next col and a short climb brings you to the top with its cairn.

The path may then be rejoined by continuing, rather steeply, down the far side to Three Tarns. Going east for Great Langdale,a broad stony path sets off down The Band. After a few yards a cairn marks the end of a narrow path which descends to the right of Buscoe Sike, past Hell Gill and Whorneyside Force. Cross the footbridge to follow Oxendale Beck down to join the track to Stool End where the fields are crossed on a lane back to the Old Dungeon Ghyll Hotel.

WALK 5.4 GLARAMARA GROUP

SUMMITS		
	Seathwaite Fell	2073 ft (632m)
	Seathwaite Fell South Top	2070 ft (631m)
	Allen Crags	2575 ft (785m)
	High House Tarn Top	2244 ft (684m)
	Red Beck Top	2365 ft (721m)
	Looking Steads	2543 ft (775m)
	Glaramara	2569 ft (783m)
	Combe Head	2411 ft (735m)
	Combe Door Top	2218 ft (676m)
	Dovenest Top	2073 ft (632m)
	Rosthwaite Fell	2008 ft (612m)

DISTANCE   9¹/₂ miles

ASCENT   3050 feet

MAPS   OS Landranger sheet 89 or 90
Outdoor Leisure - The English Lakes, North Western area &
The English Lakes, South Western area

**STARTING
POINT**   (89-235122) Seathwaite in Borrowdale. 8 miles
south of Keswick. Plentiful car parking beside
the road, toilets.

Glaramara is the highest point on the long undulating ridge dividing Langstrath from the head of Borrowdale, stretching for four miles from Allen Crags, above the major path junction of Esk Hause, to Rosthwaite Fell. There is a multiplicity of tops to be visited and several pretty little tarns along the ridge, especially a tiny one in a lovely rocky setting above High House Tarn. With so many summits surrounded by others very nearly, but not quite as high, good visibility is almost essential if you are not to suffer the nagging doubt which inevitably strikes on the way home. "We did do that top above .... didn't we?"

Seathwaite Fell, despite the prominent 601m marked on the map, and Wainwright recording it at 1970 ft, is still very much a 2000 ft mountain. It has for good measure two tops in a most attractive area of small tarns and hillocks. Sprinkling Tarn is a particular favourite of backpackers overlooked by the high cliffs of Great End. The rainfall here measures 185 inches a year, exceeding even that at Seathwaite 'the wettest place in England' which has a mere 130 inches. This drops dramatically as you go down Borrowdale to 100 inches at Rosthwaite and only 58 inches at Keswick. It does not actually have that many more rainy days than anywhere else; it just rains harder. But every cloud has

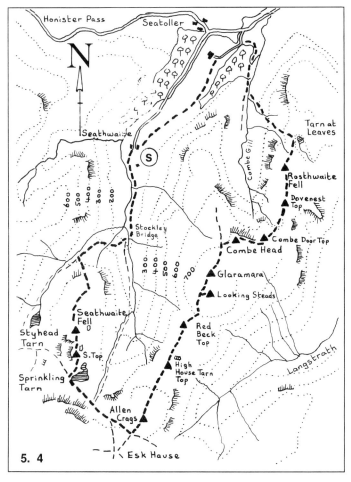

5. 4

a silver lining, Snowdonia has a much higher average rainfall and if it is raining at Seathwaite it is some consolation to reflect that it is probably a lot worse in Blaenau Ffestiniog!

In August 1966 there was a devastating flood which swept down on the head of Borrowdale, huge boulders were moved by the river and Stockley

Bridge was washed away. Even today the traces of the flood damage are visible while there are now massive fortifications which have been put in place to prevent a recurrence.

To the west of Seathwaite is the site of the old plumbago or graphite mine whose black lead was used to make pencils until the mine was worked out in 1880. The plumbago was so valuable that the mine had to be guarded night and day. The Cumberland Pencil Factory in Keswick is still open, but now the graphite comes from Sri Lanka.

ROUTE DESCRIPTION

SEATHWAITE FELL *(Sedge Clearing Fell)*
Walk past the farm buildings following the wide gated track on the left bank of the gill. Further up the valley you pass through a hummocky area, which is a glacial dumping ground, and then cross Stockley Bridge, an attractively situated pack horse bridge. The newly repaired path zigzags uphill across the front of Seathwaite Fell with Taylorgill Force on the right. About 300 yards after a small plantation, the path levels out and the top of Seathwaite Fell is reached by climbing left, a steep pathless ascent over grass to the right of a small stream. The cairned top ahead is Wainwright's summit, but it is not the highest point of the fell and does not even reach the magic height of 2000 ft. Follow the edge of the fell round to the right for about a third of a mile, over little rocky tops and tarns to pass a stone column on the top of a small cliff. Just beyond this is the highest point, a rocky knoll with a cairn on the flat top.

SEATHWAITE FELL SOUTH TOP
Passing a small tarn, head south along the rocky ridge to a larger tarn at the col. The rocky knoll to the right of this is the fell's second summit, 300 yards south and only one metre lower than the northern one, a rise of 56 ft making it a separate top. A small cairn marks the flattish rocky top and lovely Sprinkling Tarn lies ahead.

ALLEN CRAGS *(Aleyn's Crags)*
Walk to the right of Sprinkling Tarn to join the main path from Sty Head to Esk Hause. Shortly the Ruddy Gill path comes in from the left and then the path forks, the right branch climbing to the true Esk Hause. However keep left and in under half a mile the cairn is reached at the cross roads by the wind shelter below Esk Hause. Turn left up a short steep stony path to the summit. The central cairn on the flat stony top stands on the highest spot with magnificent views over to the Langdale Pikes, Bowfell, Great End, Gable, Skiddaw and of course along the Glaramara ridge.

HIGH HOUSE TARN TOP
The broad grassy ridge with many rocky knolls and little tarns leads towards the next top, about half a mile to the north-east. This is the rocky tor to the right

of the path with just a few stones making a cairn. Although only a subsidiary top, any mountain could be proud of this summit with High House Tarn set attractively among the rocks at its foot.

RED BECK TOP
The next top is about a third of a mile further on. Descending past several tarns to the lowest point on the ridge, the path then climbs up steeply to pass almost over the summit. A cairn to the left on a little rocky tor marks the highest point.

LOOKING STEADS *(Lookout Place)*
A third of a mile beyond and after a steep descent to a boggy grassy col, the next top is the high point to the right of the path, a tumble of rough boulders and stones with a cairn on a large boulder.

GLARAMARA *(Hill with the Mountain Hut by a Chasm)*
The chief summit on the ridge is now less than a quarter of a mile away to the north. Descend to a grassy col and follow the main path to the west top of the twin summits. Wainwright prefers the east top for its better position and view, but the west one is the higher of the two. The highest point is the cairn set a little back from the edge, though another cairn on the edge itself marks a better vantage point.

COMBE HEAD *(Narrow Valley Summit)*
Passing a small tarn and the east top of Glaramara with its multiplicity of cairns, it is an awkward descent north over rocks. One of the Lake District's several Neolithic stone axe factories was identified in this area in 1959. The next summit is in no doubt. Leave the path and keeping to the left of the tarns it is a short but steep pull up to Combe Head, whose rocky top is marked by a small cairn with commanding views down The Combe.

COMBE DOOR TOP *(Narrow Valley Pass)*
Although it is close, a direct line to the next top is barred by crags to the north. Descend east following the edge of the crags to find a grassy rake that most conveniently leads to the col at the head of Combe Door. Crossing a rather boggy area, aim for the leftmost of the two rocky and grassy knolls ahead which is confirmed as the summit by a little cairn on the top.

DOVENEST TOP *(Pigeon's Nest)*
The next top is one third of a mile to the north-east. Descend over rock and grass to the col and follow a faint little path to cross a bit of ruined wall. The rocky left hand knoll is marginally higher than the right, but there is no cairn on the top.

ROSTHWAITE FELL *(Heap of Stones Clearing Fell)*
This is the final summit of the walk and only another third of a mile away due north. Return to the little path and skirting a boggy section, climb to the summit

Great End from Sprinkling Tarn

which is known as Rosthwaite Cam. The best top has been left till the end of this walk and at first sight the impressive rocks appear unscaleable, but a way up can be found round the back. From here there is a good view down Borrowdale and below lies Tarn at Leaves.

Descend to the tarn to join the path which leads west, to the right of the deep red ravine of Rottenstone Gill which is much prettier than its name. Descend easily over grass to the right of the gill to cross Combe Gill near a sheep fold, joining the Glaramara path just before a gate. Follow the path down to join the lane to Thorneythwaite. Turn left along the tarmac ròad for the final 1½ miles, with Rosthwaite Cam peeping up above the trees on the left. After the notice 'Gate Ahead' leave the road, which leads to the farm, to follow the signed field path back to Seathwaite where there is a café. Providing it has been a dry day you will be able to comply with the notice on the conveniently situated drinks machine 'DO NOT USE WET COINS!'.

WALK 5.5 THE CONISTON FELLS

SUMMITS		
	Wetherlam	2503 ft (763m)
	Black Sails	2444 ft (745m)
	Swirl How	2631 ft (802m)
	Great Carrs	2575 ft (785m)
	Grey Friar	2526 ft (770m)
	Brim Fell	2612 ft (796m)
	The Old Man of Coniston	2634 ft (803m)
	Dow Crag	2552 ft (778m)
	Walna Scar	2037 ft (621m)
	White Maiden	2001 ft (610m)
DISTANCE	13½ miles	
ASCENT	4400 feet	
MAPS	OS Landranger sheets 89 or 90, & 96	
	Outdoor Leisure - The English Lakes, South Western area	
STARTING POINT		
	(96-299976) Coniston. Old Station car park, to the west of the village.	

'Any place opposite Coniston Old Man must be beautiful', wrote Ruskin when in 1871 he bought Brantwood on the shores of Coniston Water without even seeing it. Across the lake, the view from the hills from the turret room he built onto his bedroom at Brantwood must have delighted him for Ruskin, the artist, writer and critic, lived here until his death in 1900. *'Mountains are the beginning and the end of all natural scenery'* - who could have expressed it better?

There is a Ruskin museum in Coniston and Brantwood, which is open to the public, has paintings and mementos too. Brantwood also has a room devoted to the work of another artist and writer who has been an inspiration to many thousands of walkers. Wainwright's seven volume guide is the finest celebration of the Lake District ever produced. His maps, his descriptions and the lovely composition and detail of his drawings set a standard which has been imitated, but never equalled.

Swallows and Amazons, Swallowdale, Winter Holiday - these names evoke for countless people the feel of the Lake District and a longing to return again. Arthur Ransome lived at Coniston from 1930 until his death in 1967 and the books are a fictional amalgam of the places he knew and loved. No one place is exactly reflected, but Coniston Water holds a jewel. We reached Peel Island after a four mile row down the lake during our honeymoon. As we

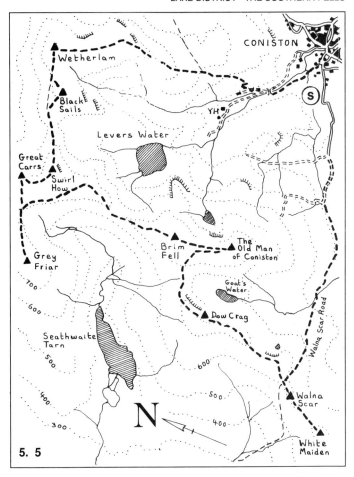

CONISTON

Wetherlam

Black Sails

YH

Levers Water

Great Carrs

Swirl How

Brim Fell

The Old Man of Coniston

Grey Friar

Goat's Water

Dow Crag

Seathwaite Tarn

Walna Scar Road

N

Walna Scar

White Maiden

5. 5

stepped from the boat onto the little beach we entered the world of John and Susan, Titty and Roger. It was Wild Cat Island. Smaller perhaps, but there was the secret harbour through the trees where John hid Swallow and here was the clearing where an arrow announced the presence of the Amazons. In Swallowdale the children climb Kanchenjunga.

'*Then indeed they knew that they were on the roof of the world, "And*

> *there's Scawfell, and Skiddaw, and that's Helvellyn, and the pointed
> one's Ill Bell, and there's High Street where the Ancient Britons had a
> road along the top of the mountains".'*

We suddenly leave the fictional world. Ransome is describing the view from
Coniston Old Man.

Fact or fiction the Coniston fells have a very special appeal. The
southernmost of the Lake District fells and bounded by the Duddon Valley,
Wrynose Pass and Coniston Water, they form a separate, compact group
whose summits can all be visited in one not overly strenuous day. Of course
Coniston Old Man is often the only objective. A friend staying at Torver ran
up and down before breakfast every day so he didn't miss his training, one
blind man has climbed it countless times, and when camping beside the trig point
we met, late in the evening, a man bringing his girlfriend up her first mountain.

Coniston's origins as a mining town are evident as soon as one leaves its
grey stone streets to climb towards the hills through the Coppermines Valley.
Mining began here in Roman times and in the sixteenth century German
miners were employed, the ore being taken by packhorse over Dunmail Raise
to be smelted at Keswick. Later it was transported by boat down the lake to
the sea at Greenodd to be shipped to Wales. The mines closed by 1890
though the spoil heaps have been worked in this century. From 1859 a railway,
used also for tourist traffic, linked the mines with Broughton in Furness, but this
closed in 1950 leaving Coniston isolated at the head of the lake.

ROUTE DESCRIPTION

WETHERLAM *(Wether Lamb)*

Leaving the station yard walk downhill towards Coniston for a few yards and
turn left to the Sun Hotel. Going to the left of the inn, signposted 'Old Man and
Levers Water', follow the track across the fields and climb beneath the trees
to the left of Church Beck to cross Miners Bridge. Continue on the old mine
road and as the Coppermines Valley opens out ahead and the whitewashed
building of the Youth Hostel comes into view, fork right up the track. Just
above the cottages turn sharp right, doubling back and then very shortly turn
off left at a quarry, up a clear stony path which climbs steadily to Hole Rake.
Just before the crest leave it for a lesser path which climbs the southern ridge
of Wetherlam wriggling through the rocks with an occasional cairn to reinforce
confidence in the route. Coniston Old Man which has been in sight for some
time is joined in view by Levers Water, Swirl How and Black Sails, but the
summit of Wetherlam stays concealed until the last moment. A false summit
is reached about 400 yards before the top and in bad weather it can be
mistaken for the true one whose flat rocky top has the larger cairn. The
prominent hills are Coniston Old Man to the south-west and Swirl How to the
west. North-west the outline of Sca Fell and Scafell Pike is easily identified,
while closer to hand are the Crinkles running up to Bowfell with Glaramara to
the right and the North Western fells in the distance. Pike o'Stickle is another

familiar outline and, almost concealed by High Raise, there are the distant shapes of Skiddaw and Blencathra. The tops of the Helvellyn range can be identified by looking for the large nick in the long skyline where Grisedale Tarn is hidden between Fairfield and Dollywagon Pike.

BLACK SAILS *(Dark Swampy Hill)*
Only about half a mile away, but bypassed by the main route heading for Swirl How, this next summit is seldom visited. Where the path crosses the shoulder of Black Sails climb south over the grass and rock of the ridge leading to the top, where the cairn on the rocky summit has a good view of Levers Water far below.

SWIRL HOW *(Windy Knoll)*
Return to the path and descend to the foot of Prison Band. A rocky scramble of 600 ft brings you to a substantial well built cairn overlooking the chasm which separates this summit from Great Carrs. To the south is Dow Crag and three quarters of the day's ascent is now completed.

GREAT CARRS *(Great Rocks)*
An easy stroll right, round the edge, passes the smashed remains of an aircraft undercarriage and a memorial cross. Some more of the wreckage lies far below on the screes. Great Carrs is really only a high point on the ridge which descends to Little Langdale. Its summit is marked by a tumble of stones.

GREY FRIAR
The ridge continues all the way down to Little Langdale Tarn, but aiming south-west directly for Grey Friar descend gently over grass to join the path at the col, which has a convenient spring. It is an out and back for this top so rucksacks may be left here and an easy ascent leads to the top. There are twin cairns about 50 yards apart, both on a rocky knoll. The one nearest Coniston Old Man just has the advantage, but from the other there is a good view into the Duddon Valley. The isolated fell to the west surrounded by trees is Harter Fell.

BRIM FELL
Return to the col and, not forgetting the sacks, contour south-east across the slope using a narrow trod which leads up to the main path at Levers Hawse. There is a lovely view of Levers Water directly below with Coniston village and the lake beyond. It's an easy stroll up onto Brim Fell whose summit has a beautiful conical cairn of which any mountain could be proud. Harter Fell stands out to the west framed by the chimneys of Sellafield on either side.

THE OLD MAN OF CONISTON *(Coniston's Hill with an Ancient Cairn)*
Even with a heavy pack no-one could complain about the ascent from Brim Fell to the Old Man. Continue following the path round the edge to the large summit cairn which, to show the importance of this top to everyone, is raised on a plinth of stone. The name 'The Old Man of Coniston' actually refers to the summit cairn and the poor insignificant trig point is fully 6 ft lower.

DOW CRAG *(Doe Crag)*

Return towards Brim Fell for 200 yards and then bear off left, descending on a path to the col of Goat's Hawse. A clear path climbs through the stones to the final rocks of Dow Crag. No cairn sits on the top which is a superb tor of solid rock poised on the edge of the precipice above Goat's Water at the north end of the ridge. Only just over half a mile away is Coniston Old Man, but the drop between is nearly a thousand feet. The cliffs below were first climbed in 1886 by W. Haskett Smith and J. W. Robinson.

WALNA SCAR

Ahead lies the ridge which is followed all the way to the Walna Scar Road, just beyond Brown Pike, in about a mile. The final two mountains are alas an out and back trip from the summit of this old road, but alternatives contemplated seem to present more problems than they avoid. It is a short grassy ascent to the top at the northern end of the fell which surprisingly has been recognised by having a low cairn.

WHITE MAIDEN

Continuing along the grassy ridge there is no path for the half mile to the isolated top of White Maiden. Just before the wall is reached a cairn in a rocky area denotes the top. The Outdoor Leisure map misleadingly gives a spot height of 608m, but this is below a 610m contour which encircles the top.

Returning to the Walna Scar Road this major track leads down to Cove Bridge and all the way back to Coniston, a distance of about 3 miles. Passing the reedy Boo Tarn go through the gate at the intake wall and the final mile on the lane descends steeply to the old railway station.

Coniston Water

WALK 5.6 HARTER FELL

SUMMITS	Harter Fell	2142 ft (653m)
DISTANCE	6½ miles	
ASCENT	1850 feet	
MAPS	OS Landranger sheet 96 & 89 Outdoor Leisure - The English Lakes, South Western area	
STARTING POINT	(96-234995) The Dunnerdale Forest Forestry Commission car park on the minor road 7 miles north of Broughton in Furness.	

Between Eskdale and the Duddon Valley Harter Fell stands isolated, a fine steep cone of a mountain rising to a rugged rocky top with one of the best summits in England. The northern flank is crossed by Hardknott Pass, a steep, narrow and very winding road, with a gradient of 1 in 3 at the steepest point. The hairpin bends soon jam with cars and it is a place to avoid on a Bank Holiday or busy weekend. Just to the north of the pass above Eskdale lie the ruins of Mediobogdum or Hardknott Castle, a Roman fort which could accommodate 500 soldiers. Built during the reign of Hadrian in the early second century it has a commanding position on the Roman road from Galava near Ambleside to the port of Ravenglass, where there was another fort, Glannoventa. Some sections of the walls have been restored by the Department of the Environment, so you can get a good idea of the ground plan. There is a bath house outside the walls and a large artificially flattened parade ground which is well seen from Harter Fell. The eastern slopes of the mountain are covered in forest with the River Duddon at their foot, one of the loveliest rivers in the Lake District. Being thus aloof from the rest of the fells, Harter Fell is best the object of an odd half day or evening with an excellent view of the higher summits from its top.

One scorching hot day when any exertion seemed too much, the ascent through the pines brought welcome cool shade, and afterwards we swam beneath the little packhorse bridge at Birks where steep rocks drop vertically into deep green pools. Another day after heavy rain the River Duddon was a boiling mass of white water crashing down the valley with the handrail at Fickle Steps only inches above the water.

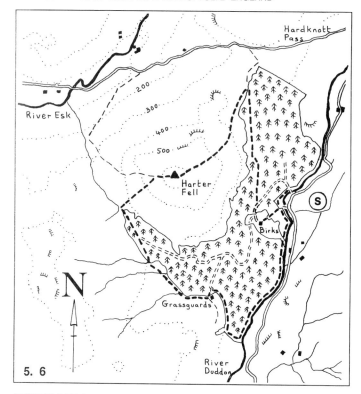

5. 6

ROUTE DESCRIPTION

HARTER FELL *(Stag Fell)*
Cross the concrete bridge over the river and turn off left downstream on the waymarked path soon joining a track to Birks. Passing the farmhouse which has been a Field Study Centre since 1985, turn right at the T-junction beyond on the forest road to enter the wood. In about 200 yards fork left along a rough and rather boggy path, which rises gradually through the forest for 1 mile, then emerges at a little gate onto the open fellside with Hardknott Pass about a quarter of a mile beyond. Turn left and follow the top edge of the forest along to a stile from where it is about 900 ft of ascent on a fair path heading south-west to the summit.

The compact mountain top consists of a grassy platform surrounded by jagged outcrops of rock. The OS trig point is obviously not the highest point which is the apex of the rocks a few yards to the east. These can only be scaled by the use of both hands and feet and from this rather isolated mountain summit the views of the high Lake District tops reach from Sca Fell all the way round to the Coniston fells.

From the grassy platform head west on the main path, but after 200 yards fork left at a cairn onto a minor path which descends to the corner of the forest. Entering the trees at a small gate, a rather muddy track leads to the end of a forest road where on a tree stump there is a carving of a squirrel. Bear right on a waymarked path which soon leaves the forest to go back onto the open hillside and across a stream. Soon this will also be forest as the hillside has recently been planted with yet more conifers. Tree planting in this forest started in 1936 and the area of fellside covered by conifers continues to increase. Follow the waymarked path beside Grassguards Gill over a forest road and down to cross the footbridge beside Grassguards farm.

Continue to follow the bridleway beside the gill, now on its left side, to the bank of the River Duddon at Fickle Steps and turn left on the permissive path for Birks Bridge. Although in places the path is rather muddy, this is one of the most interesting and also the longest 1 1/2 miles of riverside walking in the Lake District. The path picks its way over rocks and through trees, the river ever close beside with deep pools and waterfalls. Wooden walkways have been built at some of the muddiest spots, but they are only a palliative and not always present at the worst bits. Just when you think you are never going to arrive, the path climbs steeply to avoid a narrow rocky gorge, then forks right with a gentle descent and a final wander through the woods to the little packhorse bridge. Usually the river is a long way down through polished

The squirrel carving

rocks, and the deep pools and little falls make an attractive swimming place on a hot day, with brave souls jumping and diving in from the bridge. However notice the holes in the parapet designed to allow the water to pass over the bridge when the river is in spate. It is now only 200 yards back along the lane to the car park.

Birks Bridge

Striding Edge

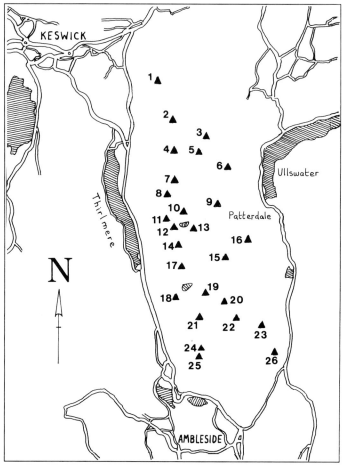

6 LAKE DISTRICT - THE EASTERN FELLS

CHAPTER 6 LAKE DISTRICT - THE EASTERN FELLS

TOP	NAME	HEIGHT	GRID REF	WALK No.
1	Clough Head	726m	90-334225 NY	6.4
2	Great Dodd	857m	90-342206 NY	6.4
3	Hart Side	756m	90-359197 NY	6.4
4	Stybarrow Dodd	843m	90-343189 NY	6.4
5	Green Side	795m	90-353188 NY	6.4
6	Sheffield Pike	675m	90-369182 NY	6.2
7	Raise	883m	90-343174 NY	6.2
8	White Side	863m	90-338167 NY	6.2
9	Birkhouse Moor	718m	90-363160 NY	6.1
10	Catstye Cam	890m	90-348158 NY	6.2
11	Helvellyn Lower Man	925m	90-337155 NY	6.2
12	Helvellyn	950m	90-342151 NY	6.1
13	Striding Edge	860m	90-351149 NY	6.1
14	Nethermost Pike	891m	90-344142 NY	6.1
15	St Sunday Crag	841m	90-369134 NY	6.1
16	Birks	622m	90-380144 NY	6.1
17	Dollywagon Pike	858m	90-346131 NY	6.1
18	Seat Sandal	736m	90-344115 NY	6.1
19	Fairfield	873m	90-359118 NY	6.3
20	Hart Crag	822m	90-368113 NY	6.3
21	Great Rigg	766m	90-356104 NY	6.3
22	Dove Crag	792m	90-374105 NY	6.3
23	Little Hart Crag	637m	90-387100 NY	6.3
24	Heron Pike North Top	621m	90-357087 NY	6.3
25	Heron Pike	612m	90-356083 NY	6.3
26	Red Screes	776m	90-396088 NY	6.3

WALK 6.1 STRIDING EDGE TO ST SUNDAY CRAG

SUMMITS		
	Birkhouse Moor	2356 ft (718m)
	Striding Edge	2821 ft (860m)
	Helvellyn	3117 ft (950m)
	Nethermost Pike	2923 ft (891m)
	Dollywaggon Pike	2815 ft (858m)
	Seat Sandal	2415 ft (736m)
	St Sunday Crag	2759 ft (841m)
	Birks	2041 ft (622m)

DISTANCE   11 miles

ASCENT   4400 feet

MAPS   OS Landranger sheet 90
Outdoor Leisure - The English Lakes, North Eastern area

STARTING POINT   (90-390161) Patterdale village at the south end of Ullswater. There is room for a few cars at the beginning of the lane to Grisedale. Car park half a mile to the east.

The mid-December sun warmed the southern flank of Striding Edge, but the shadowed side was white with hoar frost as we paused for lunch. Below us figures picked their way carefully along the narrow crest. Nightfall would see them back in the valley, but we were to spend the long hours of winter darkness on the tops. With no high intervening fells to the east the sun rises early on Helvellyn and we remembered the almost mystical experience of seeing the dawn in the early hours of a June morning from a camp on the summit. But it was too early to stop on Helvellyn; we chose instead to continue along the ridge.

With clear settled weather the temperature was way below freezing and the ground so hard that tent pegs buckled under efforts to hammer them into the turf. To the west it was still light, but to the east was darkness as the shadows crept up the cliffs. Slowly the sun sank towards the Scafells, painting the sky in rich reds and yellows and slowly the cloud in the west flowed in, filling the valleys with a white sea. The black silhouettes of the mountains rose above the sea while on the cliffs beneath us a pair of ravens croaked their evening calls as they settled for the night. With a final flash of light the sun set behind Pillar and soon the first stars appeared in the blue black of the night sky. A gentle but cooling breeze stirred the tent and drove us inside where from the comfort of our down bags we watched the stars coming out.

We woke early the next morning, but around the tent hung a thick grey

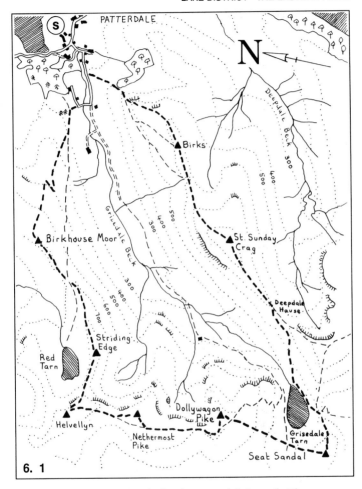

6. 1

mist. It wasn't until we had packed and were ready to leave that there was any sign of the sun which then appeared dimly, already well up in the sky. As we watched, the mist swirled aside revealing cloud filling the valley below and a bright blue sky above. The sun broke through a moment later and suddenly before us were our glories. A black shadow, ringed with the iridescent shimmering colours of the rainbow floated on the clouds. We waved, our glories waved back. We stood close together and one halo encircled us both. We watched entranced as the mist swirled about, the vision dimmed and then shone out brilliantly again, until once more the greyness closed in. We turned and descended into it. The dream was over.

On the summit of Helvellyn is a monument to Charles Gough, a visitor from Manchester who in 1805 was lost in a snowstorm on Striding Edge. He fell six hundred feet from Red Cove Crag towards Red Tarn and his body wasn't found till three months later, still guarded by 'Foxey' his Irish terrier. The same year as the tragedy, Sir Walter Scott and William Wordsworth climbed Helvellyn together and afterwards both wrote commemorative poems; Scott 'Helvellyn' and Wordsworth 'Fidelity'. When found, Gough had a 'Claude Glass' in his pocket. This was a small, convex, tinted mirror through which the visitor admired the view behind him, appearing as a picture in a frame, very similar to how a photograph would look today. This symbolised the 'Picturesque Beauty', invented by William Gilpin in 1772 and defined as '*that which would look well in a picture*'. A Claude Glass was recommended by Thomas West in 1778 in the first ever guide book to the Lakes. He planned a tour with numbered 'Stations' shown on the 'Plans of the Lakes' and the Claude Glass was to be used by every visitor. This was the standard guide to the Lake District for fifty years until Wordsworth's own guide was published. Absurd though it seems to us today, is it so very different from the modern visitor who after a hurried snapshot turns away from the view and climbs back into the car?

In 1842 Benjamin Robert Haydon painted Wordsworth's portrait to celebrate his ascent of Helvellyn at the age of seventy and inspired by this, Elizabeth Barrett Browning composed a sonnet entitled 'Wordsworth upon Helvellyn'. Wordsworth was very fond of Helvellyn and climbed it often, but it held sad memories. William and Dorothy said goodbye to their brother John on February 5th 1800 near Grisedale Tarn where William carved a few lines on a rock to commemorate the occasion. The present carving is due to Canon Rawnsley and a rusty plaque marks the faded words on the Brothers' Parting Stone. The Wordsworths never saw John again, as aged 33 and captain of his ship, The Earl of Abergavenny, he was lost at sea in 1805.

ROUTE DESCRIPTION

BIRKHOUSE MOOR *(Birch House Moor)*

Walk up the lane to the south of Grisedale Beck. After half a mile the road turns right signed 'Footpath to Helvellyn' and crosses the beck. Just beyond, go through the kissing gate at the corner of the lane and up to the trees. Turn left taking the higher path and in a quarter of a mile, just before a fence, double back on a narrow grassy path which zigzags up the hillside to a gate through the fence. Where the path flattens out beside the wall running along the ridge, cross a camouflaged step stile and continue beside the wall which after bending sharp left passes over the highest point, marked by a small cairn. This summit is really a non-event and with Striding Edge and Helvellyn ahead, few will linger here. The cairn to the north-east would be a better top, but it is lower.

STRIDING EDGE
Follow the wall along to Hole-in-the- Wall, where a broad path climbs towards Striding Edge. The highest point, High Spying How, is at the beginning of the ridge, an uncairned rocky top a few steps above the path. To the north lies Catsye Cam and Red Tarn, and to the south nearly a thousand feet below is Nethermost Cove.

HELVELLYN *(unknown)*
Stepping delicately along the very crest of the ridge, the mountain falls away steeply on either hand, but all this exposure can be avoided by a path to the right, and even the awkward rocky step at the finish can be bypassed to the left. A final easy scramble up the eastern flank of Helvellyn brings you out on the summit by the Gough memorial. Follow the edge round to the four bay wall shelter which was built in the nineteenth century and restored in 1968. A few yards above is the large heap of stones which marks the top and a little further and slightly lower is the OS trig column. It is an excellent vantage point with to the south-west the Scafells and Gable showing their distinctive outlines, to the north-west Grasmoor and Grisedale Pike and to the north Skiddaw and Blencathra, while to the east is the long ridge of High Street.

NETHERMOST PIKE *(Lowest Peak)*
Take the good path which leaves the summit heading south-east past the memorial commemorating the first landing of an aeroplane on a mountain summit in Great Britain. At the col keep by the edge where the summit is the first cairn on the northern rim, and not the next one which is surrounded by spikey rocks. It is quite an extensive plateau of stones and rocks and usually quiet as few people turn off the path to visit it despite excellent views of Grisedale far below.

DOLLYWAGGON PIKE *(unknown)*
Head west to rejoin the main path which descends to touch the edge at a col then bypasses the top of Dollywaggon Pike. Continue along the path for about 400 yards to avoid a rocky section and then climb left over grass to the summit. A cairn stands at the neck of a narrow promontory, the end of which is slightly higher and has another small cairn. It is a superb viewpoint from which to admire Helvellyn and Striding Edge with Catstye Cam beyond and from which to look over to the Eastern Fells, St Sunday Crag and Fairfield: in the far distance you can pick out Great Dun Fell and Cross Fell.

SEAT SANDAL *(Sandulf's Hill Pasture)*
Return to the path and go left to locate a solitary substantial fence post and

then head south descending steeply over grass. Aim directly for Seat Sandal following a ruined fence which becomes a wall at the boggy col. This is a much easier way down than the badly eroded path to Grisedale Tarn. A climb of 500 ft beside the ruined wall leads to the top which has a good cairn just to the right, though the ground to the left of the wall is obviously a little higher.

ST SUNDAY CRAG *(St Dominic's Crag)*
Follow the wall east down to Grisedale Hause keeping over to the left for the final section to avoid rough ground. Take the clear path down to Grisedale Tarn where just before the outflow there is an indistinct path which after crossing a small beck becomes more obvious as it climbs to Deepdale Hause. Downstream the small notice above the Brothers' Parting Stone can just be seen. The path climbs at an easy angle finally turning up a stony gully to the ridge. Follow the ridge north-east with the summit always a little further as you pass a succession of false tops. The last one has a huge cairn just to the north of the highest point. The main interest is in looking towards the eastern edges of the Helvellyn range, though far away to the south-east and beyond the Lake District fells you can see Ingleborough.

BIRKS *(Birch Trees)*
A line of cairns heads north to a fine cairn with views of Ullswater. From here the path descends the ridge steeply to a reedy col and then carries on down to Patterdale. However to reach the last top continue along the ridge on a minor path to the first unmarked grassy top which is the highest point.

The path dips and climbs to the second summit which, although it has a small cairn and is a better viewpoint, is lower. Continue along the ridge which drops down towards the end of Ullswater, ending in a little grassy path which picks its way through the scattered outcrops of the crags to join the main path just before a stile. Descend Thornhow End to another stile and cross the field back to the lane, just a short way from the start of the walk.

WALK 6.2 CATSTYE CAM TO SHEFFIELD PIKE

SUMMITS	Catstye Cam	2920 ft (890m)
	Helvellyn Lower Man	3035 ft (925m)
	White Side	2831 ft (863m)
	Raise	2897 ft (883m)
	Sheffield Pike	2215 ft (675m)

DISTANCE	9½ miles

ASCENT	4000 feet

MAPS	OS Landranger sheet 90
	Outdoor Leisure - The English Lakes, North Eastern area

STARTING POINT	(90-386170) Glenridding village at the southern end of Ullswater. Large car park (fee), toilets.

Among the highest of the Lakeland mountains, rising as an almost symmetrical cone, the sudden sight of Catstye Cam as it comes into view over Striding Edge must often prompt the surprised question "What's that peak over there?" The misfortune of Catstye Cam is to be so closely linked with Helvellyn which conceals it from the west and belittles it from the east. It's not that popular decision is wrong, given the choice Helvellyn is the finer mountain, but were it anywhere else there would be fans of Catstye Cam who would make long journeys for the privilege of standing on its summit.

The link to Helvellyn is Swirral Edge, a narrow rocky arête, not as continuous nor as difficult as Striding Edge, but in winter, when ice and snow transform the mountains, then both Striding Edge and Swirral Edge can present conditions more suited to mountaineering than walking. On one ascent by this route the upper portion of Swirral Edge was covered in hard snow which swept down to Red Tarn over seven hundred feet below. In the middle of the snow covered face to the left, the tiny figures of a pair of climbers with ice axes could be seen kicking the points of their crampons into the snow as they crept upwards. Above us on the crest of the ridge and oblivious of the consequences of a slip, a steady stream of walkers, including several young children, were teetering backwards down the hard packed snow. No doubt none of them realised how close to disaster they were.

Glenridding was a tiny hamlet before the mining village grew up around the Greenside lead mine which proved very profitable with rich veins of ore. Although the existence of the ore was known and it had been worked in a small way from as early as 1775, the main period of activity at the mine did not start until as late as 1825. A lot of money was spent on modern equipment, with

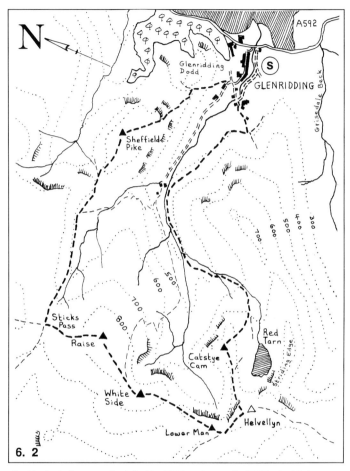

6. 2

electrical winding gear installed in 1891 and even, in 1893, electric locomotives underground. At the same time as these modern improvements however, water-wheels were still in use providing power and the remains of leats and sluices can be found on the fells. Red Tarn supplied water and was enlarged about 1860, while on the slopes of Raise there are the remains of a chimney and a mile-long flue built around 1830, which was used to collect the condensing lead from the fumes of the smelting furnace. Before this lead

124

was transported for smelting, at first by packhorse over Sticks Pass then later to Alston Moor. Lead production averaged around a thousand tons a year, reaching three times this amount in the early twentieth century. The mine eventually closed in 1959 and one of the old mine buildings is now a Youth Hostel. Glenridding has a pier for the Ullswater lake steamer, a few hotels and small shops, an enormous car park and an information centre.

ROUTE DESCRIPTION

CATSTYE CAM *(Ridge of the Wild-cat's Path)*
Opposite the Glenridding Hotel a private road follows the left bank of the river. In 300 yards fork right, signposted 'Gillside Farm Greenside' (Note not the Helvellyn one) and follow this path past the campsite. Turn left on a rough track which ascends to a ladder stile onto the open fellside signed 'Helvellyn via Greenside Mine and Red Tarn' then turn right and Sheffield Pike is straight ahead. Follow the wall on a good path high above Glenridding Beck and after a mile a metal bridge is reached leading across to the site of the old Greenside mine, an outdoor pursuits centre and the Youth Hostel. Stay on the left bank of the stream where an old road leads up beside Red Tarn Beck with Catstye Cam straight ahead until, about half a mile further on, Red Tarn Beck is crossed at a little footbridge and the path starts to climb more steeply. As it rounds the eastern end of Catstye Cam, Striding Edge comes into view with tiny figures of walkers silhouetted against the sky on the crest. The path now deteriorates and becomes rather boggy and well before Red Tarn it should be forsaken in favour of the steep slopes of the east ridge of Catstye Cam up which there is a cairned path. Red Tarn is the only tarn in the Lake District in which the schelly a kind of fresh water herring lives and it is only found in two of the lakes, Ullswater and Haweswater. On reaching the summit of Catstye Cam there is a small cairn on the rocky top with an excellent view down to Ullswater and of High Street and the Eastern fells.

HELVELLYN LOWER MAN *(Helvellyn Lower Hill with a Cairn)*
Descending to the col, the rocky ridge of Swirral Edge is seen rising ahead, but after an all too short enjoyable scramble up the rocks, the summit plateau of Helvellyn is attained. Although Lower Man is the objective of this walk, it would be gross discourtesy not to visit the summit of England's most popular mountain with its superb paroramic view of peaks from Sca Fell in the west, round through Skiddaw in the north to High Street in the east. Follow the edge westwards to Lower Man, a flat stony summit with a small heap of stones to mark its top, which is crossed by the path to White Side. In poor weather it is easy to miss the right fork, taking in error the left branch which descends by Browncove Crags to Thirlmere.

WHITE SIDE (White Hill Slope)
Head north to the col following the edge down and then easily up the path to White Side, with a cairn on its top of grass and stones. Across Brown Cove

Swirral Edge

is Catstye Cam and Swirral Edge with Striding Edge beyond.

RAISE *(Cairn)*

Half a mile away to the north-east Raise is easily reached by keeping to the ridge, but take care at the col as the clearer path goes right, descending to Glenridding. Below is Kepple Cove whose tarn was breached in 1927 by a storm, releasing a flood of water into the valley below which caused a great deal of damage. The first top attained is not the summit, which is a little further on with a cairn built on a low rocky knoll, and a line of cairns leading towards it.

SHEFFIELD PIKE *(Sheep Fell Peak)*

Descending to Sticks Pass turn right. Nearby on the slopes of Raise are the steeply pointed roofs of the ski huts. This side of the mountain retains the snow for longer and in greater quantity than most places and in winter there is a ski tow for those who don't mind the walk to reach it. Lead was carried by packhorse over Sticks Pass for smelting in the Newlands valley, the route of the pass being originally marked by posts or sticks. Sheffield Pike doesn't look very big from the top of the pass, but the further you descend, the larger it becomes. Carry on down until the quarry tips are reached where the path bends right. Leave the path heading down the valley and climb straight ahead on a small path leading directly towards Sheffield Pike. On the left an iron stake marks the boundary of two old Lakeland Estates. The summit of rock and grass has a neat little cone shaped cairn and a few feet below on the far side is a useful wind shelter. Ullswater lies spread out below and this final summit is a pleasant spot for a break now that the hard work is over.

Although if it's misty the safest descent is to retrace your steps to rejoin the path from Sticks Pass, the most interesting way down from Sheffield Pike is by the south-east ridge. Go east a short way to the next cairn, which is a magnificent viewpoint, and then descend south-east, passing some small pools, to two tiny tarns. From here an intermittent path leads down the craggy ridge with Heron Pike on the left, which has another boundary stake. Descending steeply on a fair path you get a bird's-eye view of Glenridding spread out far below. The valley fields have barrow like mounds of stones in them, collected into these piles when the land was cleared for cultivation. The path reaches a col before Glenridding Dodd and turns right, zigzagging down the slope, to join the Greenside Road to the left of a row of miner's cottages. Turn left on the track and follow this down to Glenridding, passing (or entering!) the Traveller's Rest on your way.

WALK 6.3 FAIRFIELD AND RED SCREES

SUMMITS		
	Heron Pike	2008 ft (612m)
	Heron Pike North Top	2037 ft (621m)
	Great Rigg	2513 ft (766m)
	Fairfield	2864 ft (873m)
	Hart Crag	2697 ft (822m)
	Dove Crag	2598 ft (792m)
	Little Hart Crag	2090 ft (637m)
	Red Screes	2549 ft (776m)

DISTANCE   12 miles

ASCENT   4300 feet

MAPS   OS Landranger sheet 90
Outdoor Leisure - The English Lakes, South Eastern area
& The English Lakes, North Eastern area

STARTING
POINT   (90-364063) Rydal 1½ miles north of
Ambleside. Parking on the lane by Rydal Mount.

ALTERNATIVE
START   Ambleside

Probably the most popular of all the horseshoes, the circuit of the fells above Rydal Beck is certainly one of the classic walks of the Lake District. A steep ascent at first leads to Nab Scar where Rydal Water comes into view far below then continuing on easy paths height is gradually gained with each successive rise until Fairfield is reached. Usually the return is over High Pike and the eastern cliffs remain hidden, but by taking in Red Screes, set apart and overlooking the Kirkstone Pass, the best side of Dove Crag can be seen.

If you chose a day in May with thick mist making navigation tricky on the extensive flat top of Fairfield, don't be surprised to hear a bell ringing. It isn't a summons to Sunday Service, but a call to the runners in the Fairfield Horseshoe Race to help them locate the marshall at the top. Here they collect a token to show they have passed before hurtling off down again into the mist over Hart Crag and Dove Crag, the leaders taking just over an hour to complete the circuit.

Usually the descent to Little Hart Crag is deserted, but on a recent visit the hillside was alive with runners. This was a fell race with a difference. Unlike most such races and possibly unique, the Ian Hodgson Mountain Relay has 4 pairs of runners in each team. There were 51 teams taking part and in a total distance of 25 miles with 8500 ft of ascent, a mere 6 seconds separated the first two teams at the finish.

From 1813 the small village of Rydal (Rye Valley) was the home of William Wordsworth, where he lived at Rydal Mount until his death in 1850. The field behind the church at Rydal which he gave to his daughter Dora, is a mass of daffodils every Spring and now belongs to the National Trust. Close by Rydal Church, which was built in 1824, is a handful of cottages, a couple of hotels and lovely Rydal Water, once called Rothaymere. Wordsworth would not have approved of the white-washed cottages, now so characteristic of the area. Supporting Gilpin who complained *'white destroys the gradations of distance',* Wordsworth in his 'Guide to the Lakes' says

> *'Five or six white houses, scattered over a valley, by their obtrusiveness, dot the surface...I have seen a single white house materially impair the majesty of a mountain...it is after sunset, that white objects are most to be complained of'.*

Ambleside, once a busy mill town, is now completely taken over by visitors. The streets throng with people, the shops, pubs and cafés are full to overflowing in the season, but in spite of this it is still a charming little place. The old part dating from the fifteenth century is up the hill beside the Kirkstone Road and much earlier there was a Roman Fort, Galava, on the shores of Windermere. Fortunately few people stray far from Ambleside's more obvious attractions and once the surrounding paths and hills are gained, you will have left the ice creams behind and have only fellow fell walkers for company.

ROUTE DESCRIPTION

HERON PIKE *(Eagle Peak)*

Walk up the lane beside Rydal Mount and fork left at the top at the gate to follow a rough track to the right of a barn. Waymarks guide you steeply up the hill on the newly repaired footpath to the rocky nob of Nab Scar where there is a grand view from a cairn of Rydal Water and Grasmere. The path continues north and it is a gentle climb for about a mile to the first summit of the day, the second bump on the path with a big cairn. Ahead is the rest of the horseshoe and to the right Red Screes, while to the south is a panorama of the southern and western fells.

Fell runner

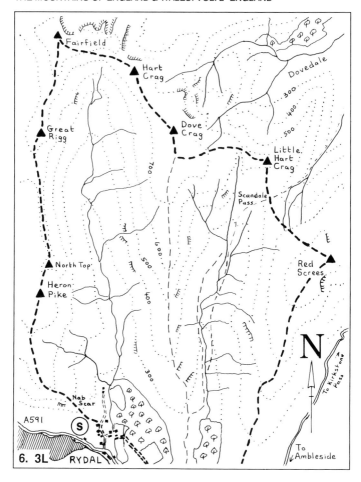

HERON PIKE NORTH TOP

The path descends then climbs again gradually to a little cairn formed from the tumbled remains of the wall coming up from the valley.

GREAT RIGG *(Great Ridge)*
Another dip is followed by a long gentle climb of a mile to the next top passing a large untidy cairn to the one on the summit. To the left Grisedale Tarn appears briefly before vanishing as you climb higher. Gable and the north western fells have now come into view and ahead is the Helvellyn range.

FAIRFIELD *(Beautiful Fell)*
It is now less than a mile to Fairfield summit on a good broad path. The flat stony top is confusing in mist with a proliferation of cairns, but the highest is a many bayed wind shelter right on the edge above the head of Deepdale. Helvellyn to the north vies for attention with High Street and the fells to the east.

HART CRAG *(Stag Crag)*
To continue the horseshoe, almost retrace your steps and following the edge round join a line of cairns heading east. A good path leads south-east to the next summit a mile away and it is marked by the first cairn to the right of the path, a second cairn at the other end of the ridge -100 yards away is nearly as high.

DOVE CRAG *(Pigeon Crag)*
A rocky descent and a grassy ascent beside the wall leads to the next top. The highest point is an obvious cairn to the left of the wall from which you can look down upon Brothers Water.

LITTLE HART CRAG *(Little Stag Crag)*
Continue beside the wall and past the boundary fence to a big cairn which marks a narrow path to High Bakestones where there is an interesting set of shepherds' cairns similar to those found in the North Pennines. Now descend steeply east to Bakestones Moss and then bearing left climb to the ridge and along to the cairned top of the first and highest rocky summit of Little Hart Crag. Dove Crag is now seen in proper proportion with rugged cliffs at the head of Dovedale, and in Scandale the many streamlets form a pattern of silver threads.

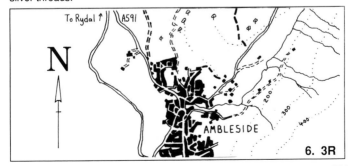

RED SCREES

Descend south from between the twin tops of Little Hart Crag to join the wall crossing the Scandale Pass and follow this for the final climb. Bear left at the cross wall to reach the stone OS trig point, cairn and windshelter on the far side of a little tarn. The best views are towards Ullswater to the north and the High Street fells to the east.

Take the path to the left of the little tarn, walking towards Windermere in the distance. Below to the left is the Kirkstone Inn and also the source of Stock Ghyll, which 3 miles downstream produces a spectacular series of falls at Ambleside. The path continues along the ridge kinking abruptly right after a mile to become a wide stone walled green lane. In another mile this lane joins the Kirkstone Road which is left after a quarter of a mile at a sharp zigzag bend to take a quiet footpath on the right back to Ambleside.

Although at first you must leave Ambleside on the main road to Grasmere and Keswick, after half a mile turn right through impressive wrought iron gates to walk the last mile back to Rydal Hall through Rydal Park.

Fairfield and Grisedale Tarn

WALK 6.4 HARTSIDE TO CLOUGH HEAD

SUMMITS		
	Hart Side	2480 ft (756m)
	Green Side	2608 ft (795m)
	Stybarrow Dodd	2766 ft (843m)
	Great Dodd	2812 ft (857m)
	Clough Head	2382 ft (726m)

DISTANCE   11½ miles

ASCENT   2450 feet

MAPS   OS Landranger sheet 90
Outdoor Leisure - The English Lakes, North Eastern area

STARTING
POINT   (90-380219) The corner of the minor road 1 mile west of
Dockray. Ample parking at the road junction.

With avalanche warnings for the lee slopes of Helvellyn, the hills which stretch northwards from Sticks Pass to Clough Head appeared a suitable choice for the day. In winter these eastern hills retain snow much longer than the higher fells nearer the sea. Sometimes rather unjustly called the boring Dodds, these rounded grassy hills were covered in a firm layer of consolidated snow and their craggy western slopes above St John's in the Vale looked quite alpine. The silver covering of the mountains seemed most approriate as it was our twenty fifth wedding anniversary, while the bitingly cold gale force winds against which we struggled in twenty yard visibility certainly made it a day to remember.

Not surprisingly we saw no-one all day, but even in summer these hills are shunned with walkers turning south rather than north at Sticks Pass. Similarly while the A66 under the slopes of Blencathra is busy with the roar of high speed traffic, the Old Coach Road on the flanks of Clough Head, once the main route from Penrith to Keswick and the north, is quite deserted.

Although the ridge is grassy it presents a steep and rugged side to St John's in the Vale, while below Watson's Dodd lies Castle Rock. Immortalised by Sir Walter Scott in his poem 'The Bridal of Triermain' it is highly prized by rock climbers with a spectacularly overhanging front face.

Rising high on Stybarrow Dodd the little Aira Beck has a short but very eventful journey to Ullswater. From Deepdale it passes through Dowthwaitehead, reputed to be the hamlet with the fewest hours of sunshine in the Lake District and then by the sleepy village of Dockray, an attractive collection of farms, cottages and a pub, whose church is half a mile up the road at Matterdale. Descending through the National Trust land of Gowbarrow

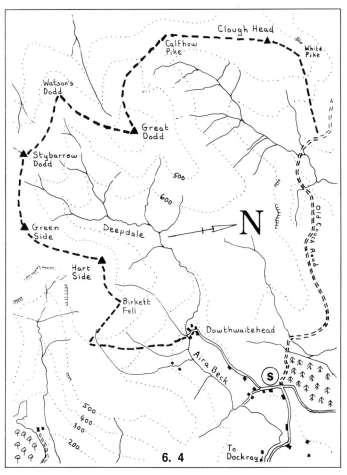

Park it finally plunges spectacularly sixty feet down a rocky gorge at Aira Force before flowing peacefully into the lake. Aira Force was the setting for Wordsworth's poem 'Somnambulist' and it was on the shores of Ullswater, below Gowbarrow Fell, that Dorothy Wordsworth saw the daffodils that inspired William's most famous poem 'I wandered lonely as a cloud'.

ROUTE DESCRIPTION

HART SIDE *(Stag Hill Slope)*

Take the metalled No Through Road which leads in a mile to the tiny hamlet of Dowthwaitehead where the path crosses the beck at a footbridge signed Birkett Fell. Waymarks helpfully indicate the direction of the old way, now long disappeared and rather boggy underfoot, which led over to the Greenside mines. After crossing the fence at a small gate continue to climb south towards Brown Hills aiming for the dip in the hills ahead from where you can look across to Sheffield Pike. Next follow the ruined wall north-west to the good viewpoint of Birkett Fell, named after Lord Birkett who died just two days after making the speech in the House of Lords which saved Ullswater from the worst intentions of the Government and Waterboard. Although there is now a pipeline to Haweswater, it and the pumping station at the head of Ullswater are concealed underground. Just to the left of the wall there is a small cairn with a plaque.

Hart Side summit is only 500 yards to the west and it is an easy walk over grass to the three cairns on the grassy and stony top. The easternmost is the highest. There is a mysterious stony ditch on the south side which was probably made by miners and to the west you can see the remaining summits of the walk.

GREEN SIDE *(Green Hill Slope)*

A path leads south-west to the next summit which is about a mile away over the rather featureless moor. After passing a prominent cairn on the ascent,

Descending from Clough Head

the flattish top of stone and grass has another cairn a few yards west of the unmarked highest point. The Glenridding lead mine in the valley is named after this fell.

STYBARROW DODD *(Round Hill by the Steep Path)*
A faint path continues west towards Stybarrow Dodd disappearing at the peaty col. Now climb directly over grass to the summit which has a small cairn with a large piece of slate in the centre on the highest point, and also a section of wall a few yards to the east which provides some shelter. The view from the top is excellent in all directions and most of the high fells of the Lake District can be seen from this point.

GREAT DODD *(Big Round Hill)*
The next summit lies just over a mile to the north, but the broad grassy ridge first kinks west, the path passing over Watson's Dodd which fails to qualify as a separate top. Continue north-east climbing to the good shelter cairn on Great Dodd whose true top with its small cairn is about 100 yards further north.

CLOUGH HEAD *(Ravine Summit)*
The ridge takes a roundabout route to Clough Head, descending at first south-west then gradually curving round to the north-west to reach Calfhow Pike which is nearly at the lowest point. With only 33ft of ascent this is not a separate top, but it is a good place to stop with a useful spring just to the west of the rocky knoll. Refreshed, the final ascent of the day, a mere 300ft, doesn't take long and the only OS trig point of the five summits is quickly reached. There is also a small windshelter on the flat grassy top and the steep cliffs of Red Screes below make this the most attractive summit of the walk with grand views of Blencathra and Skiddaw to the north-west.

Continue north along the edge of the cliffs for about 400 yards to a small cairn and then descend right over grass to the cairned rocky top of White Pike. Easy grassy slopes lead east to the Old Coach Road and then it is a pleasant walk of under 3 miles back round Matterdale Common to the starting point.

Ill Bell

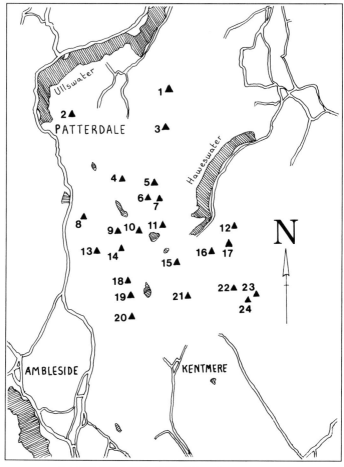

7 LAKE DISTRICT - THE FAR EASTERN FELLS

CHAPTER 7 LAKE DISTRICT - THE FAR EASTERN FELLS

TOP	NAME	HEIGHT	GRID REF	WALK No.
1	Loadpot Hill	671m	90-457181 NY	7.2
2	Place Fell	657m	90-406170 NY	7.2
3	Wether Hill	670m	90-456167 NY	7.2
4	Rest Dodd	696m	90-433137 NY	7.2
5	High Raise	802m	90-448135 NY	7.2
6	Rampsgill Head	792m	90-443128 NY	7.2
7	Kidsty Pike	780m	90-447126 NY	7.2
8	Hartsop Dodd	618m	90-411119 NY	7.3
9	Gray Crag	699m	90-428117 NY	7.3
10	High Street	828m	90-441110 NY	7.1
11	Rough Crag	628m	90-454112 NY	7.1
12	Selside Pike	655m	90-490112 NY	7.4
13	Stony Cove Pike	763m	90-418100 NY	7.3
14	Thornthwaite Crag	784m	90-432100 NY	7.3
15	Harter Fell	778m	90-460093 NY	7.1
16	Branstree	713m	90-478100 NY	7.4
17	Branstree North East Top	673m	90-488103 NY	7.4
18	Froswick	720m	90-435085 NY	7.1
19	Ill Bell	757m	90-436077 NY	7.1
20	Yoke	706m	90-438067 NY	7.1
21	Kentmere Pike	730m	90-466078 NY	7.1
22	Tarn Crag	664m	90-488078 NY	7.4
23	Harrop Pike	637m	90-501078 NY	7.4
24	Grey Crag	638m	90-497072 NY	7.4

WALK 7.1 THE KENTMERE FELLS

SUMMITS	Yoke	2316 ft (706m)
	Ill Bell	2483 ft (757m)
	Froswick	2362 ft (720m)
	High Street	2717 ft (828m)
	Rough Crag	2060 ft (628m)
	Harter Fell	2552 ft (778m)
	Kentmere Pike	2395 ft (730m)
DISTANCE	12½ miles	
ASCENT	4300 feet	
MAPS	OS Landranger sheet 90	
	Outdoor Leisure - The English Lakes, South Eastern area	
	& The English Lakes, North Eastern area	
STARTING POINT	(90-455041) Kentmere Village. 8 miles	
	north-west of Kendal. Parking for a few cars by the church.	

The delightful switchback over Yoke, Ill Bell and Froswick, the dip to the Nan Bield Pass and then, after the steep ascent to Harter Fell, the long easy ridge returning over Kentmere Pike, is one of the best high level walks in the Eastern fells and is very probably walked every day throughout the year. If like us you know the names Yoke, Ill Bell and Froswick well enough, but sometimes have difficulty in deciding which is which, remember they go in alphabetical order from north to south.

The little village of Kentmere has a fine example of a fourteenth century pele tower. This square building has thick stone walls and would originally have consisted of a basement with a low door and slit windows with a narrow staircase or ladder leading to the rooms above. The local people would have retreated there for safety during raids from Scotland. The farmhouse is a later addition to the building. The reformer Bernard de Gilpin who was born here in 1517, became the Archbishop of Durham. The Kentmere was a mile long lake south of the village. It had a natural dam of glacial moraine which was breached to drain the lake at the end of the nineteenth century. The bed of this lake is now dredged and the diatomaceous clay processed to form insulating bricks and sound proof boards in a well screened works, hardly noticable from the road. A tenth century wooden boat was found in the old lake bed in 1955 which is now in the National Maritime Museum. The village no longer has a pub but the Low Bridge Inn, which is now a private house, had the infamous distinction of being the first in England to lose its license due to the bad behaviour of the navvies who built Kentmere reservoir. The reservoir was built to maintain a constant head of water, regulating the flow of the river to the many mills downstream of which there were ninety at the beginning of the nineteenth century. Dropping a thousand feet in only twenty five miles the Kent is reputed to be the fastest flowing river in the country.

High Street to the north of the horseshoe is usually gained from the less interesting western side and the craggy face which it presents to Mardale is unsuspected by walkers traversing its flat summit. However Rough Crag, that outlying spur of High Street which looks down on Haweswater reveals the wilder side of the mountain. As it is also a two thousander this presents an opportunity for a Kentmere Horseshoe walk with a difference including a visit to the tarns of both Blea Water and Small Water as a bonus.

Street means a metalled road and High Street was named after the Roman road which ran for twelve miles over the fell tops from Brocavum near Penrith, which had a garrison of one thousand men, to Galava at Ambleside. It was built on the line of a prehistoric trackway which would have run high above the marshy and wooded valleys of the time. The summit is also known as Racecourse Hill after the custom of holding races there following the gathering of sheep and the returning of the strays to their owners. People from the surrounding dales gathered there on July 12th, barrels of ale were rolled up the hill and games and wrestling took place. The last annual fair was in 1835, but surely the weather must have been better then!

We have a particular affection for these fells as they were the scene both of our first backpacking trip and also of our first high level winter camp. It was snowing gently as we pitched our small tent at half past four, just as it was getting dark, and the long winter evening was enlivened by listening on a tiny radio to a play about a Himalayan climb. Outside the snow fell and the wind blew and it was at times difficult to distinguish which sound effects were real.

ROUTE DESCRIPTION

YOKE

From the church walk up to the end of the tarmac road. Don't go through the gate which leads to Hartrigg Farm, but continue left on the lane. Shortly a signpost 'Garburn Pass to Troutbeck' points the way right and the old packhorse route is then followed as it steadily gains height. After a mile there is a gate across the track and in the grassy bowl beyond, a minor path turns off right beside a stream to head for a notch in the skyline. This short cut is preferable to the alternative continuation to the head of the pass where the initial slopes of Yoke are very boggy. On gaining the skyline there is still a short wet section ahead before firmer ground can be followed alongside the ridge wall. When the wall bends away left, follow a good path steadily uphill to the summit of Yoke. At the far end of the ridge there is a small cairn on a little rocky rib which thrusts up through the predominating grass.

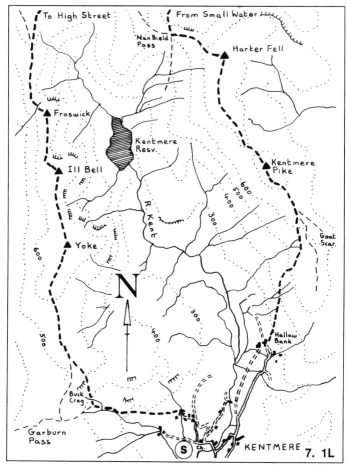

ILL BELL *(Steep Hill)*

Continuing north, easy slopes to the col are followed by the rockier flanks of Ill Bell. There are three cairns, two of which, close together, compete for the honour of being the highest. It is a dead heat. Kentmere Reservoir fed by the headwaters of the River Kent, which rises in Hall Cove, attracts the downward glance, while the long level ridge from Harter Fell to Kentmere Pike fills the eastern view.

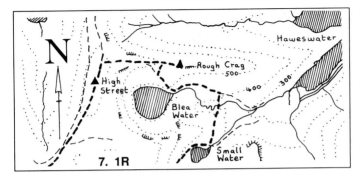

FROSWICK
Ahead lie the steep cliffs which drop into Over Cove and these must be avoided by following the path north-west down stony slopes to the col. Grass is now met again and a steady uphill plod soon brings you to Froswick's compact summit and its cairn.

HIGH STREET *(High Road)*
Although the beacon on top of Thornthwaite Crag beckons, there is still a long way to go and the next stop is High Street. The path forks right about half a mile up the ridge from the col, and the wall end appears a similar distance beyond. The Roman road which runs parallel to the wall some 50 yards or so to its left misses the top. In mist a compass is useful in ensuring that the end of the wall which runs over the top of High Street is found. This wall then leads unerringly over the summit where an OS trig point leaves one's position in no doubt. The panorama is extensive from Morecambe Bay in the south to Cross Fell in the north-east and from the Howgill Fells in the south-east to the Helvellyn range in the west.

ROUGH CRAG
A cairn 300 yards north-east of the trig point marks the top of the ridge which descends towards Mardale. This narrow ridge makes an attractive and interesting way onto High Street from the Haweswater side. It is about a mile from the trig point on High Street to the summit of Rough Crag, most of it downhill, so having reached the top which has a small cairn astride the path, don't go any further as the way on is back.

HARTER FELL *(Stag Fell)*
Re-trace your route to Caspel Gate, the col where there is a small tarn, and descending south-east a path soon appears and leads down to the dam. Blea Water is the deepest tarn in the Lake District with the slopes of High Street going straight down to a depth of 200ft. Follow the path above Blea Water

143

Beck for nearly half a mile then leave it to cross the beck and skirting the boggy marsh, climb grassy slopes southwards to cross over the ridge to Small Water. Passing to the right of a small tarn on the col go down to join the path beside Small Water near the stone shelters. An ascent of about 600ft brings you to the wall shelter at the head of the Nan Bield Pass. The classic route has now been rejoined and the climb to Harter Fell is the last major ascent of the day. The flat grassy plateau of a summit has a cairn spiked with old iron fence posts. A curiosity and much as Wainwright recorded it, unlike alas the cairns on Lingmell and Pike of Blisco.

KENTMERE PIKE *(Kentmere Peak)*

A boundary fence and then a wall follows the ridge all the way. A very easy walk over grass leads in a mile, and with little ascent, to the final mountain summit. There is a trig point on the other side of the wall.

Continue along the wall descending gradually until after half a mile the path forks just before the minor top above Goat Scar. Turn right and descend over a ladder stile to follow a cairned path down to the houses at Hallow Bank. Go through a gate, turn right onto the track and go between the houses on a rough road to drop down to join the bridleway coming from the head of the valley. Leaving the field at the corner go straight on over the stone slab bridge and along a grassy track to join and follow Low Lane with its flanking stone walls. After half a mile, a stone step stile over the wall on the right, at the brow of the hill, leads to a footbridge over the river. Turn left on the lane beyond which brings you back to St Cuthbert's Church in Kentmere. Restored in both 1866 and 1950 only the roof timbers remain from the sixteenth century.

Harter Fell

WALK 7.2 PLACE FELL AND HIGH RAISE

SUMMITS	Place Fell	2155 ft (657m)
	Rest Dodd	2283 ft (696m)
	Rampsgill Head	2598 ft (792m)
	Kidsty Pike	2559 ft (780m)
	High Raise	2631 ft (802m)
	Wether Hill	2198 ft (670m)
	Loadpot Hill	2201 ft (671m)
DISTANCE	13 miles	
ASCENT	3540 feet	
MAPS	OS Landranger sheet 90.	
	Outdoor Leisure - The English Lakes, North Eastern area	
STARTING POINT	(90-436192) Martindale Church, ½ mile south-west of Howtown on the eastern shore of Ullswater. Small car park.	

Angle Tarn to many people means that rather gloomy stretch of water under the slopes of Esk Pike, but the Angle Tarn of these Eastern fells is more open and while in less dramatic surroundings than its western namesake, is somehow a more friendly place which catches the sun and more often reflects the blue sky. On one such sunny clear and calm evening in early April we pitched the tent on the shore with our two boys and strolled over to Brock Crags to watch the setting sun. The next morning it was as though we had been transported to the other tarn; the ground was frozen hard, the sky was grey and as we made breakfast the snow began to fall.

Following High Street northwards, the Roman legions tramped over Rampsgill Head and High Raise along the grassy ridge to Wether Hill and Loadpot Hill beyond. The highest point is reached at High Raise, another twin, but while more mountainlike in its proportions than its counterpart in the Central fells, it is not quite such an extensive viewpoint being much closer to the edge of the Lake District. To the west Place Fell, with one of the most attractive lakeside walks anywhere, is set apart from the rest of the Eastern fells, facing Glenridding at the head of Ullswater.

At the centre of the area is the Martindale Deer Forest. It is a forest in the old sense of a wild open place and there are only a few trees to be found situated above Ramps Gill, but it is a sanctuary for deer and one of the few places in the Lakeland hills where the walker is actively discouraged. Collectors of 'Wainwrights' who are approaching the final total of 214 peaks may sneak into this restricted area by the back door, approaching from Rest

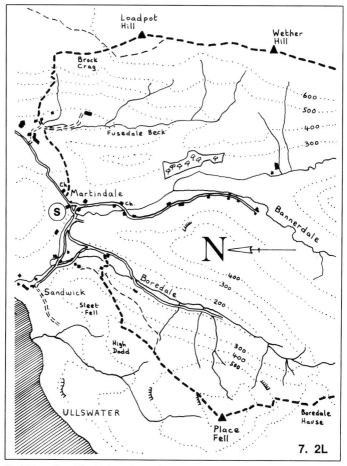

7. 2L

Dodd to collect The Nab and may be rewarded by the sight of a herd of red deer, but as The Nab reaches only to 1890 feet, consciences will not be troubled on this walk.

Martindale Church, beside which the walk starts, is condemned by some as a Victorian intrusion, though we found it well enough in keeping with its surroundings and were charmed to discover the mouse carved on the church

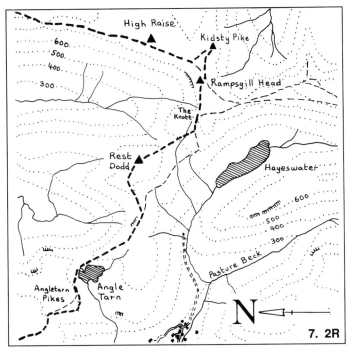

gate that is the trademark of Robert Thompson, the woodcarver who fashioned it. Although located in a sparsely inhabited valley, it is not however Martindale's only church. Half a mile south stands a chapel built in 1633, while at the head of Boredale, high on the path to High Street, is Chapel in the Hause whose ruins, indistinguishable from a tumbled sheepfold, are in fact the remains of a medieval chapel.

ROUTE DESCRIPTION

PLACE FELL *(Swampy Fell)*
Take the road south-west going gently downhill, forking right at the road junction signed 'Sandwick' and on to cross the Howegrain Beck. At the next turning, go left (signed 'Bridleway to Patterdale') up Boredale, which as its name suggests refers to wild boar, and at Garth Heads in just under half a mile turn right on the path which crosses Boredale Beck at a clapper bridge. Follow the old track to the left of the barn and over stiles onto the slopes of Sleet Fell

and climb up to join the good path which slants south-west across the fellside. Here in a boggy area grows the rare Grass of Parnassus which despite its name is not a grass but a pretty five petalled white flower. At the col, after passing a sheepfold, continue in the same direction to a prominent cairn which gives good views back to Ullswater; it is then only a short walk to the summit where a stone OS trig point stands on the rocky top. From here the line of the walk can be seen, starting from the clump of trees by the church at the start onto Place Fell, past Angletarn Pikes to the High Street ridge and the final descent to Howtown.

REST DODD *(Round Hill Moor)*
After passing a well built wind shelter the path descends gently south along the ridge with bird's-eye views of Patterdale. Boredale Hause is reached in three quarters of a mile. Pass to the left of a ruined enclosure, the remains of the Chapel in the Hause, and after crossing Stonebarrow Gill continue in the same direction on the main path climbing towards Angletarn Pikes. Keeping right where the hillside steepens, and contouring round on a little alpine path

Place Fell from Hartsop Dodd

with views down to Brothers Water far below, the path then bends left to go round Angle Tarn. The next section can be rather boggy underfoot. As you climb, Angle Tarn finally disappears from view and Hayeswater can be glimpsed down to the right. 200 yards after passing through a gate in the wall, leave the path to head east following the grassy ridge for half a mile to the summit of Rest Dodd, (in mist it is easier to continue along the main path and then follow the wall which heads east to just below the summit). The grassy dome has three small cairns of equal height. The one to the west gives the best views of Angle Tarn and the Helvellyn range, with Catsye Cam standing out most prominently, and Great Gable appearing in the dip on the skyline. Below to the north is the deer sanctuary of The Nab and eastwards are the surprisingly craggy slopes of Rampsgill Head and High Raise the next objectives. The number of fellow walkers will by now have diminished as Rest Dodd is strictly a peak bagger's mountain, it is not really on the way to anywhere, the approach is pathless and there are no obvious attractions to tempt people away from the main path.

RAMPSGILL HEAD *(Ram's Gill Top)*
Descend south-east to the col then climb beside the wall for half a mile until the main path below The Knott is reached where you turn left. The mountain rescue kit is no longer kept here, amazingly because of vandalism, surprising in this remote spot. At the wall corner leave the path and climb east over easy slopes to Rampsgill Head. A cairn stands above the cliffs with good views down into the valley, but this is not quite the highest point. A little further on, marked by a few stones, is one spot height and beyond the tiny tarns is another of equal height. High Street stretches away to the south and to the east only 500 yards away lies Kidsty Pike.

KIDSTY PIKE *(Goat's Path Peak)*
Head south-east to pick up the good path which runs along the edge, high above the Head of Riggindale. Kidsty Pike, though a prominent landmark, is really only a bump on the eastern ridge of Rampsgill Head. The pointed rocky summit, marked with a small cairn perched above the steep drop, looks out over Haweswater towards the Cross Fell range.

HIGH RAISE *(High Cairn)*
Retrace your steps for 200 yards and then fork right on a tiny path which joins the main path along the ridge at the col between Rampsgill Head and High Raise. From here it is only a quarter of a mile and less than 200ft of ascent to the summit. The cairn is to the right of the path set in the middle of a stony area with an adjacent windshelter.

WETHER HILL *(Hill where Wethers were kept)*
Return to the main path which switchbacks along the ridge for a couple of miles. The interest lies mainly in the views with Ullswater to the left and the Haweswater Reservoir to the right. The path passes over the shoulder of the

first high ground and leads to the second high point which is the official top. The ground to the right of the small cairn, which incorporates an old boundary stone, is slightly higher.

LOADPOT HILL *(Ore Hole Hill)*

The grassy path dips to a col and then climbs past the ruins of Lowther House, a shooting lodge on the Lowther Estate. The chimney collapsed in 1973 leaving only a pile of stones. On the flat grassy summit is a small cairn round a boundary stone and a trig point which is post-Wainwright, not being mentioned by him. Looking back along the ridge you can trace the route of the old Roman Road which ran all the way to High Street.

Head north along a minor path which descends to cross the Roman Road to the left of Loadpot Hole, from which stone was quarried by the Romans to metal the original High Street. Continue across an area of small tarns to Brock Crag then go north for about a quarter of a mile to the col before Bonscale Pike. Dropping steeply to the left, the end of an old trackway is picked up which zigzags down the hillside to Mellguards where you join the lane. Turn immediately left on the bridleway and cross Fusedale Beck at the clapper bridge. Go straight across the far track and take the path signed 'To Martindale' which contours round above The Coombs back to the Parish Church of St Peter, Martindale.

Dinner time

WALK 7.3 THE HARTSOP HORSESHOE

SUMMITS	Hartsop Dodd	2028 ft (618m)
	Stony Cove Pike	2503 ft (763m)
	Thornthwaite Crag	2572 ft (784m)
	Gray Crag	2293 ft (699m)
DISTANCE	6 miles	
ASCENT	2450 feet	
MAPS	OS Landranger sheet 90	
	Outdoor Leisure - The English Lakes, North Eastern area	
STARTING		
POINT	(90-410130) Hartsop village to the east of Brothers Water on the A592, 2 miles south of Ullswater. Small free car park.	

Concluding his 'little Volume', his Guide to the Lakes, Wordsworth devoted an eighty line ode to 'The Pass of Kirkstone'. *'This block - and yon, whose Church-like frame, Gives to the savage Pass its name'.* The final section of this steep pass from Ambleside was known as 'The Struggle' where passengers on the horse drawn coaches had to get out and walk. Crossing the Kirkstone Pass after a brilliantly clear weekend of blue skies and iron hard frosts we descended into a sea of thick fog which covered the whole of the southern Lake District. Winter often brings out the best in the hills with their structure shown in sharp relief by the low sun and perfect conditions unsuspected by those confined to the valleys.

At the foot of the pass opposite Brothers Water is the village of Hartsop with its houses of blue slate and picturesque seventeenth century spinning galleries. Hartsop Dodd which rises steeply behind the houses was, like the village, originally known as Low Hartsop, but low refers to its position in the valley and the summit is more than 300 ft higher than its twin High Hartsop Dodd on the other side of the valley.

Although a steep ascent, Hartsop Dodd is merely the end of a ridge which continues climbing to Caudale Moor. The highest point is Stony Cove Pike while the lower summit, known as John Bell's Banner, was named after the Reverend John Bell of Ambleside who was born in the sixteenth century. The word 'banner' means boundary and so presumably this was the boundary of his parish as three parishes met on the top of Caudale Moor. A roughly constructed memorial cairn, surmounted by a wooden cross and a plaque to Mark Atkinson of Kirkstone Pass Inn, who died 14th June 1930, is sited just below this lower summit. Mark Atkinson bought the inn, the third highest in England, in 1914. A new plaque has been added in memory of his son William Ion Atkinson who died 2nd April 1987 aged 83 years. From here you can look

151

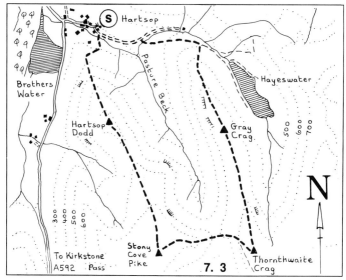

down upon the inn and on towards Windermere.

The finest summit of all though is Thornthwaite Crag. The Beacon, a magnificent 14ft high pillar of stone, is on the route of a prehistoric way and marks an old parish boundary. After the depredations which have befallen other lovely cairns it is with great relief that we look up to the skyline of the Eastern fells every year to see the familiar shape against the sky.

ROUTE DESCRIPTION

HARTSOP DODD *(Stag Valley Round Hill)*
Go through the kissing gate at the end of the village on the public footpath to Pasture Beck, crossing Hayeswater Gill at Walker Bridge which has been defaced by an unsightly metal parapet. After a very short way cross a ladder stile beside a gate and climb beside the wall to a small gate onto the open fellside. Continue steeply with old mine workings to the left to join the ridge and a good path. The highest visible point on the ridge above proves to be a false summit when reached, but there are fine aerial views with Hartsop village and Brothers Water almost beneath your feet. It is only a little further to the top which is crossed by a wall that is joined for the last few yards of ascent. The substantial cairn is not at the highest point which is a little beyond and marked by a small new pile of stones beside the wall. Ahead lies the mass of Caudale Moor while to the right the valley of Dovedale leads up to Dove

Crag and the Fairfield tops; to the left is High Street.

STONY COVE PIKE
Follow the wall for just over a mile and after about 500ft of ascent the top is reached. Several cairns on the otherwise flat top vie for the honour of being the highest, but the spot chosen by the Ordnance Survey is a few yards west of the wall, and unmarked. Eastwards lie the Kentmere Fells with the next objective Thornthwaite Crag and its prominent beacon looking close.

THORNTHWAITE CRAG *(Thornbush Clearing Crag)*
The path down the steep drop to Threshthwaite Mouth is located by returning north along the wall for a few yards to a ruined joining wall. Follow this east steeply down to the col and equally steeply up again the other side. The path diverges from the wall and misses the summit, so keep the wall in sight to reach the highest point of the fell which is unmistakably identified by its fine dry stone column. This is set in the wall above outcropping jagged rocks to the west and smooth glacier scratched rocks to the east. Thornthwaite Crag is really only a subsidiary top of High Street beyond which the fells stretch away towards Penrith.

GRAY CRAG

Follow the summit wall north, and when it bends away west to Threshthwaite Mouth keep to the ridge where a path soon appears continuing northwards for a mile. After passing over an intermediate top the highest point is reached just before a wall crosses the end of the ridge. This is unmarked and undistinguished, but a few paces to the right gives views down to Hayeswater, which supplies Penrith with water, and across to Kidsty Pike peeping out to the right of Rampsgill Head.

Beyond the wall is a cairn which is the better viewpoint for Ullswater and the Helvellyn range. Continue along a path which wiggles down the ridge and then terminates abruptly at a cairn. Continue in the same direction down steep grassy slopes finally following a ruined wall to the main track where you turn left for the short walk back to Hartsop village.

Thornthwaite Beacon

153

WALK 7.4 SELSIDE PIKE, BRANSTREE AND
THE SLEDDALE FELLS

SUMMITS	Selside Pike	2149ft (655m)
	Branstree North East Top	2208ft (673m)
	Branstree	2339ft (713m)
	Tarn Crag	2178ft (664m)
	Grey Crag	2093ft (638m)
	Harrop Pike	2090ft (637m)
DISTANCE	11½ miles	
ASCENT	2450 feet	
MAPS	OS Landranger sheet 90	
	Outdoor Leisure - The English Lakes, North Eastern area & The English Lakes, South Eastern area	
STARTING POINT		
	(90-516133) The minor road to Swindale, 2 miles west of Shap. Parking for a few cars by the side of the road just before Truss Gap.	

On the very eastern fringe of Lakeland and encircling the head of Mosedale, the hanging valley above Swindale, these fells are usually approached from the motorway and Shap. With its high limestone walls reminiscent of Yorkshire, this rural village, once sitting astride the main highway north to Scotland, now has a sleepy and decaying air. In 1745 Bonny Prince Charlie marched through Shap, retreating the same way somewhat later pursued by the Duke of Cumberland. A few farms come right up into the village, which has more than its fair share of pubs, much appreciated in winter as until the opening of the M6 in 1970, lorries were often marooned here by heavy snowfalls. Swindale, a perfect Lakeland valley gouged out by the glaciers millions of years ago, comes as a surprise after the pastoral, undulating countryside and the empty Shap Fells. As you approach, the whole character of the landscape changes on entering this unexpectedly beautiful and dramatic dale.

The fells of Selside Pike and Branstree separate Swindale, originally Swine Dale, from Haweswater, the reservoir which drowned Mardale. The hamlet of Mardale Green at its head was described by Harriet Martineau in her 'Complete Guide to the English Lakes', published in 1855. She writes of the inn being a full mile from the water and of the snug little farms. The valley was flooded by 1940, raising the level of the original lake by 50ft and drowning a whole community. The church the seventeenth century Dun Bull Inn and

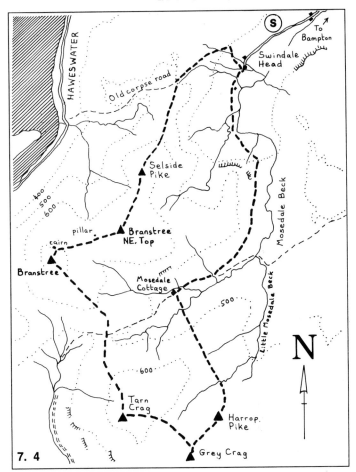

7. 4

the handful of cottages and farms were lost. The pub was rebuilt half way down the reservoir as the Haweswater Hotel, a building quite out of keeping with its surroundings. During a drought visitors come to stare at the sad remains of the village exposed in the mud. Swindale itself was once, like Mardale, under threat of flooding, but mercifully it has been spared.

Between Long Sleddale and Wet Sleddale are the three tops of Sleddale

Fell. Tarn Crag was our last Wainwright two thousander and we agreed with him, as we damply celebrated with the children beside the surveying pillar, that we had *'Passed outside the verge of Lakeland'.* The surveying pillars were built by Manchester Corporation during the construction of the Longsleddale aqueduct that carries the water from the reservoir to Manchester.

After a week of wild weather in Keswick, winter was finally losing its grip on the hills as we climbed Harrop Pike, the easternmost top in the Lakes. The snow had almost gone and toadspawn lay in the shallow pool beside the summit cairn. Descending into Mosedale a darting lizard stopped motionless at our feet while at the head of the valley a herd of deer grazed peacefully.

ROUTE DESCRIPTION

SELSIDE PIKE *(Sallow Sheiling Peak)*
In the spring the narrow lane to Swindale Head has grassy banks scattered with primroses and with few or no cars it makes a beautiful approach to these little visited hills. At Swindale Head turn right on the 'Old Corpse Road', which led from Mardale via Swindale and Keld to the parish church at Shap. Coffins were carried this way for burial until a graveyard was made at Mardale Chapel in the eighteenth century. When the valley was flooded to make Haweswater reservoir the bodies at Mardale were exhumed and also taken to Shap for reburial. Climbing steeply, the waymarked old way bends back to ford the stream and then becoming indistinct continues to climb until the angle eases. Leave the path and pick your way south across marshy grass to join Selside Pike's grassy north ridge. The ridge rises and narrows with views down into Swindale. When the ridge broadens leave the edge and climb south-west easily over short grass to the summit. The large ancient cairn, just to the west of the fence corner, has been roughly hollowed out to form a windshelter. Ahead lies Branstree with the High Street range to the west and Haweswater below.

BRANSTREE NORTH EAST TOP
Follow the fence south-west to the col and the strangely named Captain Whelter Bog, and then continuing in the same direction, climb the grassy slope following a bit of a path. A few stones mark the highest point on the tussocky moor.

BRANSTREE *(Steep Road)*
Descend west, in clear weather making directly towards the prominent cairn on Branstree's northern slope. On older maps it is marked as Brant Street. Pass between two small tarns to the old surveying pillar from which there is a good view of Haweswater. Crossing the fence climb to the fine stone beacon on Artle Crag, a good viewpoint for High Street and Haweswater. The summit is 300 yards to the south-west. In mist the fence can be followed and the highest point is marked by a ground level small circular concrete structure, rather like a bird bath. Inscribed 'Ordnance Survey Station Trigonometrical',

it lies 40 yards north of the fence wall junction. From the flat grassy top the best views are towards Harter Fell and Kentmere Pike

TARN CRAG
Follow the wall then fence leading south-east from the summit of Branstree for 1½ miles to the next summit. After crossing the head of Mosedale climb beside the fence to a bend on the flattish top. The highest point on the fell is 200 yards to the south-west, marked by a small cairn augmented with lumps

Jeremy, John and Joe on Branstree summit

of concrete; a few yards further on is another old survey pillar. The actual summit is rather boggy but it is surrounded by small rocky outcrops. The survey post is the better viewpoint for Longsleddale and looking back you can spot the top of the Branstree pillar.

GREY CRAG
Descend east to the col by the swampy Greycrag Tarn, really only a vast bog. The fence crosses the firmest bit of the area, but even this heaves and quakes as you walk over it. A further quarter of a mile of fence following leads to another helpful fence bend. The summit, difficult to locate in mist, is 250 yards to the south. There are many little tops to chose from, all crowned with a few stones, but the highest point is obvious in clear weather.

HARROP PIKE *(Hare's Valley Peak)*
Return to follow the useful fence, or in clear weather make a beeline for the last summit, only half a mile away to the north-east. The old fence has been replaced by a new one, and the old iron posts embedded in lumps of rock, stand forlornly beside it. Luckily Harrop Pike just qualifies as a summit as it is the best top visited. With a large beacon rivalling that of Artle Crag, a small tarn and a windshelter, it is a very attractive spot. The highest point is the westernmost unmarked outcrop on the other side of the fence. This top, the easternmost of the Lake District's 2000ft mountains, has extensive views towards the Pennines, and down into the three dales of Crookdale, Borrowdale and Bannisdale.

The simplest way back is to follow Little Mosedale Beck to the footbridge in Mosedale, but a more interesting route is to return via the remote Mosedale Cottage. Head north-west crossing the beck to pass over Seavy Side. With careful contouring there is no ascent, and steep but easy slopes lead down to the bridleway beside the cottage. Above Mosedale Cottage, which is used as a bothy by shepherds, is the huge and unexpected Mosedale Quarry. The 3 mile walk back is at first boggy and the waymarked path turning left down Mosedale has vanished in places. It is a lovely valley and the sudden drop into Swindale comes as a surprise with its dramatic rock scenery and fine waterfalls. The path improves and makes its way through the glacial moraines to rejoin the outward route at Swindale Head, with its one remaining inhabited dwelling, for the final walk back up the lane.

The Cheviot from Housey Crags

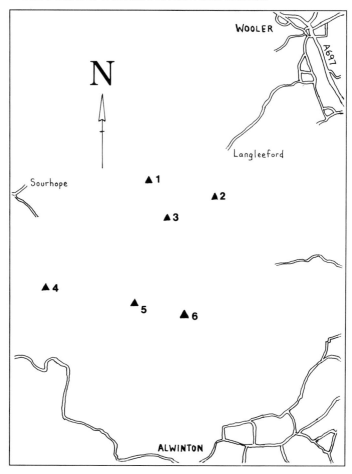

8. THE CHEVIOTS

CHAPTER 8 THE CHEVIOTS

TOP	NAME	HEIGHT	GRID REF	WALK No.
1	The Cheviot	815m	75-909205 NT	8.1
2	Hedgehope Hill	714m	80-944198 NT	8.1
3	Comb Fell	652m	80-924187 NT	8.1
4	Windy Gyle	619m	80-855152 NT	8.2
5	Bloodybush Edge	610m	80-902143 NT	8.2
6	Cushat Law	615m	80-928137 NT	8.2

John backpacking in the hills

WALK 8.1 THE CHEVIOT

SUMMITS	The Cheviot	2674 ft (815m)
	Comb Fell	2139 ft (652m)
	Hedgehope Hill	2342 ft (714m)

DISTANCE	9¹/₂ miles
ASCENT	2700 feet
MAPS	OS Landranger sheets (74 or 75) & 80
STARTING POINT	(75-954225)The Harthope Valley, 5 miles south-west of Wooler.Parking by the roadside at the confluence of Hawsen Burn and Harthope Burn, just before Langleeford.

With their western edge marking the Scottish border, the Cheviot Hills are the most northerly outpost of England's mountains. Heather moor, bilberry, rough grass and high rounded summits rise from attractive quiet valleys and although the southern part is penetrated for a long way by a narrow public road serving a few scattered farms and the military who occupy much of the area to the south, the mountains are not crossed by any road. Approaches thus involve a lengthy drive around the perimeter, but apart from the Pennine Way and The Cheviot itself, these remote hills are unfrequented and it is the very fact that access by car is so awkward that helps to preserve their beauty.

Although at first their rounded outlines suggest otherwise, these hills are of volcanic origin with outcropping tors hinting at the underlying rocks. The origins of the Cheviots lie in massive lava flows from volcanoes 350 million years ago. In subsequent ages further volcanic activity remained beneath the surface cooling to form a pinkish granite which has since been exposed by weathering. The intense heat of the intrusion of this later rock altered and hardened the earlier lava, which has resisted the weathering to form the characteristic rocky tors.

The little border town of Wooler is a quiet backwater bypassed by the busy A697 to Scotland. Well endowed with inns, the old market town is a good base from which to explore the northern part of the area.

Our first encounter with Cheviot was in the half light of a misty wet day when snowflakes mingled with the rain and the ground underfoot was a sloppy mess of wet snow and mud. It was hardly inspiring. We waded to the trig point and left again with few regrets. As if to make up for its previous sullen mood, Cheviot was transformed on a return visit. The sun shone out of a blue sky, in the clear air the view extended to the distant sea and the Farne Islands and the mountains glowed purple with the heather at its finest. Among the large,

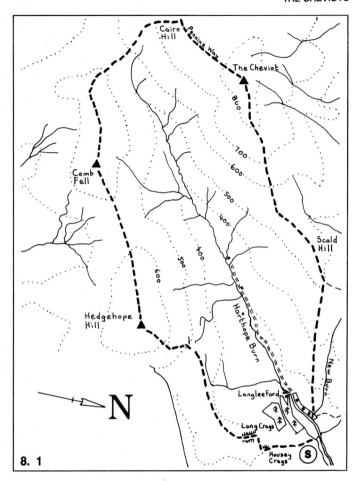

8. 1

black, finger staining bilberries were the much rarer orange fruits of the cloudberry which were once prized as a great delicacy for the king. We ate royally.

ROUTE DESCRIPTION

THE CHEVIOT *(unknown)*

Beyond the car park, 100 yards up the road, a signpost points the way to The Cheviot via Scald Hill and a good path climbs to the left of the New Burn to join the ridge. It is worth the small detour to the summit cairn of Scald Hill, on the far side of the fence, to look towards the College Valley and down upon the remote farm of Goldscleugh. After one and a half miles climbing steeply beside the fence, you gain the summit plateau. An easy stroll leads to the elevated OS trig point which stands on the other side of the fence, perched precariously on a high plinth set in the midst of a wilderness of peat. The views are disappointing as there is too much foreground, but climbing to the top of the concrete pillar improves them considerably affording distant glimpses of the sea with Hedgehope Hill in the foreground, and to the west the Auchope Cairn, named after General Auchope who was killed in the Boer War.

COMB FELL *(Narrow Valley Fell)*

Follow the fence south for about half a mile to Cairn Hill, which as the name implies has a huge ancient cairn as usual modified to form a windshelter. This is a little frequented spur of the Pennine Way, nowadays somewhat busier than when Edward Grierson wrote in the 'Companion Guide to Northumbria' *'the*

Pennine Way is little known, even to some of the farmers and landowners whose fields it crosses'. From the cairn descend first south and then south-east to cross the head of the Harthope Burn to a broad col and then climb east for half a mile. This is the only rough section of the walk as there is no path through the heather and groughs, but soon the fence from Coldlaw Cairn is joined and with its accompanying sheep trod it leads to the highest point at the eastern end of the ridge. The summit is unmarked and the view is dominated by The Cheviot to the north-west while to the south lie Cushat Law and Bloodybush Edge.

The summit of Cheviot

HEDGEHOPE HILL *(Hedge Valley Hill)*

It's an easy stroll north-east to the col, and then following the fence all the way, a final climb which is easier than it looks, leads to the fine summit with its massive ancient cairn. What a pity The Cheviot overtops Hedgehope Hill as this is much the better mountain summit. The concrete OS trig point sits incongruously on the highest stones with magnificent views of the sea covering half the horizon. To the north-east it is just possible to pick out Bamburgh Castle and the Farne Islands with the naked eye.

A steep descent north down the concession path or, in bad visibility, beside the fence, leads to a wide col where the waymarked path becomes more trodden and leads to the rocky tors of Long Crags and the striking Housey Crags. An attractive path then descends north to cross the Harthope Burn at a footbridge back to the starting point.

WALK 8.2 CUSHAT LAW TO WINDY GYLE

SUMMITS	Cushat Law	2018 ft (615m)
	Bloodybush Edge	2001 ft (610m)
	Windy Gyle	2031 ft (619m)
NOTE	Grouse moors	
DISTANCE	15½ miles	
ASCENT	2950 feet	
MAPS	OS Landranger sheet 80	
STARTING POINT	(80-920091) 2 miles north of Alwinton. Parking at the entrance to Kidland Forest, at the end of the unmade track from Alwinton which passes to the left of Clennel Hall.	

Approaching these southern summits of the Cheviots up the long narrow road beside the River Coquet where the yellow monkey flower grows in profusion, herons skulk furtively beside the streams or flap lazily into the air with a guilty backward glance as if caught in some reprehensible act.

Although the tops of these rounded hills are open heather moorland which stretches away northwards to the higher companion summits of Cheviot, the southern flanks are covered by the Kidland Forest. Here the forest tracks wind their way through steep sided valleys with colourful grassy verges of eyebright, thyme, harebells and heather.

The beautiful valley of Coquet Dale and much of the land to the south is alas marred by the presence of an Army Training Range. On his visit to Northumberland in 1910 Winston Churchill decided to purchase this land for a practice camp for the Royal Artillery and since then the area has been increased to 92 square miles. The largest training ground in Britain it amazingly takes up one fifth of the National Park. Although Otterburn is a live firing area, even when red flags are flying motorists can still drive up the quiet lane beside the River Coquet past the remotely situated Windyhaugh school (goodness knows where the children come from). The southern flank of Windy Gyle is a 'dry training area' used for troop manoeuvres. Forbidding notices warn keep to the path as there may be unexploded bombs left from when this was a target area, but fortunately correspondence with the army confirms that this area is soon to be cleared. On the summit of Windy Gyle and standing on the boundary of England and Scotland is Russell's Cairn. Dating from the bronze age it is named after Lord Francis Russell who was killed here in 1585, murdered by the Scots.

The return from Windy Gyle is along Clennell Street, a Roman road and also an old drove road making for easy walking. This too passes through the forest, but the views are open and extensive, a complete contrast to the ascent.

Named after some long forgotten battle or murder Bloodybush Edge comes as a bit of a disappointment with no bush and no edge, but on our last visit it was certainly bloody. We had just gained the summit when suddenly the sound of gunfire echoed over the purple heather moors and we walked straight into a twentieth century ambush. The Glorious Twelfth was a foolish day to chose; the book that stated *'Mercifully, grouse shooting has now been abandoned'* was patently wrong, and our descent was blocked by a line of men with guns. Beating a hasty retreat we made a detour by the forest to gain Uswayford unobserved. The shooting hut bustled with activity. Polishing their guns in readiness were numerous men, wearing deerstalker hats, green wellies, matching waistcoats and tweed plus-fours in tasteful shades of lovat green. Grouse shooting, like all other sports, has its unofficial uniform.

ROUTE DESCRIPTION

CUSHAT LAW *(Wood-pigeon's Hill)*
The ascent is an easy walk through the attractive Kidland Forest, which was once a monastic sheep pasture, following the main track beside Yoke Burn. A circular sheepfold or stell, the first of several to be seen, is typical of the area. These sheepfolds were supposedly invented by one of Nelson's captains,

Cushat Law

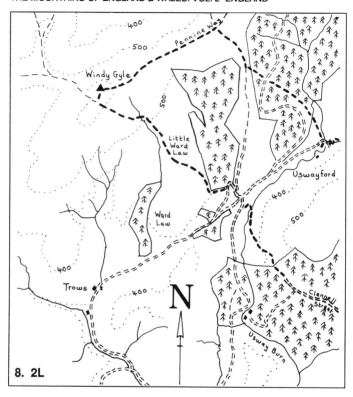

8. 2L

George Napier, who later farmed in Northumberland. After a couple of miles following the burn, the path begins to climb steeply and the summit can be seen above the trees. The path doubles back away from the hill, but in 200 yards turn right continuing to climb and contour the slope for another half mile then fork left on a minor grassy road to pass below Cushat Law, finally leaving the trees only 300ft below the summit. A tractor track through the grass climbs to a fence which has a stile opposite a small cairn, a hollowed out ancient cairn lies just beyond. To the north is The Cheviot and Hedgehope Hill and to the east the North Sea. The wide open views are a welcome contrast to the shut in closeness of the forest.

BLOODYBUSH EDGE

Follow the fence west to the col where we saw two deer, and then climb gently on a good path through the heather to the summit and a standard concrete OS trig point to the left of the fence junction.

WINDY GYLE

Continue to follow the fence west towards Yarnspath Law to join the right of

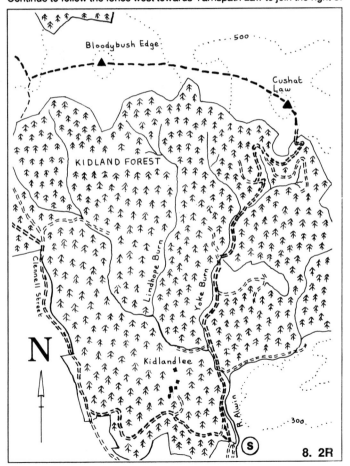

way from the forest and descend to the remote farm of Uswayford. From this isolated building a clear but narrow path leads to the left of the Usway Burn, climbing high above the stream and then up a forest ride to cross a forest road. Leaving the forest at a stile veer right to join Clennell Street for a short way and this main track on the open hillside leads to a stile on the Pennine Way at Cocklawgate. Deserting England, follow the north side of the fence climbing to a fine cairn. From here it is a further half mile of easy Scottish walking to the summit which is on the boundary between Scotland and England and is marked by an OS trigpoint surmounting Russell's Cairn. Inserted both in this and in the previous cairn is a pantomime fairy's wand, in reality a marker from the artillery range denoting something which must not be disturbed by the troops. There is a new memorial erected in 1988, a windshelter and fine views of The Cheviot.

The return route goes over the stile heading first south and then south-east to cross the burn. A large red notice alarmingly warns of unexploded bombs, so keeping to the path, whose course can best be followed by navigating from notice to notice, cross the col south of Little Ward Law and follow the edge of the wood down to the farm track where we had to contend with a large bull as well as the bombs. After a gate marking the boundary of the military training area, a short walk along the road, where there was once a drovers inn, leads to a waymarked stile and a steep descent to a footbridge over the Usway Burn by a circular sheepfold. The footpath, which is the line of Clennell Street, climbs high above the valley to enter Kidland Forest. The way back is straightforward, just keep to the main track. After about 3 miles the forest road bends left, then after another mile turn right at a T junction (don't go left to Kidlandlee). A final half mile and a waymarked path to the right on a bend cuts off the corner, descending steeply to the forest edge and the start of the walk.

Cross Fell from Meg's Cairn

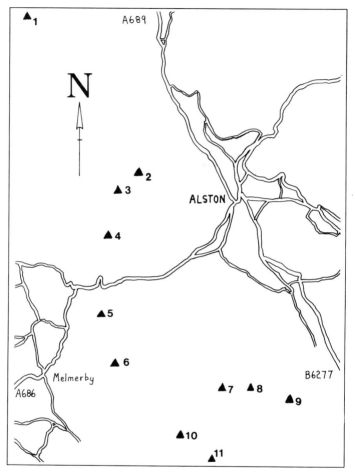

9 NORTH PENNINES - THE WESTERN FELLS

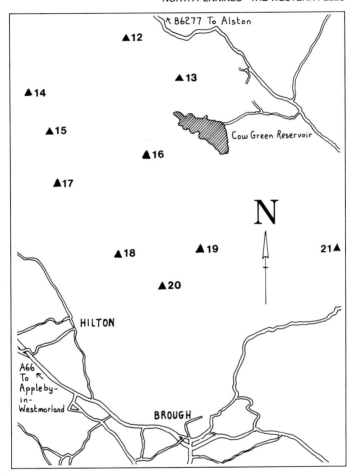

9 NORTH PENNINES - THE WESTERN FELLS

CHAPTER 9 NORTH PENNINES - THE WESTERN FELLS

TOP	NAME	HEIGHT	GRID REF	WALK NUMBER
1	Cold Fell	621m	86-606556 NY	9.7
2	Grey Nag	656m	86-665476 NY	9.8
3	Tom Smith's Stone Top	637m	86-655467 NY	9.8
4	Black Fell	664m	86-648444 NY	9.8
5	Fiend's Fell	634m	86-643406 NY	9.2
6	Melmerby Fell	709m	91-652380 NY	9.2
7	Bullman Hills	610m	91-706373 NY	9.1
8	Long Man Hill	658m	91-724373 NY	9.1
9	Round Hill	686m	91-744361 NY	9.1
10	Cross Fell	893m	91-687343 NY	9.1
11	Little Dun Fell	842m	91-704330 NY	9.1
12	Bellbeaver Rigg	620m	91-763351 NY	9.6
13	Viewing Hill	649m	91-789332 NY	9.6
14	Great Dun Fell	848m	91-710322 NY	9.1
15	Knock Fell	794m	91-722303 NY	9.3
16	Meldon Hill	767m	91-772291 NY	9.3
17	Backstone Edge	699m	91-726277 NY	9.3
18	Murton Fell	675m	91-754246 NY	9.4
19	Mickle Fell	788m	91-804243 NY	9.4
20	Little Fell	748m	91-781223 NY	9.4
21	Bink Moss	619m	91-875243 NY	9.5

WALK 9.1 CROSS FELL

SUMMITS	Great Dun Fell	2782 ft (848m)
	Little Dun Fell	2762 ft (842m)
	Cross Fell	2930 ft (893m)
	Bullman Hills	2001 ft (610m)
	Long Man Hill	2159 ft (658m)
	Round Hill	2251 ft (686m)

NOTE	Grouse moors
DISTANCE	15 miles
ASCENT	2660 feet
MAPS	OS Landranger sheet 91
	Outdoor Leisure - Teesdale
STARTING POINT	(91-714309) 7 miles north of Appleby-in-Westmorland at the end of the road from Knock to the Radar Station on Great Dun Fell. There seems to be no objection to driving as far as the locked gate where there is space for a few cars. Starting lower down from the quarry (685288) adds 4 miles and 1200 ft.
ALTERNATIVE START	From the east (757384) 2 miles south of Garrigill. Parking at the road end. Walk up the bridleway to join the route adding 2½ miles but no extra ascent.

Highest of all the mountains in England outside the Lake District and birthplace of the River Tees, Cross Fell is visited by thousands every year, but it is not this high, wild and remote moorland mountain that has brought them here. Approaching along the switchback of Great Dun Fell and Little Dun Fell, the Pennine Way marches up to the summit and then sets off resolutely for Alston.

Although infamous for the violent Helm Wind which rushes down the western slopes and like many high places often covered in cloud, Cross Fell with under 80 inches of rain a year, is less than half as wet as the central Lake District fells. There is however considerably more snow, which can linger in the gullies till midsummer. Once called Fiend's Fell, legend has it that Saint Augustine erected a cross on the summit to drive out evil spirits. They haven't gone far though as there is a Fiend's Fell only five miles to the north-west. During the nineteenth century the summit was the site of more secular

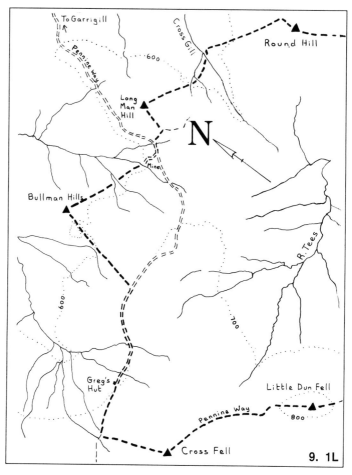

9. 1L

revelries with political meetings, sports and even in 1832, massed brass bands when 50 bands assembled on top to celebrate the passing of the Reform Bill. The weather must have been much better then; it is always windy, cloudy and freezing cold when we are there.

From a distance the glistening white dome of the radar station on Great Dun Fell, looking rather like a mountain top observatory, is not wholly

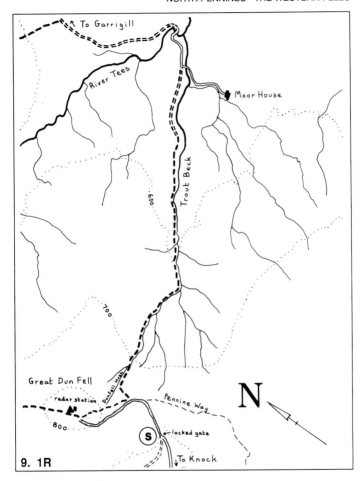

To Garrigill

River Tees

Moor House

Trout Beck

600

700

Great Dun Fell

radar station

Dunfell Hush

Pennine Way

N

800

S

locked gate

To Knock

9. 1R

unpleasing. Closer at hand though it feels more like a military camp than a mountain summit with its long range radar station and meteorological station. Grey shapes of buildings loomed out of the mist as we approached. Struggling with the wind and a Heath Robinson pyramid of equipment was a physicist from Manchester University. His team were taking measurements to determine the amount of sulphur dioxide in the air. Apparently the droplets of water vapour in the mist which floats around the fell tops are very acidic. There was plenty to keep them happy that day.

Much of the surrounding fellside is a National Nature Reserve. Managed by the Nature Conservancy Council, whose work is generally commendable, they seem at the Teeside Mine to have suffered a rush of blood to the head. In a profligate gesture they have provided not one, but two identical large notices proclaiming that this is a 'Biosphere' (the only spherical object hereabouts is the radar dome on Great Dun Fell) and this notice prohibits just about everything one could think of to do and a few more beside. With one notice for each of us and no-one else within miles it seemed an excessive precaution.

ROUTE DESCRIPTION

GREAT DUN FELL *(Great Hill Pasture Fell)*
Go up the tarmac road and past the locked gate. To the left is the Silverband lead mine where barytes and galena were once carried on an aerial ropeway to a processing plant below, though nowadays the ore comes down the hillside in lorries. In half a mile at a bend, after emerging from the confines of the enclosing valley, leave the road in favour of a footpath. This runs north-west above Dunfell Hush directly towards the dome and masts of the radar station, though in mist the road, which is the highest surfaced road in England, may be preferred. The radar station has been recently modernised, and the resulting differences from the map make it difficult to be precise about the exact spot of the summit. It appears to be just to the right of the waymarked path which passes to the left of the buildings, and can easily be missed by walkers distracted by identifying the outline of the Lake District fells to the west.

LITTLE DUN FELL *(Little Hill Pasture Fell)*
After crossing the stile at the boundary of the radar station there is little evidence of a path although this is the Pennine Way, and one is usually more concerned with avoiding the juicier parts of the bog than following the posts marking the way. A line north-west for three quarters of a mile and with only about 200ft of ascent brings you to the flat grassy top of Little Dun Fell where the first cairn, of gritstone slabs, marks the summit.

CROSS FELL
A little beyond is a stony area with a couple of windshelters and then the path, still faint, goes gently downhill to Tees Head where the River Tees begins its 75 mile journey to the North Sea. Veering more westerly and starting to climb beside a small stream, the ground now becomes stony and firmer and occasional cairns guide you to a tall currick and then on to the flat summit of Cross Fell. There is a whitewashed concrete trig point with a protecting wall of stones and close by a cross shaped substantial wind break with space enough for a dozen or more people to eat their lunch in its shelter. On a clear

Greg's Hut

day you can see as far as both the Irish and the North Seas.

BULLMAN HILLS *(Bull Hills with a Cairn)*

Heading just west of north for a quarter of a mile you come to a steeper section with Crossfell Well, a small spring, rising under a stone wall just beside the path. In about another quarter of a mile the Pennine Way turns right on a track and descends gradually among old spoil heaps to Greg's Hut. This restored mineworker's cottage, a popular bothy in the care of the Mountain Bothies Association, is a neat stone building with real glass windows and was opened in 1972. Continue on the path, which is now a stony track, an old corpse road, for about a mile past Greg's Hut to Backstone Edge and then leaving the Pennine Way head north across the rough pathless moor towards the twin topped Bullman Hills three quarters of a mile away. Although the southern top is the higher it is joined to Cross Fell by a high col and fails to achieve separate summit status. Its twin however, slightly lower and with a tiny cairn, has been carefully checked and rises by nearly 60ft. In the spring mountain pansies can be found here.

LONG MAN HILL *(Long Hill with a Cairn)*

Return south-east across the rough moor towards old mine workings made colourful by the blue-purple crystals of fluorspar. The Cashwell Mine workings were very large and with four levels extended underground for one mile. From the mine a track leads back to the Pennine Way where you turn left, but after only a couple of hundred yards turn right on a minor track which leads up to a gate just to the south of Long Man Hill. Here we met a shepherd who was convinced we were lost and kept telling us helpfully that the Pennine Way was "over there". From the gate, head north-east up over the pathless moor to the extensive flat top which is quite unremarkable, undistinguished and unfortunately uncairned. Careful back bearings on Cross Fell may convince you that you have found the exact spot, but in mist there is nothing to help.

ROUND HILL

Leaving Long Man Hill to the grouse, set off eastward to follow a line of shooting butts down to Cross Gill. This is a very attractive and remote valley with a small waterfall where Doups Burn tumbles down to join the main stream. Fording the gill, climb steeply until a line of shooting butts comes into view and these can be followed up across the moor to continue on a grassy line to a gate in the wall a quarter of a mile north of the summit. Turn right and follow the wall on the far side to its junction with a fence almost at the grassy top of Round Hill where there is a boundary stone. The highest point is about 100 yards south of the junction and like the last top is uncairned.

If returning towards Garrigill descend north-east to the ruins of Cocklake to rejoin the valley track, but for Dun Fell descend south-east passing the grassed over remains of old mines to join the bridleway, an old drove road, and walk up this by the claimed source of the River South Tyne. In a mile the wide stony track comes down to the River Tees at a substantial bridge beside the Teeside Mine. Over the bridge the track, almost a road at this point, runs beside Trout Beck. Moor House, on the other side of the beck, which was used as a shooting lodge from 1842, now belongs to the National Nature Reserve. At one time this house was permanently occupied with experts carrying out

Trout Beck

research, but perhaps their work is now done as it has looked very deserted on our visits. The track gradually deteriorates as the beck is followed upstream, but is easy enough. Around 3 long miles after leaving the bridge the gradient steepens and it climbs beside the desolation of Dunfell Hush to come out on the radar station access road. The end of the walk is now only an easy half mile downhill.

WALK 9.2 MELMERBY FELL

SUMMITS	Melmerby Fell	2326 ft (709m)
	Fiend's Fell	2080 ft (634m)
NOTE	Grouse moors	
DISTANCE	9 miles	
ASCENT	1250 feet	
MAPS	OS Landranger sheets 86 & 91	
STARTING POINT	(86-678424) On the A686 Penrith to Alston road, 2 miles east of Hartside Cross which is the top of the pass. Parking for a few cars by the roadside.	

Descending north-west from Cross Fell, Pennine Way walkers soon forsake the high ground taking the old mine track down to Garrigill. The ridge, however, continues for another six miles over two unfrequented tops to meet the A686 trans-Pennine road at Hartside Cross. To the east of this ridge is an area of quiet sheep and grouse moor, while westwards the land falls steeply in the typical Pennine scarp slope.

Nestling at the foot of these western slopes is Melmerby, Melmer's village, named after a local landowner and one of the most picturesque in the area. There is a large green, once used for cock fighting, a pub and the village bakery where stoneground wholemeal flour, milled at nearby Little Salkeld, is baked in a wood-fired brick oven. Trees planted round the green are a windbreak against the Helm Wind. Helm means hilltop and this very fierce, cold and violent wind howls down from the western slopes of these fells with a loud rushing noise. Caused by the temperature difference between the top of the fells and the Eden Valley it usually blows for three to four days each spring and sometimes for longer.

Just south of Melmerby Fell and providing a useful track for shepherds and

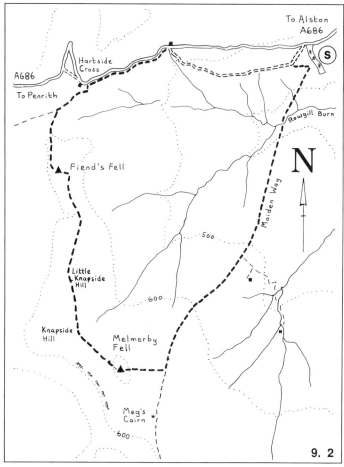

9. 2

gamekeepers is the Roman road of Maiden Way. Known as Maydengathe, the maiden's road in the twelfth century, it crosses the ridge on its way from Bravoniacum at Kirkby Thore via the fort at Whitley Castle to the Stanegate on Hadrian's Wall. Probably one of the principal routes by which Roman lead was transported, it is also an old drove road down which cattle were driven from Scotland to market in the south of England. Until the 19th century and the start of the railway age, herds of up to two hundred beasts would progress at a rate of about ten miles a day along these routes.

It is a quiet area and despite the connection with the Devil in the naming of Fiend's Fell, has given us superlatively good walking weather. On one winter day with hard frozen ground and a fresh covering of snow, we enjoyed brilliantly clear views of Cross Fell which looked close enough to touch. Returning in May we basked in the first heatwave of summer and chatted with a shepherd driving a herd of Swaledale yearlings down the Maiden Way. Swaledales are the most common breed of sheep in these parts, easily identified by their black faces, white muzzles and curly horns.

ROUTE DESCRIPTION

MELMERBY FELL *(Melmer's Village Fell)*

Leaving the A686, built by Mr Macadam in 1823, take the old road to the right of the plantation as far as the corner and turn left through a gate. Follow the track which winds downhill to ford the Rowgill Burn and then keeps to the line of Maiden Way climbing over the shoulder of Melmerby Fell. The track provides access to the shooting butts which were being repaired by a couple of men on our last visit. When the track turns left towards Melmerby Shop keep straight on, following a line of cairns over the moor. Once used by the miners to lodge in during the week, Melmerby Shop is neatly furnished including even a settee and a bit of carpet. A note on the door reminds *'No council collection here, take your empty tins and bottles away with you, thank you'*. After about another mile near an old kiln, leave the Maiden Way, which continues to Meg's Cairn and then descends to the Eden Valley, to climb west up easy slopes. From the pointed cairn on the flat grassy summit there is a good view of Cross Fell and far away to the west the Lake District mountains form the skyline.

FIEND'S FELL

Heading north-west it is an easy walk along the ridge to the cairn and wind shelter on Knapside Hill. Continuing north over Little Knapside Hill to the col before Fiend's Fell a gate on the west side of the ridge leads to a track which climbs past a ruined sheepfold to the OS concrete trig point on the sunmmit, set in the centre of a circle of stones. On the western slope of the fell, known also as Gamblesby Allotments, is a miniature version of the Great Dun Fell masts.

Hartside Cross looks very close and the track continues, curving gently down past a currick to a gate and on to the café. Turn right beside the main road and in half a mile, at a little empty house, the old road leads back to the starting point.

WALK 9.3 DUFTON FELL

SUMMITS	Backstone Edge	2293 ft (699m)
	Knock Fell	2605 ft (794m)
	Meldon Hill	2516 ft (767m)
NOTE	Grouse moors	
DISTANCE	15 miles	
ASCENT	2290 feet	
MAPS	OS Landranger sheet 91	
	Outdoor Leisure - Teesdale	
STARTING POINT	(91-690250) Dufton village, 3 miles north of Appleby-in-Westmorland. Roadside parking.	

Just north of Appleby-in-Westmorland, Dufton Fell lies mid-way between Cross Fell to the north and Mickle Fell and the Warcop Artillery range to the south. On its northern slopes is the Moorhouse Nature Reserve, and guarding the western edges of this vast plateau stand Knock Pike and Dufton Pike. While these isolated conical hills on the rim are of volcanic rock, Dufton Fell is layered with limestone beds, sandstone and shale and although the high moorland is typical Pennine heather and bog, occasionally the limestone breaks through creating a vivid green oasis on the moor.

Above Dufton and visible for miles is the unique High Cup Nick, a splendid example of a glaciated valley and probably the finest in England. The vertical horseshoe shaped crags at its head are hard and weather resistant rocks known as the Whin Sill, a volcanic intrusion of blue-black crystalline quartz-dolerite which has been cut right through by the torrents of melt water from retreating glaciers which during the Ice Age formed this long U-shaped deep and narrow channel.

Dufton, which until the late seventeenth century was surrounded by forest, is a quiet village with cottages clustered round the village green and its distinctive fountain. In the nineteenth century, with mines at Knock and Dufton and those at Threlkeld Side reaching up to 2000ft, Dufton's importance grew and it became the administrative centre for the London Lead Company which improved and extended the village. Dufton Hall, an imposing building, is built of red sandstone and dates from the sixteenth century, with the additional wing being added in 1779 although its matching counterpart was never built.

As we toiled up the lane past Dufton Pike, three landrovers sped by, their occupants wearing camouflage jackets and determined expressions. The

Dufton

friendly shepherds gathering their flock made reassuring comments "You're bigger than the grouse, they'll be able to tell the difference", but as we neared the first summit, shrouded in mist with visibility down to 50 yards, the sound of guns got louder and closer. Nervously we stood close to the protective concrete pillar of the OS trig point; surely they couldn't be shooting in this? It was December and long past the usual season for grouse, but not wanting to participate in a game of Blind Man's Buff, the fell had to wait. On the second attempt in snow and what the weather forcaster described as 'brisk' winds, the map was torn from our hands and was last seen heading towards Cow Green Reservoir. Thus delayed till the spring, Meldon Hill became the last top to be reached on our explorations for this book.

Dufton Fell is wild and wet and the crossing from Knock Fell on the western edge to Meldon Hill will test navigational abilities in all but good weather. The centre of the plateau is drained by a series of rivulets which feed the headwaters of Maize Beck, but instead of making west for the precipitous drop of High Cup Nick, the cliffs are left high and dry while Maize Beck turns abruptly east to join the Tees and thence to the North Sea.

ROUTE DESCRIPTION

BACKSTONE EDGE

From Dufton Hall Farm and its adjacent cottage, dated 1648 and inscribed 'Lane Foot' in Old Westmorland dialect, take the lane signed 'High Scald Fell'. Very shortly the waterlogged Pennine Way departs left and it is an easy 2 mile walk on the bridleway past Dufton Pike as far as the gate that leads onto the unfenced fellside. Ahead is Threlkeld Side mine where although lead mining ceased in 1898, barytes was mined until 1924 and then from 1981 extracted from the spoil heaps. Turn right up the wall and pick up an old mine track which

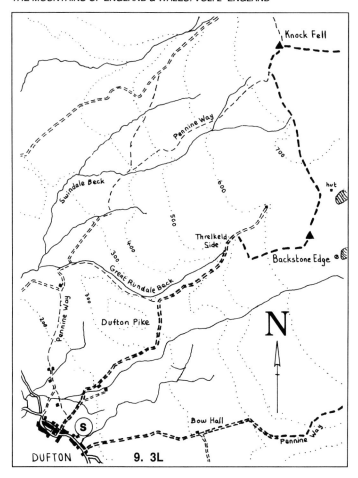

comes in at a gate on the right and zigzags up the ridge to peter out in an area of disused shafts and levels at around 1800ft. As the ground steepens, climb to locate the stone OS trig point on the flat grassy top near the edge of the fell. From here the summit cairn which is slightly higher, is about 200 yards to the north-east. From this vantage point Cross Fell and Great Dun Fell can be seen to the north-west and Mickle Fell and Little Fell to the south-east, while to the

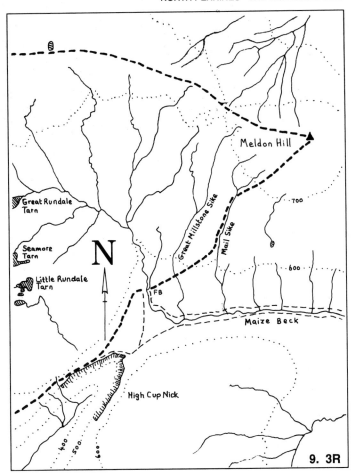

west lie the Lake District fells.

KNOCK FELL *(Hillock Fell)*
First aim north-east towards the shooting box near Great Rundale Tarn which supplied water to the mines, and then head just west of north, passing the site of a crashed aircraft, to the cairns on the summit. The highest point is marked

by a conical pile of stones some 250 yards north-east of Knock Old Man, a fine square stone currick. The top which lies just within the Moor House National Nature Reserve is crossed by the Pennine Way which ascends from Dufton and continues towards the dome on Great Dun Fell.

MELDON HILL *(Hill with a Mark)*
Over 3 miles of pathless moor must be covered to reach the final summit and navigation in mist can be tricky. Walk east for a couple of miles keeping to the highest ground and passing to the south of a large tarn and to the north of the coal pits. The broad ridge of the high ground gradually swings round to the south-east and passing a second aeroplane wreck declines to a col. The final mile steepens, but it becomes easy underfoot and on the slopes by a sheepfold, is a good roofed shelter. The summit has an OS stone trig point, a pointed cairn, a wind shelter just beyond and a good prospect of Cow Green Reservoir.

It is another 2 miles of pathless walking, this time downhill in a south-westerly direction, aiming just to the right of the gap in the hills above High Cup Nick. Following the sikes, the Pennine Way is met where it crosses Maize Beck by a footbridge over the black limestone gorge. Half a mile further and suddenly there is the dry valley of High Cup Nick, an awesome spectacle. The isolated column of rock on the northern edge is known as Nichol Chair after a local cobbler who is supposed to have seated himself on top and mended a shoe.

From High Cup Nick the Pennine Way hugs the western edge to descend gently for a mile and a half via Narrow Gate to a disused quarry with a fine lime kiln. A field track then leads the 2 miles back to Dufton becoming a metalled road just before Bow Hall, one of the largest sheep farms in the area.

WALK 9.4 MICKLE FELL

SUMMITS	Little Fell	2454 ft (748m)
	Mickle Fell	2585 ft (788m)
	Murton Fell	2215 ft (675m)

CAUTION

Most of the walk lies within the bounds of the Warcop Artillery Range and even on public rights of way access is only possible when firing is not taking place. At the time of writing this was on Mondays, but it is advisable to follow the recommendations of the warning notices and check first with the range officer (Tel. Brough 661). This is a military training area and you walk there at your own risk. As the notices say, 'Do not touch anything, it may explode and kill you.' It is also a grouse moor.

DISTANCE   15 miles

ASCENT   2550 feet

MAPS   OS Landranger sheet 91
              Outdoor Leisure - Teesdale

STARTING
POINT   (91-735207) Hilton village, 3 miles east of
              Appleby-in-Westmorland. Ample parking at the
              road end at the start of the walk.

South and east of High Cup Nick is a high wild deserted moor of around forty square miles ringed by red flags and warning notices. The northern boundary is skirted by the Pennine Way as it passes Cow Green Reservoir, while along the southern edge lies the reason for the warnings in the tank and gun positions of the Warcop artillery range. The moor, which apparently resembles the Falklands, was used, according to locals, in training troops for their mission in the South Atlantic. The highest point is reached in the centre of the area at Mickle Fell, Yorkshire's highest mountain before being appropriated by County Durham. Nearly four miles from the nearest road, we have had the summit to ourselves in both good weather and bad.

"It's very dangerous round here", said the young soldier. He and his heavily armed mates with blackened faces were straggling back down the path at the end of a night exercise. Firing the occasional round of what we hoped were blanks they looked tired after their long night out and several muttered "You do this for fun?". We glanced apprehensively at the shells which lay beside the path. It was a right of way, surely these rusting objects

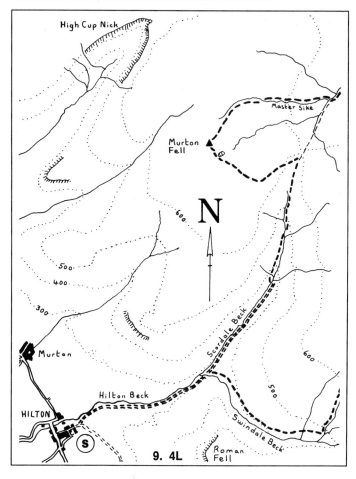

9. 4L

were not about to explode and how did the troops manage to avoid them in the dark? "You have to keep a good lookout", continued the soldier, "there's lots of unfenced mineshafts about".

Keeping a cautious eye open for mineshafts as well as the shells we climbed on into the dank mist and low cloud. Intent on our survey we didn't notice the next group of soldiers until we were hailed by a group of menacing

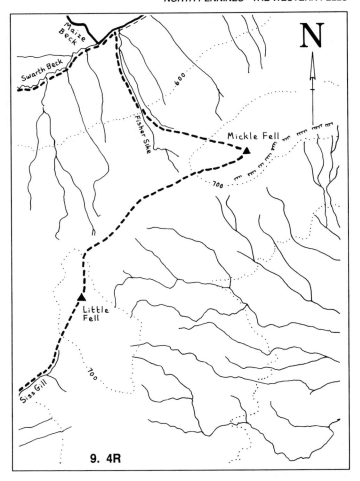

9. 4R

shadowy figures with guns at the ready. "Is that the track down there?" they asked as they crowded round us. Our aprehension was gone in an instant and after a friendly chat they continued on their way. Soon the cloud lifted, the sun began to dissolve the mist and for the rest of the day we were in complete solitude. In the evening we returned down the ravine of Scordale Beck, where mines were operating from the mid seventeenth century, to Hilton which

24 hour exercise

developed as a mining village. This was the birthplace of Cardinal Christopher Bainbridge who became Bishop of Bradford and later York in the early sixteenth century.

ROUTE DESCRIPTION

LITTLE FELL

Take the riverside track that follows Hilton Beck for just over a mile, passing the site of a smelt-mill and an old lime kiln, then turn right on the far side of Swindale Beck. The grassy path slants up the fellside climbing quite steeply above the deep ravine which moat-like separates Roman Fell. There are many violets beside the path which, when the angle eases, abruptly disappears with only the odd cairn to guide the way. Until the top of Little Fell there is a fair scattering of practice shells so, taking great care not to tread on any doubtful objects, continue along the right of way to Christy Bank and the little ravine of Siss Gill, where there is an old mine and the additional hazard of an unfenced shaft. The left branch of the gill makes a beeline for Little Fell with easy though pathless walking in the same direction beyond the stream source. We were lucky enough to see two fell ponies here with a tiny foal. The grassy flat top has an OS trig point at the southern end, but the northern is fractionally higher. No cairn graces the highest point which is impossible to determine with any great accuracy. There are numerous shake holes and the odd shell decorates the summit. The next top, Mickle Fell, looms impressively in the distance while to the north is a vast expanse of open moor. The minor tops of Long Fell to the south are littered with shells and fortunately fail to qualify as separate summits.

MICKLE FELL *(Large Fell)*

A direct route to Mickle Fell would cross some very rough and tough country, but by keeping to the high ground the way is remarkably easy. Remembering that the rest of the walk is also through the shelled area and that you must continue to be careful where you put your feet, head north along the ridge. The highest land gradually veers round to the north-east and about half way, at a stony area scattered with cairns, there is a collapsed shelter. On either side stretch vast bogs. The climb up Mickle Fell seems more than the 300ft shown on the map. The OS trig point is well over a mile along the curved ridge but thankfully the huge cairn on this western grassy end marks the highest point. If you are lucky enough to have a good seeing day it may be possible to glimpse the North Sea 42 miles away, as well as the nearer Irish Sea.

MURTON FELL *(Moor Village Fell)*

The direct route to the next summit is very rough, pathless and boggy, however unless you have masochistic tendencies it is possible by walking just that little bit further to follow a way which is both pleasant and comparatively easy. Descend north-west over the moor, crossing the boundary fence to join Fisher Sike, which is then followed down to the right of way beside Maize Beck. Turn left and when Maize Beck bends away continue up Swarth Beck. The path shown on the map is a figment of the imagination, but as the ground anywhere else is worse the stream makes a good line to take. After hopping from side to side of Swarth Beck, turn up Master Sike just before a ruin where the valley narrows. This is in fact much easier going and leads magically through the peat hags with no effort, right to the grassy summit of Murton Fell which is just north of the shallow lake. The jumbled blocks of the cairn are approximately at the centre of the ring contour, though purists may notice that it is not exactly at the highest point which is a few yards away to the north-east. Here you can relax and admire the views as you are temporarily just outside the shelled area. Behind the fine curricks above High Cup Nick are Great Dun Fell and Cross Fell while to the east lies Mickle Fell. Closer at hand Murton Pike and Roman Fell are prominent.

Passing to the south of the pool between Murton Fell's twin tops and back into the shelled area, walk almost over the other top to avoid the peat hags. The direct descent is very steep so slant down east to the head of the huge ravine of the Scordale Beck and then follow the right of way, which is a good path, down this spectacular valley, which has much evidence of mining. After passing a lovely waterfall the main track is joined which leads down to Hilton Beck and back to the village.

WALK 9.5 BINK MOSS

SUMMITS	Bink Moss	2031 ft (619)m
NOTE	Grouse moors	
DISTANCE	10½ miles	
ASCENT	1100 feet	
MAPS	OS Landranger sheet 91	
	Outdoor Leisure - Teesdale	
STARTING POINT	(91-885287) The High Force Hotel, 5 miles west of Middleton-in-Teesdale on the B6277. Car park, toilets	

Bink Moss is the end of a long ridge of high ground extending east from Mickle Fell. The northern slopes above the River Tees are on the edge of the Upper Teesdale National Nature Reserve and most of the fell is managed as a grouse moor. It is possibly named after John Binks, a miner from Middleton-in-Teesdale, who at the beginning of the eighteenth century supplemented his income by supplying the local druggist with wild herbs. Mr Binks discovered many Teesdale rarities which he gave to a clergyman in Middleton who claimed the credit for these discoveries. In 1974 this side of the dale was amalgamated into County Durham, but by special dispensation those born here can still play cricket for Yorkshire.

The climax of the walk, High Force waterfall, is saved till the end. It is reputed to be the largest waterfall in England, and when in spate is a fearsome sight. Usually the river flows only to one side of the central rocky column but in conditions of flood this is isolated and the sound of the falls can be heard over a mile away. In extreme conditions, last occuring in the 1880s, the central rocks submerge completely. These freak occurrences are unlikely to ever happen again as Cow Green Reservoir now controls the flow of water down the river. In 1929 the fall froze solid, which must have been a most spectacular sight. The river has two other falls close by. Upstream, just below the reservoir dam, is Cauldron Snout, the longest cascade in England, while downstream lie the pretty falls of Low Force. Just below these falls is Wynch Bridge. The original bridge, built in 1704, was the first suspension bridge in Europe. Built so that the Holwick miners could get to work at Newbiggin on the other side of the river, it was swept away by floods in 1830 after which the present bridge was built.

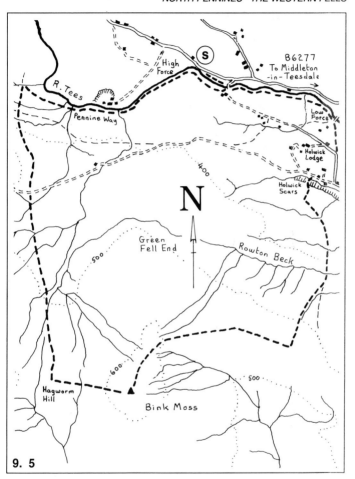

9. 5

ROUTE DESCRIPTION

BINK MOSS *(Bink's Bog)*

A new flight of steps near the entrance to High Force on the B6277 leads down to the River Tees. Walk beside the river to the railway sleeper bridge and then continue downstream on the other side to Low Force and Wynch Bridge. Fork

High Force

right at the suspension bridge and cross the fields to join the lane to Holwick.
Turn right at the T junction below Holwick Scars and pass between the houses
on a track to the ravine where Scar Beck is forded to climb a rocky stairway
beside a minor stream. A stile leads to a well cairned path over the fields which
crosses tiny streams. After about a mile, at Rowton Beck, the right of way
becomes indistinct and veers off left to cross the ridge wall at a gate. By
crossing the fence at the beck and climbing to the right of the wall beside
Easter Beck a large chunk of rough walking can be avoided with a short cut
into the bargain. Follow the ridge fence for nearly 2 miles of easy walking past
Green Fell to its highest point at a corner. 100 yards further on in the same
direction, beyond a grough and a ditch is the unmarked summit, an expanse
of recently burnt heather through which the new shoots of the cloudberry are
growing prolifically. A short distance away to the east is a post beside an OS
marker, a brass stud set in concrete. This now obsolete point gives better
views to the south of Selset Reservoir and the Yorkshire Dales. To the north-
west you can just see the puff ball dome of the radar station on Great Dun Fell
and the twin topped Mickle Fell to the west.

Continue along the fence west to the summit of the charmingly named

Hagworm Hill. There is a good windshelter here and the ridge continues to Long Crag, now demoted from its separate mountain status. A magnificent much cairned and clear path sets off boldly downhill back to Teesdale, but enjoy the easy walking while you can, for this path deserts the right of way and heads off through a gate towards Green Fell End. Leave it at the gate to navigate cross country in a northerly direction, over a series of cunningly concealed ankle twisting ditches, to the Nature Reserve notice which stands where the path would be if it were here. Proceeding with more confidence, because you are after all on the path which is shown on the notice, cross a good track, skirt round Noon Hill and cross Skyer Beck to a second notice where a clear path leads straight on to a gateway in the wall. A few yards beyond, turn right to join the Pennine Way. This leads beside the River Tees, past Force Garth Quarry where the hard Whinstone rock is quarried for road stone. The flower filled meadows lead to the climax of the walk, High Force, the largest waterfall in England. Here the river falls from the Whin Sill which erodes more slowly than the sedimentary rock beneath, cutting a deep gorge. There are many juniper bushes on the hill slope and core samples taken from the peat in Teesdale show that juniper has grown in this region for twelve thousand years. From here it is only a short walk back to the railway sleeper bridge at the start of the walk.

Teesdale

WALK 9.6 BELLBEAVER RIGG AND VIEWING HILL

SUMMITS	Bellbeaver Rigg	2034 ft (620m)
	Viewing Hill	2129 ft (649m)
NOTE	Grouse moors	
DISTANCE	6 miles	
ASCENT	600 feet	
MAPS	OS Landranger sheet 91	
	Outdoor Leisure - Teesdale	
STARTING POINT	(91-784354) Beside the B6277, 8 miles south-east of Alston. Ample parking.	

From Yad Moss, the highest point on the Alston to Middleton-in-Teesdale road and so called because the peat or moss is a yard thick, Bellbeaver Rigg doesn't look like a summit at all; it is only 75 feet higher than the main road. To the north-west is the valley of the South Tyne, while skirting the lower slopes to the south is the infant River Tees.

Approaching these hills up the lovely Teesdale valley, the fields in spring are a brilliant golden yellow with marsh marigolds and as the season progresses other beautiful and often rare flowers are a delight.

Widdybank Fell is one of the most renowned sites among botanists and it was with consternation and almost disbelief that the news was received in the late 1960s that a reservoir was to be built in the middle of all this. Efforts to reverse the decision failed and an army of helpers in desperation set to and moved the plants instead. Around seven thousand plants were transplanted in this life saving operation. The almost unique habitat results from the rock, a sugar limestone, produced by crystalisation of the limestone by the intense heat of an intrusion of volcanic rock. This is the home of the Spring Gentian which flowers between April and June and is one of a very few sites where it is found. About 20 acres of arctic alpine vegetation were drowned by Cow Green Reservoir and Cauldron Snout, England's longest and largest cataract, is now tamed and controlled by the regulated overflow from the reservoir.

The cultivated fields high in Teesdale owe their origin to the miners who supplemented their wages by working at weekends on their tiny upland farms. Especially on sunny days the scattered farms and cottages in Teesdale stand out brilliantly as nearly all of them are whitewashed. What is not so obvious is that most belong to the Raby Estate and this indirectly explains their curious uniformity. An early Lord Barnard, separated from his hunting party at nightfall

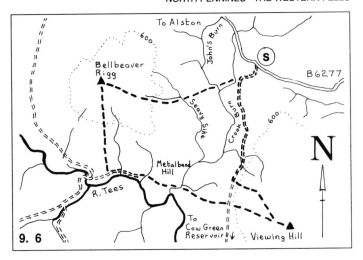

was refused lodging on an isolated farm. Wrathfully he returned the next day to find that it was not part of his estate. In order to recognise his properties in future he decreed they should all be whitewashed. They were certainly all whitewashed by 1848 for Francis Cockshott wrote in 'A Journey on foot through Teesdale' '*The houses are for the most part rude in their construction, but their being whitewashed partly redeemed the poverty of their aspect, and this operation is said to be always performed, with becoming loyalty, on the approach of the Duke to the moors in the hunting season.*'

ROUTE DESCRIPTION

BELLBEAVER RIGG *(Beaver Hill Ridge)*

Walk down the mine road for 300 yards and then follow the Crook Burn south-west to the old mine workings on the far bank where a ruined bridge and a covered shaft remain beside the spoil heaps. A 500 yard trek west across rough heather moor leads to Seavy Sike which is then followed west beside a line of grouse butts to a large flat eroded area. The fell top is only a short way to the north-west, a flat heathery expanse with two cairns, 300 yards apart, the north-western one being the highest. From this rather undistinguished spot you are surrounded on all sides by much higher tops; to the south lies Meldon Hill and Mickle Fell, to the west Cross Fell and to the north-east the ski tow ironmongery on Burnhope Seat stands against the skyline like a pit's winding gear. On the slopes of Round Hill to the north-west, in a dark green patch of improved land, sit the ruined cottages of Calvertfold. In the nineteenth century these were some of the highest inhabited dwellings in England.

VIEWING HILL *(Lookout Hill)*

Descend south aiming for Meldon Hill in the distance. Moor House on the other side of the Tees belongs to the National Nature Conservancy Council. After an initial rough crossing of an area of peat groughs, an easy walk over grass leads to a mine track above the River Tees which is followed east. When the track ends continue in the same direction over the col at the end of Metalband Hill, cross Crook Burn and climb past a ruined mine reservoir to the mine road. Another 200 ft of ascent over easy grass leads to the flat peaty top. The summit cairn is towards the far end, on the edge of a large flat stony area. The views are similar to those from Bellbeaver Rigg though with Cow Green Reservoir much nearer.

Return north-west to rejoin the mine road and this is then followed north back to the starting point.

Marsh Marigolds

WALK 9.7 COLD FELL

SUMMITS	Cold Fell	2037 ft (621m)
NOTE	Grouse moors	
DISTANCE	5 miles	
ASCENT	1200 feet	
MAPS	OS Landranger sheet 86,	
STARTING POINT	(86-588585) 4 miles south-east of Brampton. Roadside parking beyond Clesketts on the road from Hallbankgate where the track forks into three.	

At Hartside Cross the trans-Pennine A686 hairpins its way up to 1900 ft on its lonely journey from Penrith to Alston. To the north rough, tough, wild and deserted moorland stretches for ten miles to isolated Cold Fell, the northern-most mountain in Cumbria. At its foot lies Tindale Tarn, where seagulls wheel and call above its quiet waters, and close by are the remains of fast disappearing mines and quarries. One of the earliest railways was built here to link the Tindale mines with Brampton and for a time George Stephenson's famous locomotive 'The Rocket' ran along the line. Talkin Tarn a little further to the west is a country park with boating and other watersports on its 65 acre lake, but Cold Fell is aloof, its summit and ridges marked with ancient cairns, it sees few visitors.

ROUTE DESCRIPTION

COLD FELL

At the three way fork, take the centre track which crosses a cattle grid and, heading straight towards Cold Fell, leads to the Howgill Miner's Cottages. Cross the Howgill Beck to the left of the houses and climb the track past old coal mines. Continue up the hill to the left of the stream on a rough stony shooting track which deteriorates and becomes indistinct higher up. Rejoin the stream above a little waterfall and cross over to follow a line of new shooting butts which head south-east towards the summit. At first there are faint traces of a path and then, when a stone currick appears ahead, aim just to the left of it over rough tussocky grass for the highest point. The grassy top is crowned by an ancient cairn with the OS trig point perched on top. A tall wind shelter has been built out of the cairn stones and a little tarn and a new fence lie between the summit and the currick. There are wide views across the

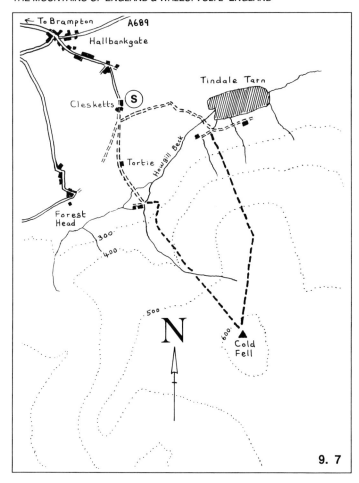

9. 7

border counties to Scotland.

The quickest descent is to retrace your steps from the summit of Cold Fell, but a far more attractive way is to return by Tindale Tarn. Heading north straight for a prominent currick, the going is rough but easy as it is mostly gently downhill. This currick is also built on top of a huge ancient cairn and standing by it you are in a very commanding position perched right on the end of the Pennines. The low border country stretches ahead, with Wark forest below and Talkin Tarn to the left. Carry on descending north over rough grass and Tindale Tarn soon comes into view, then the going is easier to where more curricks stand in a line looking down on the tarn. Aim for the road at the west end of the tarn, crossing the remains of old mines, to descend finally to the left of a fence and down over little outcrops. Join the right of way at a gate and follow the lane back to Clesketts.

WALK 9.8   GREY NAG AND BLACK FELL

SUMMITS	Grey Nag	2152 ft (656m)
	Tom Smith's Stone Top	2090 ft (637m)
	Black Fell	2178 ft (664m)
NOTE	Grouse moors	
DISTANCE	10½ miles	
ASCENT	1450 feet	
MAPS	OS Landranger sheet 86,	
STARTING POINT	(86-702485) Lay by on the A689, two mile north-west of Alston by the bridge over the Gilderdale Burn.	

These tops, to the west of the quiet South Tyne valley, are typical Pennine moors with gently rounded summits rising gradually amid an expanse of tussocky grass and heather. With no roads intruding upon over sixty square miles of wilderness much of the appeal lies in the quiet and remoteness, with hill succeeding hill above deserted long valleys.

It was here that we came after cutting short a very wet weekend in Scotland. Grey Nag and Black Fell looked to be only a short distance from the summit of the Hartside Pass, but unfortunately our map of the area was at home and Penrith failed to yield another copy. Tracing the route from our 3 miles to the inch road map onto the only paper we had, the back of a supermarket receipt, and armed with a compass, we set off into the thick mist. After less than an hour's walk we celebrated our arrival at Black Fell only to find the true summit, with its OS trig point, looming out of the mist 5 minutes later. Continuing towards Grey Nag in a grey fog and floundering through peat hags, we met a party of ramblers who materialised from nowhere, but this was the only time we have ever seen anyone else on these hills.

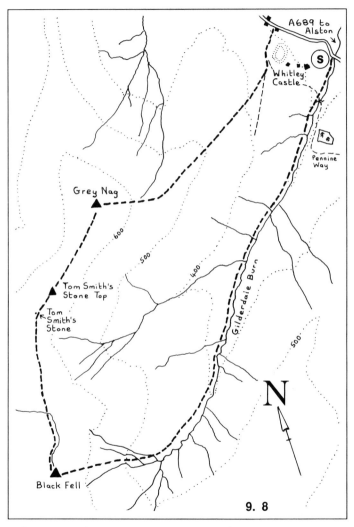

Downstream from the road bridge over the Gilderdale Burn there is a second bridge which at one time carried the Alston to Haltwhistle branch line.

It was opened by the Newcastle and Carlisle Railway Company in 1852 and closed by British Rail in 1976. It is now the route of England's highest narrow gauge railway. The South Tynedale Railway Preservation Society has constructed a 2ft gauge line along the old trackbed from Alston to a temporary terminus at Gilderdale, which was opened in 1984 and there are plans for the line to be extended to the lovely village of Slaggyford in the future.

Nearby is Whitley Castle, the site of a Roman Fort which was perhaps built to defend the lead mines and is the best preserved of this type in the country. Now only grassy banks show the outlines of the foundations which cover nine acres consisting of earth ramparts and ditches round a large platform. The Maiden Way linked the fort to others north and south and this Roman road, which can be traced on the map, is now followed by a modern army on foot as Pennine Way walkers tramp towards Hadrian's Wall.

ROUTE DESCRIPTION

GREY NAG *(Grey Horse)*
Walk north up the A689 to where the Pennine Way crosses the main road by a telephone box. Turn left past the farm to follow the Pennine Way across a field to a ladder stile in the far corner, but as it bends left downhill above Whitley Castle leave it and follow the rough track uphill past some old mine workings to a well preserved lime kiln in the next field. The track becomes indistinct climbing gently to pass through another gate onto the open moorland of the ridge. Ahead you can see the summit of Grey Nag. Keep to the left of the ridge above the valley on a well managed grouse moor. The heather, which has been burnt, is short and the walking is easiest here. The valley to the left is that of the Gilderdale Burn. Cross a fence at the corner at its highest point, then head up a grough to easy grass. At a stony area cross the next fence where it joins a wall and follow this wall uphill for a few yards to the summit. The highest point is crowned by a large ancient cairn. Some of the stones from this have been used to build a big cone shaped cairn which has subseqently been incorporated into the massive stone walls which cross the top. A concrete OS trig point stands on the other side of the wall and there are a couple of square sturdily built sheep pens with stone walls at least 5ft high. This is a good place for lunch as it is sheltered from the wind from any direction. The views are extensive with much of the North Pennines to be seen. To the south Great Dun Fell's dome peeps over the shoulder of Cross Fell and to the west the double topped peak of Blencathra is the nearest of the Lake District's higher fells.

TOM SMITH'S STONE TOP
Following the wall south-west over easy moorland it soon ends abruptly and becomes the more usual fence which after a mile crosses the next top. Featureless and unmarked it will be passed unrecognised in all but perfect conditions. Tom Smith's Stone is 400 yards beyond, a large four sided

gritstone pillar at the fence bend with the letters A.C.K.W., one on each side. This stone, which marks the junction of three parishes on three ridges and is on the Cumbria Northumberland boundary, also bears an OS bench mark.

BLACK FELL
The going now becomes very rough, climbing in and out of peat groughs and avoiding the bogs with difficulty. The fence, which is a useful guide in bad weather, leads south all the way. After about half a mile you pick up the upper reaches of Croglin Water which amazingly rises only a stone's throw from the summit. The grassy top is beside the fence and crowned with a concrete OS trig point. There are extensive views in all directions with southwards a wall marching along the ridge towards Cross Fell.

The return is down the remote and deserted Gilderdale. Descending east over easy grass into the valley it is 4 miles down to the road and you experience a sense of isolation walking here. As we turned the corner into the main valley we were surprised to discover a well preserved building, probably a mine shop now used by shepherds, with the remains of a four poster bed upstairs. Nearby are beehive shaped cairns which cap old mine shafts. From here it is still a long walk back down the wide deserted valley with no habitation as far as you can see and that's a long way. Keep to the north bank of the burn taking the easiest line. A ruin is passed on Watchers Hill and after this the river flows through a limestone gorge with a very fine waterfall to the confluence with Woldgill Burn. Follow the burn, staying on the north bank, and passing more old mine workings and a level, to meet the Pennine Way which crosses the river at an inappropriately blue painted footbridge. Don't cross the bridge but continue downstream on the left bank to reach a stile at the road bridge beside the lay-by.

Below Black Fell

Great Stony Hill

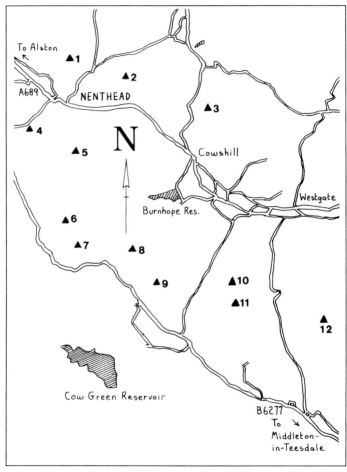

10 NORTH PENNINES - THE EASTERN FELLS

CHAPTER 10 NORTH PENNINES - THE EASTERN FELLS

TOP	NAME	HEIGHT	GRID REF	WALK No.
1	The Dodd	614m	87-791458 NY	10.2
2	Killhope Law	673m	87-819448 NY	10.2
3	Middlehope Moor	612m	87-862432 NY	10.2
4	Flinty Fell	614m	87-771423 NY	10.3
5	Dead Stones	710m	91-794399 NY	10.1
6	Burnhope Seat	746m	91-788375 NY	10.1
7	Harwood Common	718m	91-795363 NY	10.1
8	Great Stony Hill	708m	91-824359 NY	10.1
9	Three Pikes	651m	91-834343 NY	10.1
10	Chapelfell Top	703m	91-876346 NY	10.4
11	Fendrith Hill	696m	91-877333 NY	10.4
12	Westernhope Moor	675m	91-923326 NY	10.4

WALK 10.1 BURNHOPE SEAT

SUMMITS	Three Pikes	2136 ft (651m)
	Great Stony Hill	2323 ft (708m)
	Harwood Common	2356 ft (718m)
	Burnhope Seat	2447 ft (746m)
	Dead Stones	2329 ft (710m)
NOTE	Grouse moors	
DISTANCE	13½ miles	
ASCENT	1700 feet	
MAPS	OS Landranger sheet 91	
	Outdoor Leisure - Teesdale	
STARTING POINT	(91-848388) The dam of Burnhope Reservoir, 1 mile west of Ireshopeburn village which is on the A689 11 miles south-east of Alston. Cars may be parked on the road which crosses the dam.	

The long high ridge of heather moor that divides Weardale from Teesdale reaches its highest point at Burnhope Seat which until demoted by county re-organisation was the highest point in County Durham. In a distance of over sixteen miles the ridge is only crossed twice by roads, both of which are unfrequented and marked by the Ordnance Survey with the arrow symbol denoting steep gradients. Nevertheless steepness is not one of the characteristics by which one remembers this area, it is rather for the high, wild pathless moor. Here the song of the lark and curlew rise overhead, the red grouse sits camouflaged on her nest in the heather or starts up suddenly from beneath one's feet with staccato calls of complaint, lizards scurry away through the grass and above is a huge expanse of sky reaching to the far horizon where yet more moorland hills stretch away into the distance.

Although these moors are quiet enough now, except perhaps following the 'glorious twelfth', and long days may be spent without meeting another person, there is plentiful evidence that it was not always so. Conical depressions in the ground may be shake holes, but often they are collapsed bell pits where miners worked along the lead veins from shafts dug in the moor until the air gave out and another shaft had to be made. Other and deeper shafts were dug and lined with stone and some of these can still be found on the slopes of Scaud Hill. The mines, principally for lead, and also barytes, were both productive and extensive, but all had closed by the early nineteen hundreds. The Lodgegill Mine produced ten thousand tons of lead and one of the mine levels is thought to have extended right under the fell, a distance of two miles, with an entrance on opposite sides of the hill. This incidentally provided the miners with a quick under cover route to work in bad weather.

The villages strung out along Upper Weardale, date back to the fourteenth century while above them Burnhope Reservoir, which destroyed the hamlet of Burnhope, impounds the water from the eastern slopes of these hills. It is a late comer, finished in 1936.

ROUTE DESCRIPTION

THREE PIKES *(Three Peaks)*

From the reservoir dam climb the steep gated road going south and turn right beside an old limekiln towards the moors on the minor road of Grasshill Causeway. The road climbs steadily, passing through a gate. Soon the 2000ft contour is passed and for the next 10 miles the walk is above this height. The

Stonewaller at work

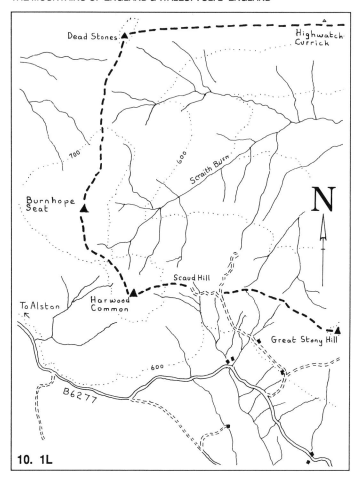

10. 1L

surface gradually deteriorates to a rough track up Galloway Hill which was named after the Galloway, a sturdy little packhorse of about 12 hands. These were used until late in the nineteenth century in strings of 25 animals, each of which could carry around 2cwt. After about a mile and a half of rather dull but very easy walking there is a shooting cabin on the left, which although shuttered has one room at the end open and available as a shelter. Shortly

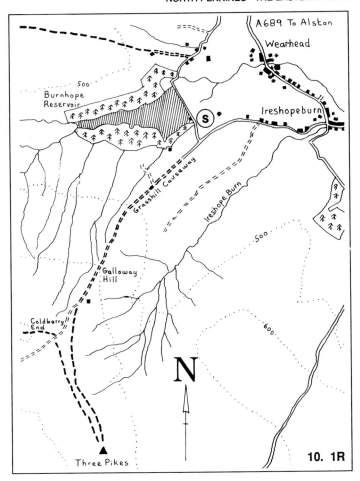

A689 To Alston

Wearhead

Burnhope
Reservoir

Ireshopeburn

S

Grasshill Causeway

Ireshope Burn

500

500

Galloway
Hill

600

Coldberry
End

N

10. 1R

Three Pikes

after and nearing the summit of the pass at Coldberry End, with its disused mines, short grass appears beside the track. Members of the party who are not peak baggers should use this opportunity for a nice long rest while the others turn off left and weave a way through the tussocks and groughs across the pathless moor south-east to a col. This bit of the moor is much the toughest and the moors later are, though still pathless, fortunately much easier. A short climb brings you to a z bend in a fence and beyond there is a boundary stone. Although the moor now appears flat, the summit is slightly higher and some 500 yards beyond to the south over rough heather. There is a cairn on the edge overlooking Upper Teesdale which the OS have chosen for their spot height, but a small pile of upright stones about 100 yards east of this marks the highest point of the fell.

GREAT STONY HILL
Return north to the summit of the pass keeping to the left of the outward route as this provides slightly easier ground and it is then only a short ascent to Great Stony Hill. Though hardly great and stony by say Lake District standards it is nevertheless unusual for these moorland hills to find so much stone scattered about the summit. Beside the trig point there is a new-looking large cairn and the remains of mining activities. To the south Cow Green Reservoir can be seen while westwards are the easily identified triple summits of Cross Fell and Great and Little Dun Fells.

HARWOOD COMMON *(Hare's Wood Common)*
Heading west then north-west the moor is pathless, but nowhere near as difficult as over Three Pikes. In just over a mile after passing the grassed over bell pits of old mine workings an area of mine spoil is reached. An old mine track can then be used below Scaud Hill, an outlying top of Harwood Common, which takes you beneath the southern slopes past unfenced mine shafts. Finally a short tussocky section of heather, crowberry and cowberry is crossed to the small summit cairn. A mile away to the north-west the trig point on Burnhope Seat gleams whitely.

BURNHOPE SEAT *(Stream Valley Hill Pasture)*
Descending gradually north-west across the moor straight towards the next summit, a fence corner is passed where a grand boundary marker, fashioned from two interlocking blocks of stone, lies tumbled on the ground. When erect it must have stood nearly 6ft high, its three visible faces are marked EC, GH and DC. Following the fence the trig point is reached at a three way junction where in order to give it a better view of the surroundings the trig point has been placed by its builders on a concrete plinth. From this comfortable seat, complete with back-rest, due east is Burnhope Reservoir and exactly opposite away to the west lies Cross Fell.

DEAD STONES
The fence makes a beeline for the next summit and it is mostly easy going beside it for the mile and a half of moorland that separates the two. There is a tall cairn beside the fence, but the attention is caught by a small drystone hut a few yards downhill. This provides excellent shelter with a seat, a paved floor and even a small fireplace fuelled by discarded fenceposts, but alas no door.

The return to Burnhope Reservoir traverses the eastern ridge following a fence for 1½ miles to Highwatch Currick and a trig point from which there is a lovely view down into Upper Weardale. Here a grassy tractor track is joined and this leads down to eventually turn left through a fence. Leave the track now and trending right away from the fence go down towards a new corrugated iron barn where a walled track is joined. Here we paused to chat with a contract stone waller restoring one of the intake walls. These walls provide not only a boundary, but also shelter for the sheep and as a grant is available, repair is more often undertaken now. The track leads down to the road where you turn right and the dam is only a little further.

WALK 10.2 KILLHOPE LAW

SUMMITS	The Dodd	2014 ft (614m)
	Killhope Law	2208 ft (673m)
	Middlehope Moor	2008 ft (612m)
NOTE	Grouse moors	
DISTANCE	13½ miles	
ASCENT	1900 feet	
MAPS	OS Landranger sheet 87	
	Outdoor Leisure - Teesdale	
STARTING POINT	(87-808432) 6 miles east of Alston on the A689 in Weardale at Killhopehead Bridge. Parking beside the road.	

At Killhope Cross the A689 reaches a height of 2044ft, the highest main road in England or Wales and higher in fact than two of the three mountains on this walk. The road was built in 1823 by Mr MacAdam who was employed by the mine proprietors to improve the roads which he thought *altogether the worst that have yet come to my knowledge*. Although winter clings longer to this high pass, with snow frequently remaining for over six months of the year, not just straggling trees, but a whole forest is found on Killhope Law at the remarkably high level of well over 2000ft. This is close to the theoretical limit in Britain for trees. Above this height the temperature fails to exceed 50°F for the minimum two months required to maintain growth.

Just north of Killhope Cross is the meeting of the three counties of Cumbria, Northumberland and Durham and for the whole of the high level

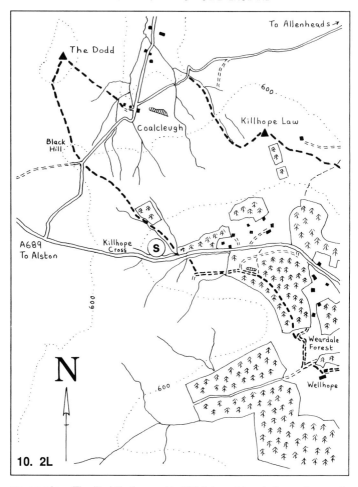

10. 2L

traverse from The Dodd in the west to Middlehope Moor in the east a county boundary is straddled. Killhope Law the highest of the three summits is, at 2208ft, fully 164ft higher than the road. Much of the county boundary is marked by a shallow ditch which seems a prodigiously difficult method of demarcation, but for most of the way there are very few stones on the extensive heather moor.

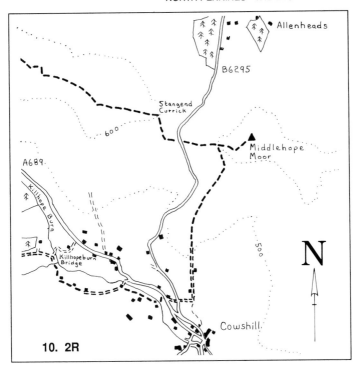

10. 2R

The return up Weardale makes a pleasant contrast to the wild windswept moors. Reported until recently to be a gaunt abandoned structure, the huge Killhope Wheel, 34ft in diameter, set in the Weardale Forest which was planted in 1966, has now been restored as the star attraction of a lead mining museum. Built in 1860 to provide power to the lead mines, the aim is to show it and the surrounding area as it would have looked around 1870 when the mines were at their height. In 1821 there were 36 mines in Weardale and although there was a rapid decline at the end of the century, some mines persisted for a time and as late as 1910 the Weardale Lead Company was reported to have extracted 3700 tons from its five remaining mines.

ROUTE DESCRIPTION

THE DODD *(Bare Rounded Hill)*

Of the three streams which meet at the bridge, follow the middle one north-west up the hillside and beside the small plantation of dead trees until the peaty top of the moor is reached. A new fence, with an old mine road on its left, leads north-west down to Black Hill, the highest point on the minor road. To the left, on the slopes of Knoutberry Hill above Nenthead, stands the chimney of the smelting mill. It has a half mile long stone built flue and was built high on the moor to carry the lead fumes away from the valley bottom.

From the road cross the hummocks of the old quarries to the north-west corner where a fence may be crossed at its junction with the wall, and then follow this north across the moor. There is no trace on the ground of the several rights of way at the boggy col and as the ground becomes firmer and starts to climb, the fence is replaced by a wall. This wall leads to a ruined stone platform within 300 yards of the summit and when it turns left continue in the same direction over the moor to reach the small conical cairn, set amid the heathery peat hags. The views are extensive with the familiar outlines of Great Dun Fell, Little Dun Fell and Cross Fell to the south-west with Blencathra beyond, to the north lie the Cheviots, but the view to the south-east is blocked by the bulk of the next objective.

KILLHOPE LAW *(Narrow Valley Hill)*

Descending south-east over the moor the whitewashed house at Coalcleugh is reached in three quarters of a mile, where a mine road leads out to the minor road. This was an important lead mine and the site of the Barneycraig Horse Level, the first horse-drawn waggon way along an underground level. Started in 1760, by 1765 it was a mile long. After lead mining ceased in 1880 the mine was worked for zinc until 1921, but the hamlet is now almost deserted. Turn left and then immediately right, signposted Allenheads. The unfenced road climbs steadily and at the second bend leave it to follow Bridge Cleugh south-east up the hillside. This provides the easiest line up to the ridge passing a disused quarry where the stream is stained a bright orange. The summit is clearly indicated by its 30ft high wooden pole. The trig point and a substantial beehive cairn, which was restored in 1969, seem almost unnecessary additions. The view south-east now opens out to give a wide panorama in all directions.

MIDDLEHOPE MOOR *(Middle Valley Moor)*

The dividing line between Northumberland on the left and Durham on the right is marked for most of the way by a ditch which provides a good guide for the 3 miles of rough moorland walking to the final top beyond the B6295. Two small open sheds a third of a mile to the east of the summit afford shelter in bad weather. After about three quarters of a mile a line of posts crosses the route and shortly after that the sunken path of the Weardale Way. The ditch,

The Dodd from Coalcleugh

mostly but not always in evidence, tacks its way along the broad ridge and Stangend Currick seems the only thing to look forward to, but alas it is no more, merely a low pile of stones remain. The road is now close at hand and a small gate at the corner of the wall permits an exit. Durham has snow poles lining the road with fluorescent tops but those in Northumberland are only black and white plastic and are definitely not so smart. The Weardale Way which is 46 miles long, comes in perversely up the road and is joined for the next section. Go through an iron gate and up the fellside beside the wall meeting your old friend the ditch again. Soon however the Way turns off right and while it provides a useful route to the valley, there is one more top to be visited first. A fence continues in the same line with a final tack to join a ruined wall. A few stones adorn the highest heathery hummock to the left of the fence and after the wall. The OS pick a point some 20 yards away to the north-west for their spot height and have built the trig point a further half mile to the east.

Return now along the fence to rejoin the Weardale Way and follow it south, down an easy grassy path which later becomes a rough track as it descends towards Cowshill. After passing the rubbish of farm machinery at Cogley and an attractive cottage confusingly called 'Coglea', turn right as obviously does most of the traffic on this lane, to emerge again onto the B6295 and go straight across. At this point the quickest return would be up the main road, but a much pleasanter alternative is available, so continue across the A689 down a lane to the compact group of cottages at Low Allers. Going between the houses follow the lane and then across the fields to Heathery Bridge. Although this is the route of the Weardale Way, it appears that the way has been neglected by its creators and the line is neither waymarked nor easy to trace on the ground. Finally losing patience with it, we chose instead the track from Heathery Bridge which passes the deserted farmhouse at High Rush before descending via Blakeley Field to Killhopeburn Bridge. You again have the choice of a quick return along the main road with a grandstand view of the Killhope Wheel Lead Mining Centre, but for a more sporting route however don't cross the bridge, but turn up the farm road leading west to Wellhope. Go past the farm and turn right up beside the left edge of the wood to cross a forestry track. Follow the track beyond past Cuthbert's level and climb up to a stile into the forest just at the top of the mine workings. There is a right of way at the bottom of the forest too, but the owner has different ideas as evidenced by the discouraging notice. In our explorations we opened the gate and were startled by the deafening explosion of a shotgun cartridge, his first line of defences; his second is to build his smart new residence over the line of the path.

The higher path through the woodland however has no such problems and makes a very pleasant route back, contouring along a wide ride. On reaching Kidd's Dam the right of way turns right, but a new forest track continues past the lake to emerge onto the open moor at a gate. It continues until almost above Killhopehead Bridge which is reached in a few minutes descent across the moor, where an ancient notice warns 'Beware of Adders'.

WALK 10.3 FLINTY FELL

SUMMITS	Flinty Fell	2014 ft (614m)
NOTE	Grouse moors	
DISTANCE	4 miles	
ASCENT	600 feet	
MAPS	OS Landranger sheet 86, Outdoor Leisure - Teesdale	
STARTING POINT	(86-781437) The old mining village of Nenthead, 4 miles south-east of Alston. Car park and toilets.	

An ascent of Flinty Fell could, if one wished, be accomplished and a return made to the road in no more than half an hour. The extent of the exercise would amount to less than a mile with around a hundred feet of ascent. But what would be the point? The village of Nenthead would be missed, so would its mellowed industrial archaeology, Dowgang Hush once ravaged by miners, but now a delightful wooded ravine, would remain unseen and anyway it's cheating!

Between Garrigill in the valley of the South Tyne to the west and Nenthead to the north, Flinty Fell was already a noted mining area in the fourteenth century, but it was the arrival of the London Lead Company in the eighteenth century which turned Nenthead from an isolated sparsely inhabited area into a thriving industrial complex with over 2000 inhabitants in the 1861 census. Attracted by the opportunity to acquire the large smelt mill built speculatively some eight years previously, this Quaker owned company had taken leases on most of the mines in the area by 1753. In an effort to drain the mines as well as explore new veins, a level five miles long was driven all the way from Alston to Nenthead. This work was initially directed by John Smeaton who was later to build the Eddystone Lighthouse. The lower section was a canal which was a popular excursion in Victorian times.

After building a few houses for their workers, the Company soon began the construction of an entire village. The chapel and church were well attended and the Reading Room, built by the Company in 1833, was the first free library in England. Study of engineering and chemistry was promoted while the innkeeper bemoaned his vanishing customers who preferred study to drinking. The miners, whose cottages were provided with large gardens, were also encouraged to work on smallholdings, and reclamation and cultivation extended right up onto the moors; the enclosures reaching almost to the summit of the fells date from this time. Compulsory schooling for children, the

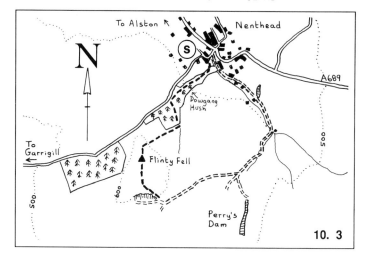

10. 3

first in the country, was an innovation of the Company which also brought to an end the widespread use of women in the crushing and washing of the ore. Mining finally came to an end in 1936 and now Dowgang Hush, where once miners released torrents of water to scour the ground in search of minerals, is a quiet and attractive little valley.

ROUTE DESCRIPTION

FLINTY FELL

From the car park take the mine track beside the River Nent, passing the entrance to Dowgang level on the right and on the left Rampgill horse level, which ran for 3½ miles underground. The track goes through an iron gate by the Nenthead Smelt Mill, now an ancient monument, which has largely been demolished, but you can see the laboratory and assay house which is a two storey building with a tall chimney and the men's barracks. Keeping to the main track a high bank on the left hides a disused reservoir whose waters powered a waterwheel, at the time the second largest in the world, and then, at a bend in the track, there is an old mine building with a stone bridge concealed behind it. Half a mile beyond fork right, taking the higher track. Walk along high above the valley with Perry's Dam away to the left and passing through a couple of gates to the recently reopened Flinty Quarry, where stone was quarried for the mines. Across the valley to the left the pylons of the ski tow on Burnhope Seat appear on the skyline. Skirting the quarry to the right head north over the moor. There are two tops of almost equal height. The first is marked by an iron post and a couple of stones, while 250 yards

222

north across a flat featureless grassy moor covered with drainage channels is the fractionally higher top, unmarked amid old mine workings with a mineshaft capped by concrete posts at the highest point. Nearby at the head of Brown Gill, the London Lead Company first started its operations in 1706. To the south-west is the familiar outline of Cross Fell and Great Dun Fell with its radar dome.

The descent follows a wall down north-east and past a conifer plantation. At the forest corner, where there is a disused coal mine, take the track north, then just before the road, turn right down the ravine of Dowgang Hush to join the Dowgang Burn. Once ravaged by mining, this whole area is now attractively wooded and it is difficult to imagine it as it must once have been. A right of way joins the path beside this pretty little burn, while below you can see the village of Nenthead, which is quickly reached on a good path.

Fountain at Nenthead

WALK 10.4 CHAPELFELL TOP TO WESTERNHOPE MOOR

SUMMITS	Chapelfell Top	2306 ft (703m)
	Fendrith Hill	2283 ft (696m)
	Westernhope Moor	2215 ft (675m)

NOTE	Grouse moors

DISTANCE	7¹/₂ miles

ASCENT	1200 feet

MAPS	OS Landranger sheet 91
	Outdoor Leisure - Teesdale

STARTING POINT	(91-895347) On the minor road between Newbiggin in Teesdale and Westgate in Weardale, at the bridge over Swinhope Burn. Car parking beside the road.

Above the Weardale villages of Eastgate and Westgate which once marked the limits of the Bishop of Durham's deer park, rise Swinhope Moor, Westernhope Moor and Snowhope Moor topped by the three summits which are at the eastern end of the Teesdale Weardale watershed.

Nearly two miles from the road over pathless heather the trig point on Westernhope Moor must be seldom visited except by dedicated peak baggers or those intent upon following the Teesdale Watershed Walk. This gruelling trek follows the high ground which gathers the waters of the River Tees and at 49 miles must be an extreme test of endurance as for most of the way it lies over pathless moor. After such a walk an appetite for heather moorland might well be satiated!

The railway in Weardale began a steady retreat in 1953 with the withdrawal of the passenger service, but the remaining line is still in regular use for the cement works whose chimney, nearly 300ft high, reminded us of the Hope Valley in Derbyshire. Also at Eastgate is a Roman altar built into the wall by the phone box and dedicated to Silvanus the god of huntsmen. Modern huntsmen are now taken up to the moors by landrover and have the birds driven towards them by beaters, so perhaps they have no need of Silvanus; his monument is only a copy anyway.

Snowhope Moor hints at expectant skiers, but it is the fellsides of Swinhope Moor where the Weardale Ski Club have their ski tow and where they are now building a new club hut. Understandably reluctant to share their snow with anyone, a notice announces that they do not accept day members. Not having brought our skis, for the good reason that it was May and the only snow left was a very small patch on Cross Fell, we did not feel deprived.

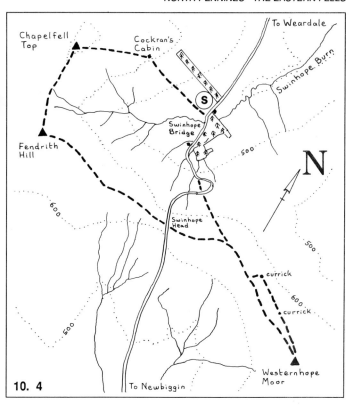

The moors are common land on which each farm has the right to graze a certain number of cattle or sheep. Grassy flanks rise to undulating tops of peat and heather where boundaries which have long lost their territorial importance are marked by ditches following much of the ridge and these provide good guides and often easier walking. The summits themselves are, like many moorland ones, incidental on a high level walk. As usual though the first one, which requires most of the day's ascent and is here reached after a steep climb of nearly a thousand feet, feels very much a mountain.

ROUTE DESCRIPTION

CHAPELFELL TOP *(St John's Chapel Fell Top)*
Go through the gate on the west side of the road and then straight up the hillside aiming for the ruined cottage, Cockran's Cabin, almost on the skyline. It is a steady climb over grass to reach its tumbled walls and beams. Above the angle eases and the ground underfoot changes to typical rough moorland. It is about half a mile from Cockran's Cabin to the summit, but as the top of Chapel Fell is crossed by a boundary ditch this provides a good guide in the final stages (the ditch is marked on the Outdoor Leisure map with the same symbol as a fence). The small cairn is about 40 yards to the north of the ditch, 150 yards before it turns a sharp corner to head south to Fendrith Hill. While this is not exactly the spot marked by the Ordnance Survey, it would be pedantry to deny it recognition as the alternative is certainly no higher. The view is extensive in all directions and the distant horizon is all of mountains with the characteristic outline of the Cross Fell range easily identified to the west.

FENDRITH HILL
The boundary ditch provides a useful guide and an easy route south across the rough moor; it is both wide and deep and must have taken a long time to dig. In a mile the trig point is reached with an ascent of fractionally over 50ft. Set on the edge of the slope, this is much the best viewpoint on the walk with Cow Green Reservoir to the west beyond Teesdale.

WESTERNHOPE MOOR *(Western Valley Moor)*
The ditch at this point turns through a right angle and heads east. Follow it down to meet fencing above the top of the ski club tow where overlooking the grassy bowl of Swinhope Moor, a small rock outcrop provides a walled shelter and in an emergency there is the ski club's wooden hut. The cables and pylons have the usual messy look of all ski slopes when there is no snow. Continue beside the following wall over the rise of Dora's Seat and down to meet the road at Swinhope Head, the highest point on the pass. Sections of this high substantial wall have recently been repaired and it is interesting to admire the craftmanship and notice the slight differences that have been used in walling techniques. The wall continues for a short distance on the other side of the road to be followed by a new fence climbing gently to reach the flat topped moor, where the remnants of a broken wall have been used to build two new cairns. The fence, a useful guide in mist, leads all the way to the concrete trig point less than 2 miles after leaving the road and while the going is pathless it is quite easy. There are distant views and the nearest points are Chapelfell Top to the west and to the east Outberry Plain, which you will be relieved to learn it is not necessary to visit as it hasn't even a single ring contour.

Rather than returning by the same route, although this may be the best option in mist, the return can be varied by descending to visit the pair of tall stone curricks which stand proudly north of the path. On reaching the second of these there is a fence just beyond and this should be followed up to rejoin the ridge fence. In under half a mile where the twin cairns are met again at the fence corner, head north-west down over the moor to cut across the road at the hairpin bend and then follow it back to Swinhope Bridge.

Currick on Westernhope Moor

Cautley Crag from Low Haygarth

CHAPTER 11 YORKSHIRE DALES - THE NORTHERN FELLS

TOP	NAME	HEIGHT	GRID REF	WALK No.
1	Randygill Top	625m	91-687001 NY	11.1
2	Yarlside	639m	98-686985 SD	11.1
3	Fell Head	640m	97-650982 SD	11.1
4	Bush Howe	623m	97-659981 SD	11.1
5	The Calf	676m	98-667971 SD	11.1
6	Bram Rigg Top	672m	98-668965 SD	11.1
7	Calders	674m	98-671960 SD	11.1
8	Wild Boar Fell	708m	98-758988 SD	11.2
9	Swarth Fell	681m	98-756967 SD	11.2
10	Knoutberry Haw	676m	98-731919 SD	11.2
11	Baugh Fell	678m	98-741916 SD	11.2
12	Nine Standards Rigg	662m	91-825061 NY	11.4
13	Water Crag	668m	91-929046 NY	11.3
14	Rogan's Seat	672m	91-919031 NY	11.3
15	High Seat	709m	91-802012 NY	11.5
16	Archy Styrigg	695m	91-802004 NY	11.5
17	Hugh Seat	689m	98-809991 SD	11.5
18	Little Fell	667m	98-808971 SD	11.5
19	Great Shunner Fell	716m	98-849973 SD	11.6
20	Lovely Seat	675m	98-879951 SD	11.6

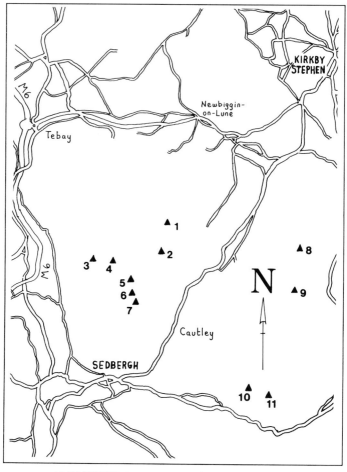

11 YORKSHIRE DALES - THE NORTHERN FELLS

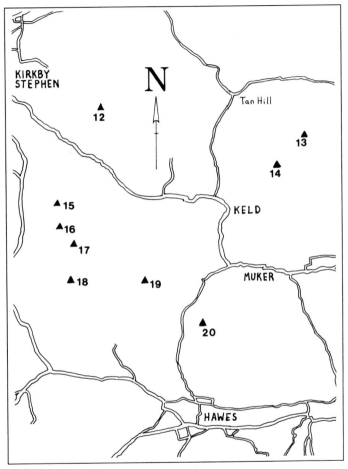

11 YORKSHIRE DALES - THE NORTHERN FELLS

WALK 11.1 THE HOWGILLS

SUMMITS	Yarlside	2096 ft (639m)
	Randygill Top	2051 ft (625m)
	Fell Head	2100 ft (640m)
	Bush Howe	2044 ft (623m)
	The Calf	2218 ft (676m)
	Bram Rigg Top	2205 ft (672m)
	Calders	2211 ft (674m)
DISTANCE	12 miles	
ASCENT	4300 feet	
MAPS	OS Landranger sheets 97, 98 & 91	
	Pathfinder SD 69/79 (except Randygill Top)	
STARTING		
POINT	(98-698969) The Cross Keys Hotel on the A683 about 4 miles north-east of Sedbergh. Parking in the lay by.	

Travelling north on the M6 and just after passing the turn off for southern Lakeland, the view changes, closing in from the rugged distant skyline of the Lake District to sheep pastures and the lower hills on its fringe. Eastwards however the land climbs again to high rounded hills, grassy domes which must often provoke the resolution - "Must have a look there someday". That not many follow this resolve is evident when one does turn off through Sedbergh to visit these hills as apart from Cautley Spout it is a very peaceful and unfrequented scene. Even this fine series of waterfalls which totals 600ft in height had attracted a bare half dozen cars to the lay by at the Cross Keys on our last visit, a brilliantly sunny Bank Holiday in May.

Sedbergh too is a quiet backwater seldom visited by tourists and though it is the largest town in the Yorkshire Dales National Park it now belongs to Cumbria. Famous for its public school which was founded in the sixteenth century, there are a couple of bookshops and the odd tea room. The oldest part of the town is near the church and the earliest Quaker meeting House in the north of England, which dates from 1675, stands at Brigflatts beside the River Rawthey. The local industry was hand knitting in which practically everyone took a turn, even the men, a fact that was commented on by Daniel Defoe in the 18th century. Lead miners and the navvies on the Carlisle railway line knitted, but eventually the 'terrible knitters' were replaced by mechanisation, mills and machines. Earlier civilisations seem to have shunned this area and there are no ancient settlements or roads and even the National Park Information Centre which distributes leaflets on the surrounding dales has

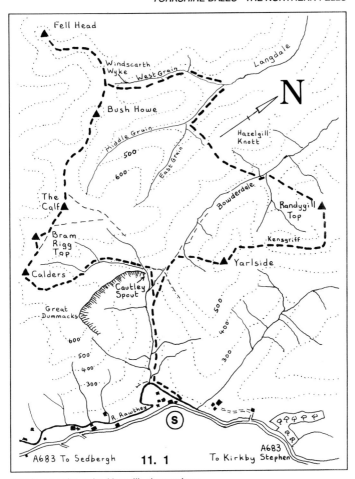

little to say about the Howgills themselves.

Strangely bisected by the boundary of the Yorkshire Dales National Park, which passes over the summit of The Calf the highest of these fells, this area of around twenty square miles is a complex series of ridges separated by radiating valleys where careful navigation is needed to avoid unwanted extra miles at the end of the day. Crossings from one valley to the next usually

233

involve the ascent and descent of some very steep grass slopes which pack a great deal of effort into a short distance. This radial pattern with even the name Langdale for one of the valleys recalls Lakeland, but although like the Skiddaw fells these hills are predominantly of slate, which explains their rounded shape, there is very little rock to be seen apart from the shattered cliffs of Cautley Crag. However it is a good place to go when the Lake District is busy with people and a visit then will be rewarded by green hills, by larks singing high in the spring air and a day very probably spent completely alone.

ROUTE DESCRIPTION

YARLSIDE

Cross the footbridge over the River Rawthey, signed Cautley Spout and after the little gate on the far side, no more gates or stiles are met on the entire walk as these hills are unenclosed common land with open grazing shared by several farmers. Cattle, including often a docile bull, graze by the footpath beside Cautley Holme Beck which is followed for about a mile nearly to the foot of the falls where a gill comes in from the right. Climb beside this to Bowderdale Head and from here aim north-east straight for Yarlside summit. The steep climb over grass is only 600ft, but with no path it seems a lot more. However this is the biggest of the several pathless grassy ascents, which is some small consolation. The summit when finally attained is in no doubt and is crowned with a small cairn. The views to the east are of Wild Boar Fell and Baugh Fell while along the ridge to the north lies the next objective, Randygill Top, inconsiderately situated on the far side of an intermediate and substantial looking hill.

RANDYGILL TOP

Walk north-west for a short way and then descend steeply north-east to a col. The following ascent of Kensgriff fortunately isn't as big as it looks and after descending more easily to the col beyond, you climb north-west for 370ft over more pathless grass to another obvious summit with quite a big cairn. From here the main bulk of the Howgills dominates the view ahead, separated from these subsidiary tops by Bowderdale.

FELL HEAD *(Fell Summit)*

To avoid a long out and back trek over The Calf an interesting cross country route can be taken over the little frequented northern valleys of the range. Unfortunately a high ridge lies in the way, but after a straightforward descent to the confluence of Randy Gill and Bowderdale Beck and another grassy slog over the shoulder of Hazelgill Knott, with a simple descent to the confluence of Middle Grain and East Grain, most of the hard work of the day is done. Spurning the grassy end of Cobles (you can have too much of a good thing) follow the stream round the northern end of the fell to visit Langdale. From the head of this wild and empty valley West Grain leads with very little effort to its source at Windscarth Wyke, only half a mile from Fell Head. This valley is a good spot for wild flowers and in the spring Marsh Marigolds bloom right up high on the col at the source of the stream. Turn right and follow the ridge path along to the furthest highest point, marked by a post in the middle of a cairn. This is the M6 motorway's very own 2000ft mountain with the cairn a mere 2 miles away and 1500ft above it. The Lake District fells look very close with the Scafells, Gable and Pillar all on show in clear weather, but whatever the weather, there will certainly be a lot more walkers on those tops than there are here.

BUSH HOWE *(Bush Knoll)*
Returning to the col at Windscarth Wyke, it is a short ascent of only 200ft south-east to the next summit whose highest point is rather vague as the gently rounded grassy top has no cairn.

THE CALF
A descent of only just over 50ft is succeeded by an easy climb south-east to the OS trig point of the highest of the Howgill Fells set on a wide grassy expanse grazed by the black and white faced Rough Fell sheep. There are grand views of the Lake District fells, Morecambe Bay and the Yorkshire Three Peaks.

BRAM RIGG TOP *(Broom Ridge Top)*
This area can be confusing in mist so be sure to locate the path south from the trig point which dips to a col, the haunt of black fell ponies, and then climbs to the left of the unmarked and unremarkable summit where you must tramp about a bit to find the highest point, about 120 yards to the right of the path.

CALDERS *(Rapid Stream)*
Return to the path which dips shallowly and climbs again to a big cairn, decorated with a metal fence post. This final summit is crossed by a fence high above the dramatic Hobdale, the only enclosed land on the Howgills. There are good views over the Rawthey valley to Baugh Fell and the main ridge continues south, down over Winder to Sedbergh.

The quickest return now is to turn left along the fence and over Great Dummacks to descend steep grassy slopes to the footbridge over Cautley Holme Beck near its junction with the River Rawthey. However to return by Cautley Spout is much more attractive. Taking the left fork at the fence corner, the path fades out like the Cheshire cat before it reaches Red Gill Beck. Continue following the beck down to reach a sheepfold where a stony path materialises and this leads steeply down beside Cautley Spout, with superb views of the falls, and thence back to the Cross Keys. This is a Temperance hotel, donated to the National Trust on the condition that it remains one, so any thoughts of a pint of ale will have to wait.

WALK 11.2 WILD BOAR FELL AND BAUGH FELL

SUMMITS	Wild Boar Fell	2323 ft (708m)
	Swarth Fell	2234 ft (681m)
	Baugh Fell	2224 ft (678m)
	Knoutberry Haw	2218 ft (676m)
DISTANCE	12 miles	
ASCENT	2700 feet	
MAPS	OS Landranger sheet 98	
	Pathfinder SD 69/79	
STARTING		
POINT	(98-728972) At the end of the minor road to Uldale east of the A683, 6 miles north of Sedbergh. Parking by the roadside.	

Just to the east of the Howgills and very similar in area, these fells are completely different. Although like their neighbours they too are grass covered, this is a tough moorland grass, the underlying rock is gritstone instead of slate and the area strongly evokes the feel of the Pennine moors. Rather than the abrupt upthrust of the steep fellsides that radiate from The Calf, the land rises gradually with far fewer separate tops, though here all of them attain the 2000ft contour, but despite the moorlike landscape there is no extensive heather and hence although half expected, we have never heard the familiar call of the grouse.

This is mainly unenclosed moorland with only a few stone walls extending beyond the valley, but where the Howgills are bereft of tarns, here there are several, all situated high on the moor. Sand Tarn beneath the slopes of Wild Boar Fell was the site of millstone quarrying and the sand itself, which forms a silver beach beside the tarn, was once used in sharpening knives and other implements. Perhaps the last wild boar in England met his fate on these moors as is claimed, killed in the fifteenth century by Sir Richard Musgrave, but it is a popular belief in many other places too. However Sir Richard took the evidence with him to the grave and his tomb at Kirkby Stephen was found to contain the tusk of a wild boar when it was opened in the mid nineteenth century.

On our walks here we have seen only one other person, a solitary runner in a white sun hat. Miles of moorland, a distant skyline of yet more hills and shared only with the long coated Rough Fell sheep whose yearlings' fleeces ripple like ankle length dresses as they trot sedately out of one's path. If the Howgills are quiet then these hills are deserted.

Wild Boar Fell from the head of the Eden Valley

ROUTE DESCRIPTION

WILD BOAR FELL

Aiming for the cairns on the edge of the Wild Boar Fell plateau, climb north-east over the unfenced grassy moor to the left of the stone wall which flanks Needlehouse Gill. Follow the line of shake holes and limestone outcrops leading to the source of Grain Gill, then continue north-east keeping below the steep summit slopes to visit Sand Tarn. A final scramble east over rough gritstone boulders leads to the flat grassy fell top with a short stroll to the stone OS trig point with its encircling wall. The OS give 2 other spot heights on the far edge which equal this point, and though they are not separate tops they give good views down into Mallerstang and over to Great Shunner Fell. From this mile long millstone grit plateau which overtops all the surrounding fells, except for the aptly named High Seat, there are wide views in all directions. To the north-west are the Lake District fells and to the south-east the Yorkshire Three Peaks

SWARTH FELL *(Black Fell)*

Head south, crossing a new fence, to join a good path which goes all the way to the next summit, first to the tarn at the col and then climbing beside a high wall. It is an ascent of only 200ft to the substantial cairn which is about 100 yards east of the wall, set amid rocks overlooking the Eden valley.

BAUGH FELL

Continue along the wall for about a quarter of a mile, then where it turns right, cross a stile to enter the Yorkshire Dales National Park. Swarth Fell Pike, with a rise of only 40ft does not qualify as a separate top, so follow the wall down

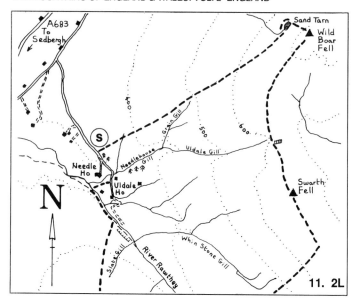

to Rawthey Gill Foot. The valley of Rawthey Gill narrows as it climbs and the stream tumbles down enchantingly with many little waterfalls over the flat rocks. The sheep who usually find the easiest line have made an intermittent path on the right bank and this hidden valley is followed up to Gill Head where the left fork climbs to the vast expanse of East Baugh Fell. The huge flattish top with its collection of small tarns is a complete contrast to the first two summits and there is a great feeling of space and solitude here. A small roughly roofed stone shelter stands on the valley rim to the east of Gill Head. Fork right to the source of the gill and then head south to a stone wall which crosses the highest point of the fell. Twenty yards east of a little kink at a wall junction is Tarn Rigg Hill, the summit of Baugh Fell, pronounced Bow to rhyme with go. Ingleborough peeks out from behind Whernside, but the main interest is the group of tarns scattered on the moor and the fell top itself, so huge and empty.

KNOUTBERRY HAW *(Cloudberry Enclosure)*
Walk west along the wall for half a mile to the OS trig point which is 6ft lower than Tarn Rigg Hill. The name Knoutberry is derived from the local word for the cloudberry, Cnoutberry or Knotberry, *Rubus chamaemorus.* Rather like a sprawling blackberry its orange fruit was considered a delicacy in times when,

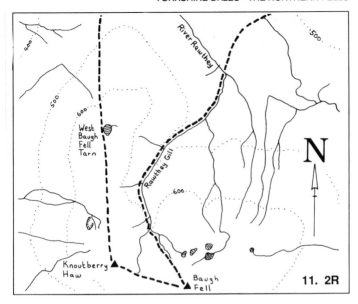

not grazed by the sheep, it was more plentiful. Ingleborough has now disappeared completely behind Whernside but the eye is drawn by the smooth slopes of the Howgills which lie serenely to the west with the little town of Sedbergh below in the valley.

Go north along the wide grassy ridge for about a mile, passing to the right of the ruined Baugh Fell Quarry which was quite extensive and still has the remnants of a few buildings affording a little shelter from the wind. Keep over to the right to be sure and find West Baugh Fell Tarn for this quiet sheet of water recalls the tarns of the Lake District for beauty as well as for its unspoilt loneliness. A large cairn to the west of the tarn marks the end of the high ground and from here it is an easy descent north over grass for about a mile passing to the right of a group of small tarns. From here head just east of north to a large sheepfold to avoid the steep cliffs of the disused Rawthey Gill Quarry and then descend an easy slope to the old quarry road. Turn left and follow the river downstream with its deep pools and little weirs, to a footbridge where a stony track leads uphill to the lane, and then left along this back to the starting point.

WALK 11.3 ROGAN'S SEAT

SUMMITS	Rogan's Seat	2205 ft (672m)
	Water Crag	2192 ft (668m)

NOTE	Grouse moors

DISTANCE	14½ miles

ASCENT	1750 feet

MAPS	OS Landranger sheet 98 & 91
	Outdoor Leisure - Yorkshire Dales, Northern & Central areas

STARTING POINT	(98-910978) Muker village in Swaledale, car park on the far side of the river.

Although the heyday of shooting at Gunnerside was in the 1930s, these heathery moorland tops are still very active grouse moors belonging to The Earl Peel who owns 32,000 acres of shooting rights. Rough tough heather defends the summits making an approach from the Tan Hill Inn to the north rather arduous, but the southern side is almost excessively easy with a land rover track to within a few yards of the cairn. Although outside the season all is quiet and the valleys of Swinner Gill and Gunnerside Gill now attractive and peaceful, in the eighteenth and early nineteenth centuries with over twenty smelt mills and at least eight hundred miners, Swaledale was one of the most important lead mining centres in the country and lead has been mined here since Roman times. The first miners searched the stream beds for likely looking pebbles and then by hushing, that is building peat dams high up the hillside and releasing the collected water, gouged out the hillside to reveal the galena: there are many examples of this in Gunnerside Gill. The ore was crushed by women and boys in crushing mills and then smelted in a furnace before being transported, originally by packhorse, to the river at York. There is much evidence of the mining activity in these hills with many old workings, tunnels, shafts and spoil heaps, ruined smelt mills and flues. The industry collapsed towards the end of the nineteenth century when cheaper foreign lead was imported.

The villages in the upper reaches of Swaledale were originally Norse settlements and these farming communities were enlarged by miners' cottages in the eighteenth century. Muker, which was built on a knoll at the foot of a south facing slope, means meadow and to this day it is surrounded by meadowland which in early summer is covered with wild flowers. Each field

The Tan Hill Inn

has its own small barn in which hay was stored and the cattle over-wintered. One of the most attractive villages in the Dales, with its narrow ginnels and outside staircases, Muker caters in a small way for visitors with a pub, teashop and craft shop, village store and post office. At one time each of these dales villages had its own band and although most have now disappeared, there is still the 'Muker Silver Band' which was founded in 1879.

The riverside track up Swaledale follows the line of the Corpse Way which ran from Keld to Grinton church. Beside Ivelet bridge, a single span packhorse bridge, is a large stone upon which the bodies were rested. After 1580, when the chapel and burial ground was consecrated, local burials took place at Muker. Many of the bridges over the Swale have been washed away by floods and the two encountered on the walk are set safely high above the stream. One dark bonfire night, following optimistic waymarks, we arrived on the banks of the Swale just to the east of Muker. There was no bridge but our torches illuminated a yellow arrow pointing the way straight into the deep swift flowing black water. Daylight or a dry summer may make this less daunting, but we opted for a detour to the safety of Ramps Holme Bridge a mile upstream.

The famous Kearton brothers who lived 2 miles away at Thwaite went to school in Muker. Richard, born in 1862 and Cherry 9 years later, were pioneers in popularising natural history. They photographed and wrote about their subjects and were the first to use a portable hide, concealing themselves inside a stuffed cow. In later life Cherry travelled all over the world photographing

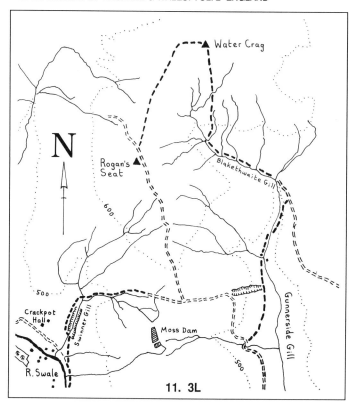

wild animals and Richard gave lantern slide lectures and wrote many natural history books illustrated with photographs .

ROUTE DESCRIPTION

ROGAN'S SEAT (Rogan's Upland Pasture)

Walk up to the left of Muker's Literary Institute and between the houses to take the field path, signed 'Gunnerside & Keld'. This passes through a series of squeezer stiles separating the meadows which are a mass of wild flowers in early summer. On arriving at the River Swale, cross the narrow footbridge set high above the water on enormous stone piers, and turn left to walk upstream beside the river on a broad track, the old Corpse Way. Ahead high up above

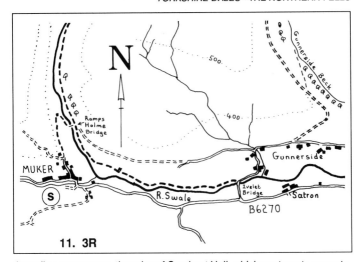

11. 3R

the valley you can see the ruins of Crackpot Hall, which contrary to expectations means the hollow of the crows; this was inhabited until 1953. The lovely vale of Swaledale is typical of the area with a wide valley bottom, steep hillsides, the remains of lead mines and many small barns dotted about. Just before Swinner Gill, turn right beside a fenced enclosure and up a path which climbs steeply and then levels out high above the gill. Descending briefly to cross the stream, it climbs again steeply on the left bank to avoid the gorge. Reaching a little bridge at the disused Swinner Gill Lead Mine there are the ruined buildings of the smelt mill which worked from 1769 to 1820. Upstream, at the head of a narrow gorge, is Swinner Gill Kirk, a hidden cave where religious meetings took place. Follow the clear path beside East Grain to join a newly bulldozed shooting road. High on the moor, after a gate where there is a good view across to Gunnerside Gill, turn left off the right of way up a track for a mile and a half, heading north straight for the summit of Rogan's Seat. Two knolls to the left vie for this honour and the second smaller peat hag has won with the trophy of a small cairn on its top. The foreground is dull, but in the distance to the south-west you can identify the Butter Tubs Pass flanked by Lovely Seat and Great Shunner Fell and beyond are other distant hills of the southern Dales.

WATER CRAG
Though appearing to be a long way to the north-east, distances are deceptive and it is only just over a mile to this next top. Return to the shooting road and after a few yards turn right along the fence. It is an easy stroll, with little loss of height, following the fence until it turns sharp left. Aim north-east for 100

yards to a prominent wall-like structure and from here a faint path leads east for 150 yards to the concrete OS trig point and wind shelter. The view across the Stainmore Gap to the northern Pennines is most extensive and the town of Barnard Castle is framed by the windshelter entrance.

Descending southwards over rough and pathless moor to join the head-waters of Blakethwaite Gill, the going soon becomes easier as a narrow trod develops. Follow the gill on the left through this beautiful and deserted valley passing the waterfalls and the ruined Blakethwaite Dams which stored water to power the mines below. Continue to follow Blakethwaite Gill keeping below Lord Peel's shooting cabin and above a dramatic limestone gorge on a narrow but clear path to the ruined buildings of Blakethwaite Lead Mine. From here a broad grassy track leads along the hillside with a bird's-eye view of the arches of the peat store, and on the other side of the gill are the remains of the furnace house with its cast-iron supports, and a well preserved lime kiln. The line of the flue runs straight up the hillside opposite to a now vanished chimney. The smelt mill was opened in 1820 and closed in 1878. Descend to the buildings, then cross the stone slab over the gill to take the wide green road that slants gently uphill to the west side of Gunnerside Gill. Follow the gill for 3 miles on this good track passing many old mine workings and hushes, then turn right on the unfenced road to Gunnerside Lodge, the home of The Earl Peel. Fork left to the small hamlet of Ivelet and then right to Ivelet Bridge, where the riverside path signed 'Muker' is followed for 2 miles back to Ramps Holme Bridge and the start.

Swinner Gill

WALK 11.4 NINE STANDARDS RIGG

SUMMITS	Nine Standards Rigg	2172 ft (662m)

DISTANCE	5 miles

ASCENT	500 feet

MAPS	OS Landranger sheet 91

STARTING POINT	(91-812041) The summit of the B6270 Kirkby Stephen to Keld road. Lay by at the National Park Boundary.

Nine Standards Rigg is not a hill to be underestimated. There are no cliffs or crags, no peaks or pinnacles and were it not for the fine summit cairns, the Nine Standards, it would pass without notice, an easy stroll for an off day. Or so we thought. After a frustrating day on Dufton Fell surveying in thick mist which maddeningly cleared as we reached our car, we decided to retrieve the day. Pausing only to purchase a large scale map of the area, with blue cover and last fully surveyed in 1910, we set off at high speed for Kirkby Stephen. It was getting a bit late and the sunshine had vanished into a murky gloom, but Nine Standards Rigg is only a little hill; we would soon nip up and back. We had misgivings straight away, our smart new map didn't seem to bear much resemblance to what little bit of the ground we could see, but we hurried on into the thick mist checking the compass at intervals. After a very long time to our surprise a wall appeared and a much used muddy path, but where were we? The wall didn't look as if it had been built after 1910 and with a certain amount of muttering and consultation we made a good guess at our position, dismissed ideas of retreat and pressed on. It was a good path and we set off uphill into an area of black peat bog where a churned mess of footprints led unerringly to a trig point. This was another surprise as it wasn't marked on our map. Abandoning ideas of an afternoon tea break and a survey of White Mossy Hill as we could only just see each other and it was getting dark, we set off briskly back the way we had come. Ten minutes later there we were on White Mossy Hill. Suppressing feelings of alarm we turned west over rough tussock grass, our torches reflecting blankly from the enveloping grey mist. Counting our paces and watching the compass we located a stream and this brought us, after what seemed like hours of stumbling through reedy bogs, back to our wall. A further eternity and we felt rather than saw the road under our feet. After a short dispute as to whether the car was to the left or to the right, we arrived back as the mist lifted. We had been gone little over two hours, but it had reinforced the lesson that no mountain, no matter how small, should be taken lightly.

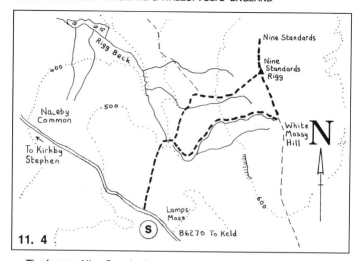

The famous Nine Standards are a set of cairns or stone men, which were originally some 12 feet high. There are various theories as to why they are there. Were they built by the miners in their spare time or, more improbably, constructed to deceive the Scots into thinking an army awaited them on the ridge? They may well be boundary markers, but there are many groups of these cairns in the North Pennines and no one really knows why they were built.

ROUTE DESCRIPTION

NINE STANDARDS RIGG *(Nine Cairns Ridge)*
About a quarter of a mile west of the lay by where the grassy limestone meets the rough moorland is a line of sink holes, some delicately fluted and surprisingly deep. These are an unsuspected hazard under snow and our first visit saw us rescuing a sheep which had fallen in. After half a mile of easy walking north along the edge of the limestone, turn right and follow the path beside the stone wall encircling the head of Dukerdale. Climb by the wall until it turns north by a ruin at the highest point and then take the path that diverges from the wall to cross a stream. Follow the stream up and then slant left to a prominent cairn, a ruined building, and a few yards further east the old road to the coal pits from Hartley is joined. Soon deteriorating to a rather boggy path, part of the Coast to Coast Walk, this is then followed to the OS stone trig point. To the north stands the group of cairns after which the summit is named and a topograph erected by the Kirkby Stephen Fell Search Team to

commemorate the wedding of Prince Charles.

With a rise of only 30ft White Mossy Hill does not qualify as a separate top, but the return route can be varied by taking the Coast to Coast path south to its summit before descending west over the pathless and boggy moor to the limestone and back to the road.

Nine Standards Rigg

WALK 11.5 HIGH SEAT AND HUGH SEAT

SUMMITS	High Seat	2326 ft (709m)
	Archy Styrigg	2280 ft (695m)
	Hugh Seat	2260 ft (689m)
	Little Fell	2188 ft (667m)
NOTE	Grouse moors	
DISTANCE	9½ miles	
ASCENT	1800 feet	
MAPS	OS Landranger sheets 91 & 98	
STARTING POINT	(91-782015) Outhgill village on the B6259 5 miles south of Kirkby Stephen. Roadside parking.	

To the west of Great Shunner Fell the moor stretches away for mile upon mile of rough grass, bog and heather, with the staccato calls of the grouse and in the distance the ground rises gradually to gently rounded summits astride the boundary between North Yorkshire and Cumbria. From the Eden Valley side however these hills present a completely different aspect. Approaching from Garsdale one follows the route of the Settle to Carlisle railway to reach the highest point on any main line in Britain at 1169 feet before descending again to the Eden valley. On the left is the massive bulk of Baugh Fell, Swarth Fell and Wild Boar Fell, while to the right steep slopes rise to the vertical rocky scars on the skyline of the three mile long escarpment of Mallerstang Edge.

Three grand rivers rise on Hugh Seat, the Ure, the Eden and the Swale, and the head of Eden Dale is on the main Pennine watershed of England. The highest of the summits is High Seat, meaning simply high pasture, but Hugh Seat is named after Sir Hugh de Morville of Pendragon Castle. Sir Hugh was one of the four knights who murdered Thomas à Beckett in Canterbury cathedral on December 29th 1170.

The local blacksmith at Outhgill (from Old Norse meaning desolate ravine) was the father of Michael Faraday, the famous scientist. This attractive small village also has a replica of the Jew Stone, a column erected in 1850 by William Mounsey, an eccentric and linguist, to commemorate his journey from the mouth to the source of the River Eden.

Another local character was Lady Anne Clifford. Born in 1590, she fought for many years to obtain her inheritance, but was thwarted on all sides until at the age of 53 she received the title and her estates, simply by outliving all

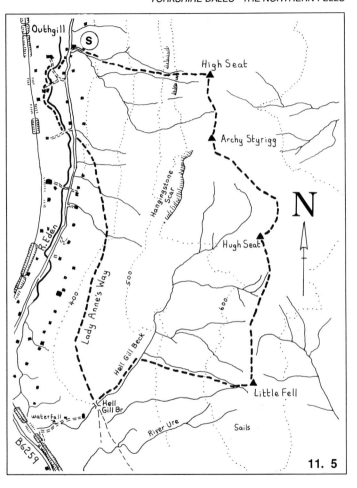

11. 5

the other heirs. Her lands extended from Skipton to Broughton. Pendragon Castle was built originally as a pele tower in the twelfth century as a stronghold against the Scot border raiders, the castle was twice burnt down, the second time in 1541. Lady Anne repaired and renovated the building in 1660 and also the other castles and churches on her land. An indomitable old lady she lived to the age of 86 travelling around her estates by horse litter surrounded by

249

servants and posessions, *'Where I think coach never did went before'.* Until the modern road was built in 1825 Lady Anne's High Way was the only road up the valley. Originally a Roman road, which would have been built on the line of a prehistoric trackway, it was used by farmers and drovers in the eighteenth century and crosses the dramatic limestone ravine of Hell Gill. Pendragon Castle is now ruined and though it is on private land, it can be well seen from the road.

ROUTE DESCRIPTION

HIGH SEAT *(High Upland Pasture)*
Take the lane past the Jew Stone and the old school house heading straight for the summit of High Seat, less than 2 miles away. An old track, a right of way to the coal pits, sets off across the common and crosses a stream but soon becomes indistinct. Climb east beside the stream over rough grassland, almost to the spoil heaps. Ahead on the skyline a solitary cairn marks a way through the crags of Mallerstang Edge between two gills. It is a short steep ascent to the shepherds' cairn and then an easy walk continuing in the same direction to the flat summit. Three cairns ornament the top, but the highest point, the centre of the ring contour on the map, is unmarked. There are panoramic views in all directions, from Mickle Fell in the north to the characteristic stepped shape of Ingleborough in the south. Closer and to the west is Wild Boar Fell while to the east the large sheet of water, Birkdale Tarn, was artificially created to serve the lead mines.

ARCHY STYRIGG
A path now leads south along the broad ridge for half a mile with grand views of Hangingstone Scar. The OS choose the uncairned northern bump for the spot height, though the southern bump which has a few large stones on the top is equally as high. The big cairn, marked Gregory Chapel on the large scale map, is slightly lower.

HUGH SEAT *(Hugh's Upland Pasture)*
The ridge path wanders south-east to a fine stone pillar and circular wind shelter and then continues along the eastern edge of the wide ridge high above Little Sled Dale to another cairn by a new fence. Follow the fence south to a sharp corner which is the highest point on the grassy summit of Hugh Seat. A few yards to the west is Lady's Pillar originally erected by Lady Anne Clifford in 1664 in memory of Sir Hugh de Morville. The pillar also bears the date when it was rebuilt, FHL1890, and an OS bench mark.

LITTLE FELL
South-east a wide ridge leads to Great Shunner Fell, but head south over the empty moor rejoining the fence at the col for the easiest way through this boggy area. When it turns away, continue up easy grass to the summit, which despite appearances is one metre higher than Sails, half a mile further on. A

few stones mark the beginings of a cairn, and there are views over West Gill with its shooting hut to Great Shunner Fell. Just to the south is Ure Head which although an undistinguished looking spot is the birthplace of the River Ure. Starting life by flowing west, the Ure soon swings south then east through Wensleydale on its long journey to the North Sea while the adjacent rivulet only a step or two away, becomes the River Eden which flows north to the Irish Sea.

A stone man to the west indicates the direction of descent to Hell Gill Beck. If the water is low enough cross the stream and follow it down to the gorge and Hell Gill Bridge, but if the beck is in spate stay above the fence hugging the gill to the bridge which spans the deep narrow limestone ravine. If there is time, Hell Gill Force should be visited. It is a half mile detour downstream to this very dramatic waterfall.

From Hell Gill Bridge go north along Lady Anne's High Way, at first across a field. Soon the line of the old road appears which leads down Mallerstang, with the steep slopes of Wild Boar Fell above on the left and to the right the shattered cliffs of Mallerstang Edge. At the main road take the track opposite which descends to cross a tiny bridge. Turn right staying close beside the River Eden and at the farm go to the left of the buildings, following the field footpath to the bridge just before Shoregill. The path then leads back to Outhgill at St Mary's Chapel which was rebuilt by Lady Anne Clifford in 1663.

Hell Gill Falls

WALK 11.6 GREAT SHUNNER FELL

SUMMITS	Great Shunner Fell	2349 ft (716m)
	Lovely Seat	2215 ft (675m)
NOTE	Grouse moors	
DISTANCE	12 miles	
ASCENT	2050 feet	
MAPS	OS Landranger sheet 98	
	Outdoor Leisure - Yorkshire Dales, Northern & Central areas	
STARTING POINT	(98-866912) Hardraw, 1 mile north of Hawes. Parking by the roadside at the west end of the village.	

One of the surprisingly few summits crossed by the Pennine Way, Great Shunner Fell is a fine moorland mountain typical of the Pennines, but while the Pennine Way is very distinct, even eroded in the softer places, away from the route other people are a rarity. On the path, although there seems to be a rush hour when walkers leaving Hardraw and Hawes congregate for lunch by the cairn on the summit, at other times it is quiet enough. The broad track leaving Hardraw once saw a very different form of traffic as it served the coal mines on the slopes of the fell.

The Butter Tubs beside the narrow mountain road which divides Great Shunner Fell from Lovely Seat and which give the pass its name are deep, vertical sided potholes with pinnacles and delicately sculpted fluted sides which have cut right through the limestone. Lovely Seat, the highest point of Abbotside Common, lies less than a mile from the summit of the pass. The bulk of the mountain is gritstone moorland with just enough heather to support some grouse, as the shooting butts on the western slopes testify.

As we climbed the slopes from the road a pair of grouse flew up from beneath our feet, but it was not their grumbling calls that made us stop and listen intently. Above, high on the hill, came a faint music, the tune fragmented by the wind, but unmistakeably the Scottish skirl of the pipes. Outlined against the sky a solitary figure could be seen with a companion seated beside him. Had he perhaps been banished to practice up here or was he like us most at home among the hills and the wild places?

One of Yorkshire's celebrated waterfalls and the highest in England, Hardraw Force must be the most easily reached, requiring merely the payment of a small fee at the Green Dragon Inn. Wordsworth visited it in 1799 with his sister Dorothy and describing it in a letter to Coleridge writes

*'We found the rock which before had seemed a perpendicular wall
extending over us like the ceiling of a huge cave, from the summit of
which the water shot directly over our heads into a baisin and among
fragments of rock wrinkled over with masses of ice, white as snow, or
rather as D. says like congealed froth'.*

Despite several trips to Hardraw and the large number of wet days we have
spent in Yorkshire, we have still to see the fall in spate. The gorge into which
the stream is precipitated, falling clear from the lip of the cliff 96ft above, was
for many years the setting of an annual brass band competition. The first took
place in 1881 and in 1884 six bands competed. After a long lapse the
competition was revived in 1989 and coincided with the weekend we had set
aside for this walk. Twenty bands each took their turn on the stand in a seven
hour programme to delight the hundreds of enthusiasts seated on the steep
grassy bank below the falls with the resounding sounds of the brass.

ROUTE DESCRIPTION

GREAT SHUNNER FELL *(Big Lookout Fell)*
Take the track at the west end of Hardraw, signposted 'FP Thwaite (PW)'
which leads steadily uphill between stout stone walls to emerge after a couple
of miles at a stile onto the open hillside. Taking the signposted right fork just
beyond, the Pennine Way carries on climbing, now more gradually for another
2½ miles to reach the pile of stones which buttress the stone trig point. This
section of the path is rather boggy, even during a dry spell. On one visit the

The summit of Great Shunner Fell

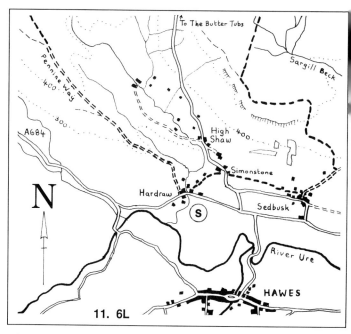

11. 6L

cairn had almost disappeared beneath the snow and we sat in the lee of a snowdrift to eat our lunch with two winter Pennine Way walkers, but other visits have always been in mist and cloud. To the west is the remote ridge of High Seat and Hugh Seat, while to the south-east is Lovely Seat.

LOVELY SEAT

Ignoring cries that you're going the wrong way, follow the fence south-east across the pathless moor. A little south of the fence is an enigmatic collection of cairns, a veritable army of stone men which when seen suddenly appearing through the mist have a rather menacing appearance. Continue down the fence and the following stone wall to meet the upper reaches of Fossdale Gill and then using this as a rough guide, head south-east on the left side of the gill to the distant white blur of the fences flanking the cattle grid on the road. The edges of the complicated system of drainage ditches provide firmer footing than the moor, but seldom are they found going in exactly the right direction. The key to the next ascent is the cattle grid where the fence may be followed on a faint path, climbing south-east to its highest point which is within a few steps of the summit of Lovely Seat. The going is very much easier and

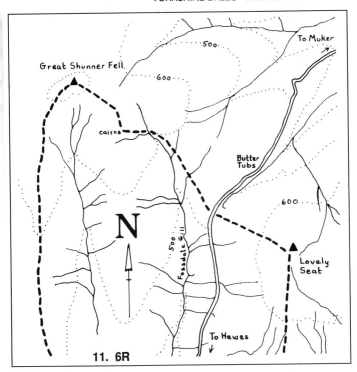

11. 6R

the cairn is soon reached, an untidy heap of stones just big enough to provide shelter for two. To the south and south-west are Pen-y-ghent, Ingleborough and Whernside, while the rest of the horizon is of more distant Pennine moorland hills. A short distance to the west, above the ruins of a building, is a tall stone man overloking the pass, one of the distant relations of those on Great Shunner Fell.

Descending south over rough moorland to the rocky edges of High and Low Millstones, the limestone fringe of the mountain is reached just beyond. The going is now very easy and the right of way is joined and a clear path followed east over short almost lawn-like turf until it turns abruptly right to descend steeply towards Hawes. The path is waymarked down to join the walled track of Shutt Lane at a gate where you turn right down into the little hamlet of Sedbusk. A path between the houses opposite the phone box, signed 'Simon Stone', leads through a series of squeezer stiles, crossing eighteen narrow fields to Simonstone. The dog owner whom we met here lifting two large overweight labradors over the first stile was not at all discouraged to be told that there were a lot more to follow! Go up the drive of Simonstone Hall opposite, signed 'FP Hardraw' and left through the stile just at the hotel main gate. The path is then quite clear over the fields as it descends into Hardraw.

Ingleborough

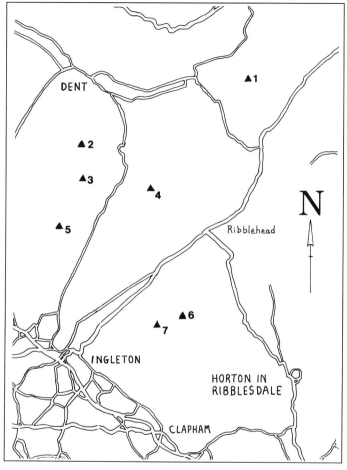

12 YORKSHIRE DALES - THE SOUTHERN FELLS

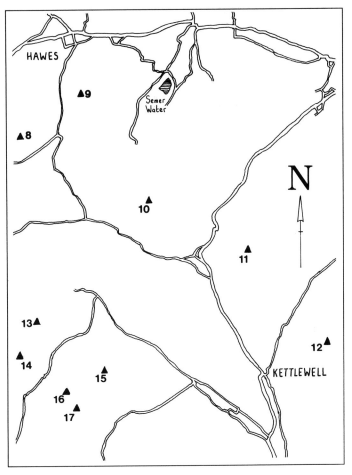

12 YORKSHIRE DALES - THE SOUTHERN FELLS

CHAPTER 12 YORKSHIRE DALES - THE SOUTHERN FELLS

TOP	NAME	HEIGHT	GRID REF	WALK No.
1	Great Knoutberry Hill	672m	98-789872 SD	12.3
2	Great Coum	687m	98-701836 SD	12.2
3	Green Hill	628m	98-702820 SD	12.2
4	Whernside	736m	98-738814 SD	12.2
5	Gragareth	627m	98-688793 SD	12.2
6	Simon Fell	650m	98-755752 SD	12.1
7	Ingleborough	723m	98-741746 SD	12.1
8	Dodd Fell Hill	668m	98-841846 SD	12.5
9	Drumaldrace	614m	98-874867 SD	12.5
10	Yockenthwaite Moor	643m	98-909811 SD	12.7
11	Buckden Pike	702m	98-961788 SD	12.6
12	Great Whernside	704m	98-002739 SE	12.6
13	Plover Hill	680m	98-849752 SD	12.4
14	Pen-y-ghent	694m	98-838734 SD	12.4
15	Darnbrook Fell	624m	98-885728 SD	12.4
16	Fountains Fell	668m	98-864716 SD	12.4
17	Fountains Fell South Top	662m	98-869708 SD	12.4

WALK 12.1 INGLEBOROUGH

SUMMITS	Ingleborough	2372 ft (723m)
	Simon Fell	2133 ft (650m)
DISTANCE	11½ miles	
ASCENT	2100 feet	
MAPS	OS Landranger sheet 98	
	Outdoor Leisure - Yorkshire Dales, Western area.	
STARTING POINT	(98-745692) Clapham village, large car park by the Yorkshire Dales Information Centre, honesty box, toilets.	

Although overtopped by Whernside and hence only the second highest mountain in the Dales, Ingleborough is undoubtedly the finest of Yorkshire's peaks, indeed for some enthusiasts the finest mountain anywhere. Superlatives have long been used about Ingleborough and while local claims that it was a mile in height may have been long disproved, it still has in Gaping Gill the deepest shaft, the biggest cave and the highest waterfall in Britain.

Designated a site of special scientific interest, the crags, gorges and limestone pavements host a variety of rare plants especially on the cliffs out of reach of grazing sheep and deep in the sheltered grikes of the limestone pavement. The layered geology of the mountain with alternating bands of gritstone and limestone has resulted in a necklace of caves and potholes that encircle Ingleborough and a circuit of the fell to visit them is a fascinating walk.

While Ingleborough and its satellite Simon Fell can be quickly ticked off by ascending from the Hill Inn on the much frequented route of the Three Peaks walk, this does not do justice to the mountain which deserves more time and a longer expedition. Approaching from the delightful village of Clapham divided by its little beck, one passes through the grounds of Ingleborough Hall where Reginald Farrer, botanist and plant collector was born in 1880. Bringing back from his travels abroad over a hundred different species he planted thousands of trees in Clapham Gill. His classic book 'My Rock Garden' set an Edwardian fashion for rockeries.

The tremendous chasm of Gaping Gill was first descended by a Frenchman, Edouard Martel in 1895. Using a rope ladder and assisted by his wife, the 340 ft descent into the huge Great Chamber took 23 minutes and the re-ascent surprisingly very little longer at 28 minutes. A couple of times a year local potholers set up a winch with a steel cable and bosun's chair to lower visitors into the depths. Fell Beck disappears down Gaping Gill and reappears as

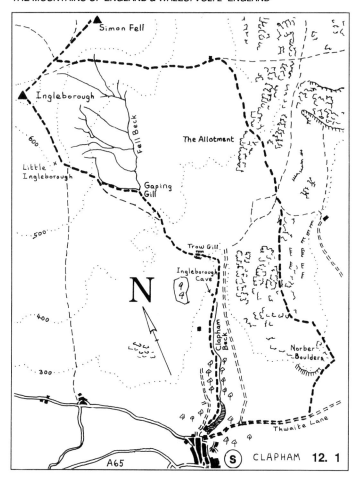

Clapham Beck at Ingleborough Show Cave which was first entered in 1837 when a large stalagmite barrier was destroyed by the brothers, James and Matthew Farrer, releasing an underground lake. The passages behind were explored over the years by cavers and cave divers but it took until 1983 to find a link with Gaping Gill.

The flat grassy summit plateau of Ingleborough provided an excellent site for our tent and tired at the end of the day we relaxed against the cairn to watch the sunset. As we sipped the wine brought to celebrate the completion of a walk round all of Yorkshire's mountains, a final group of walkers joined us. The smallest, a little girl of only eight, announced "I must be the youngest person ever to do the Three Peaks" and compared with the exhausted walkers we had passed tottering downhill on our ascent from Horton in Ribblesdale, she was also one of the fittest, skipping happily about the summit showing no signs of tiredness. We returned to our tent wondering whether we would see again the apparition of our previous visit when close to dark a procession crossed the summit carefully carrying between them a long canoe.

ROUTE DESCRIPTION

INGLEBOROUGH *(Hill Fort)*
Walk north through Clapham village, past the church and turn right after crossing Clapham Beck, following the signs to Ingleborough Cave. There is a small charge to walk through the private grounds which are laid out as a nature trail. The broad track of Clapdale Drive follows the beck through the woods, first beside the lake, then high above the stream passing an ornamental grotto. After a mile the track emerges from the wood and Ingleborough Cave lies a quarter of a mile further on.

Continuing past the show cave the path goes up a little rocky valley with Foxholes cave to the left and then narrows into the rocky defile of Trow Gill. The walls of the limestone gorge press in until there is only a narrow exit up a steep path at the end. Shortly after leaving the ravine which was formed by glacier meltwater, the wall on the left is crossed at a stile. Ingleborough now appears ahead and Bar Pot is at the bottom of the large shake hole to the left. The path continues past Flood Entrance Pot on the right and Disappointment Pot on the left to reach the awesome partially fenced chasm of Gaping Gill into which Fell Beck disappears. The path becomes less distinct, but with the immediate objective of Little Ingleborough, the end of the summit ridge, now in view. Head north-west, making a bee-line for it. The summit of Little Ingleborough is crowned with a very fine circular windshelter and numerous smaller ones. To the left of the ridge is a memorial cairn to AAS 1928 now in a rather precarious state. The path continues north over the boggy plateau to a final climb of 300ft through a narrow band of limestone and past a line of sink holes to the top.

The large flat grassy summit of millstone grit has an OS trig point, a neatly constructed four bay wind shelter with a topograph, and a big untidy cairn situated mid way between the two. There are also the remains of a circular tower built in 1830 which was damaged by local yobbos on the opening day and never repaired. To the east the enclosing walls of the ancient fort and the foundations of hut circles can clearly be seen. This is the highest hill fort in England and Wales and probably dates from the Iron Age when the Brigantian leader Venutius built a fortified settlement against the Roman invaders in the first century. The view indicator, which was erected by the Ingleton Fell Rescue team to commemorate the Coronation in 1953, tells you that on a clear day you can see from Scafell Pike to Pendle Hill. Snaefell on the Isle of Man is 84 miles away.

SIMON FELL *(Sigemund's Fell)*
To reach Ingleborough's companion top, Simon Fell, follow the north edge of the escarpment east, then keeping to the left, descend on the main path to a wall corner by the National Nature Reserve notice board. Squeezing through the stile, follow the wall on its left side for half a mile to the summit, which is a grassy mound beside the wall, marked with a few stones and an old iron post.

   Unfortunately the unstable and newly barbed wire topped wall does not have a stile, so you must retrace your steps to the notice board and then head south-east to join the main path to Horton in Ribblesdale. The path descends gradually for a mile and a half to twin ladder stiles, passing an area where attempts are being made to re-vegetate the eroded peat. The unsightly board walk beyond, which hopefully is only temporary, leads to a now ruined shooting box. After another twin ladder stile there is a signpost. Ignoring its pointing finger, helpfully labelled 'footpath', fork right and follow the track south. A short detour over a ladder stile to the right leads onto The Allotment, a moor which possesses the strangely beautiful 430ft deep Juniper Gulf pothole, well worth a visit if time permits. The cart track follows a cleared way through the limestone pavement and after crossing a ruined wall continues south past Long Scar and then turns right for Clapham at a confusing section with many tracks all leading in different directions. Continue south along a

Norber Erratic

faint path rising to an obvious cairn and follow the ridge for about a mile, then descend left down a small grassy valley between two cairned tops. Cross the wall at a ladder stile to enter the field containing the Norber Boulders. These are Silurian erratics which have been carried by a glacier and dumped on the limestone. Many now stand on limestone plinths, the surrounding unprotected limestone having been eroded away. Slant down across the field to the lower wall and turn right to reach a ladder stile below Robin Proctor's Scar, named after a farmer disappointed in love who leapt from the top. Another field is crossed and then the path joins Thwaite Lane which is followed for a mile back to Clapham. As the lane descends through the grounds of Ingleborough Hall, now an Outdoor Education Centre, there is the unexpected excitment of two very dark tunnels, made in 1833 to hide the old drove road from the hall, before suddenly emerging into the centre of the village.

WALK 12.2 GRAGARETH AND WHERNSIDE

SUMMITS	Gragareth	2057 ft (627m)
	Green Hill	2060 ft (628m)
	Great Coum	2254 ft (687m)
	Whernside	2415 ft (736m)
NOTE	Don't forget a torch for the visit to Yordas Cave.	
DISTANCE	15 miles	
ASCENT	2500 feet	
MAPS	OS Landranger sheet 98	
	Outdoor Leisure - Yorkshire Dales, Western area	
STARTING POINT	(98-706791) The minor road to Dent, 4 miles north of Ingleton below Yordas Cave. Ample roadside parking.	

The western boundary of North Yorkshire and the Yorkshire Dales National Park march in tandem over the massive bulk of Gragareth claiming within their grasp all of the eastern slopes, but the Red Rose is fighting back. Having lost The Old Man of Coniston and the fells of the southern Lake District to the new upstart county of Cumbria, Lancashire still retains a foothold in the mountains with the summits of Gragareth and Green Hill just within its borders. This is a three counties walk as after crossing the Lancashire summits one enters Cumbria which has claimed Great Coum, while Whernside is the highest of the Yorkshire Peaks overtopping Ingleborough by 43ft. High rounded fells

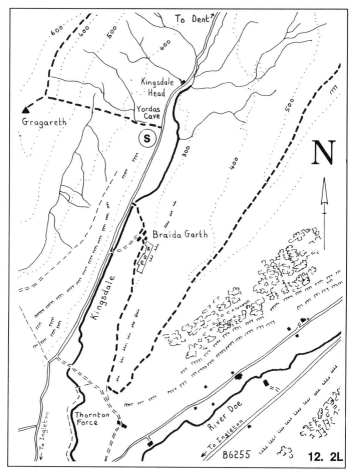

12. 2L

with gritstone moorland tops, the excitement of these mountains is all hidden from view, for in the limestone heart of Gragareth and Whernside are some of the finest caves in the country. Marble Steps Pot, Lost John's Cave, Jingling Pot, are all among the famed underground systems, while in the valley of Ease Gill to the west is Britain's longest cave. The beauty of this underground world will only ever be seen by the caver, and though show caves are well lit

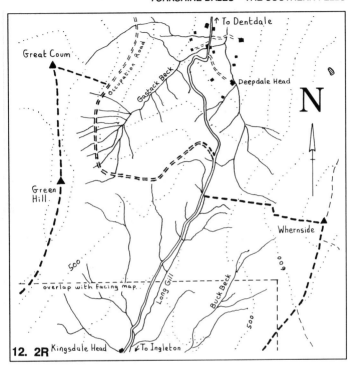

and supplied with guides, they have no excitement at all. Much better to visit Yordas cave, in Victorian times a show cave, but never developed, and here with the aid of a torch one stoops through a low arch to enter the huge cavern, 30ft high and 130ft long. The muddy entrance slopes down to the gravel floor of the main chamber which is washed in wet weather by a shallow stream. Following the sound of a waterfall through the cave, a small ante room leads into the Chapter House. The sound rises to a roar as the chamber is filled with the thunder of the waterfall crashing down and lit by the faint light from a torch one feels the thrill and power of the underground.

Approaching Ingleton, Kingsdale Beck which separates Gragareth and Whernside, becomes the River Twiss. In the middle of the town the waters of the Twiss join with the River Doe to form the Greta, meaning like its namesake at Keswick, the rocky river, but the best rock scenery is above Ingleton where the two rivers leap and splash over a fine series of waterfalls. The walk which takes in Beezley Falls, Snow Falls, Pecca Falls and the biggest of them all

Thornton Force, is one of Yorkshire's star attractions.

The eastern flanks of Whernside are crossed by the Settle to Carlisle Railway, the last line to be constructed entirely by hand, and the 165ft high Batty Moss viaduct at Ribblehead has for many years had the threat of closure hanging over it. Constructed in the 1870s a series of shanty towns were built to house the navvies and other workers; the largest of these at Ribblehead had 3000 inhabitants. In the nearby church at Chapel-le-Dale is a tablet set up in 1876 in memory of those men who lost their lives during the railway's construction; over one hundred died from accident and disease while building the viaduct.

On the slopes of Gragareth we were pursued relentlessly by a tractor. A tiny speck in the distance it drew nearer and nearer. There was no escape, only a decidedly shaky wall on one side and bare open moorland on the other. Chugging loudly it drew to a halt beside us. In the trailer a dog eyed us doubtfully. The cab door opened. "Want a lift?" asked the farmer. He was, he told us, born in Dent and on marrying a local girl moved to an isolated farm in the valley. He had never been to London and had no wish to go, adding "If I could have my time over again I'd do just the same".

St. Leonard's Church, Chapel-le-Dale

ROUTE DESCRIPTION

GRAGARETH

Go through the field gate below the trees and take the path to the right of Yordas Gill, a dry ravine. Opposite the arched entrance to the cave the path goes up to the right and then a little further on descends to cross the dry bed of the gill. Above, the stream disappears down deep fissures to emerge inside the cave and the path passes Yordas Pot, which was not discovered until 1963, when a tree growing over it blew down. Continue up the hillside to the left of the gill to a gate and then follow a faint path beside the wall towards the skyline. The ground steepens after the sheepfold and the path fades but soon the ridge wall is reached at a ladder stile. The concrete OS trig point is 200 yard to the south-west from which you can look across the secluded valley of Ease Gill, famous for its potholes, towards Calf Top which is just 3 feet below the magic 2000. You feel right on the edge of the mountains with extensive views westwards over Morecambe Bay and southwards to the Forest of Bowland.

GREEN HILL

Return to the wall and follow it north for a couple of miles with Lancashire to the left and North Yorkshire to the right. As you climb to Green Hill, the County of Cumbria meets the other two. "You'd think they'd put a marker up" said the farmer. The summit is uncairned, a green knoll at the far end of the ridge to the left of the wall.

GREAT COUM *(Big Narrow Valley)*

Descend to a gate in the cross wall which meets the ridge at the County Stone, marking where the three counties of Lancashire, Westmorland and Yorkshire's West Riding used to meet before they were messed about. Continue to follow the wall along the ridge and where it turns left cross over at the corner to a bit of a cairn with a surprise view of the Howgills. The stone man in the field to the west is in fact lower.

WHERNSIDE *(Millstone Hill Slope)*

Follow the east wall down, crossing to its right side over a fence near the bottom to reach a gate onto the old Occupation Road, so called because it ran between the newly enclosed or occupied fields of Dentdale. Turn right, and after a couple of miles turn right again onto the modern road. In a quarter of a mile a faint path beside a fence leads left uphill and veers right to an obvious cairn above the escarpment. The path then continues at an easier angle straight to the OS trig point of Whernside. Beyond Great Coum to the west are the Howgills, the Lake District and the sea, but crossing through the summit wall at a little stile the scene changes. Below are the Ribblehead, Dent Head and Artengill viaducts while Great Knoutberry Hill, Lovely Seat, Great Whernside and Pen-y-ghent lie in an extensive panorama with of course Ingleborough in the foreground. This is the least popular of the Three Peaks and the majority of its visitors will be doing the challenge walk, racing over this top about lunch time.

Following the wall south on its left side the main path to Ingleborough soon departs abruptly and with grass underfoot again, continue uneventfully beside the wall for another long three miles. A huge boulder has been incorporated into the wall and further on is a little shelter. Finally descend through the limestone, but before the final drop to a track cross a ladder stile on the right. Below are the famous Ingleton Waterfalls but a visit to the 40ft Thornton Force adds on an extra mile. The path doubles back beneath the limestone scars of Whernside, then passes below Braida Garth Wood and to the left of the farmhouse crossing Kingsdale Beck at a footbridge. From here half a mile of road walking leads back to the start of the walk.

WALK 12.3 GREAT KNOUTBERRY HILL

SUMMITS	Great Knoutberry Hill	2205 ft (672m)
DISTANCE	3½ miles	
ASCENT	700 feet	
MAPS	OS Landranger sheet 98 Outdoor Leisure - Yorkshire Dales, Western area	
STARTING POINT	(98-780881) 1 mile east of Dent station on the minor road between Garsdale Head and Cowgill. Cars can be parked on the roadside at the bridleway junction.	

Unfrequented Widdale Fell lies sandwiched between its namesake Widdale which joins Wensleydale at Hawes, and Garsdale to the west. The summit of the fell, Great Knoutberry Hill, is named like its neighbour Knoutberry Haw on the other side of Garsdale, after the cloudberry. To the west lies Dentdale, one of the most beautiful of the Dales where in spring and summer wild flowers abound and on a short walk over the fell to Hawes we once counted seventy different species. The head of the dale is very quiet and much of the traffic on the narrow road is pedestrian as this is part of the Dales Way. There are scattered cottages offering accommodation, a pub and a Youth Hostel which was originally a shooting lodge. Once known as Dent Town, though now no more than a cluster of houses, Dent is one of Yorkshire's most picturesque villages. This was the birthplace in 1785 and also the early home of Adam Sedgwick the celebrated geologist who became Professor of Geology at

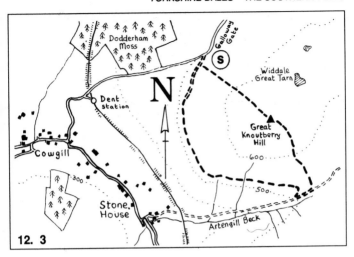

12. 3

Cambridge. The phrase 'the terrible knitters of Dent' was coined by the poet Robert Southey in 1830 to describe the hard working people of the dale, men, women and children, who knitted stockings at every spare moment to supplement their meagre income. With its narrow cobbled streets it is still firmly rooted in the past and little affected as yet by tourism. One feels quite out of place arriving by car.

The Settle to Carlisle railway which runs along the western slopes of the fellside was opened by the Midland Railway in 1876, surely the most scenic line in England. During the construction of the railway 400 workers lived in a shanty town close to the present Dent station which at 1139ft is the highest main line station in England, nice and handy for Dent town nearly 5 miles away! For many years the threat of closure hung over the line, but in April 1989 the fight was won and the line saved, a fitting memorial to the many navvies who lost their lives in its seven year construction. Dent station is again open for passenger traffic, but the reprieve was too late for the eastern branch line which once ran round the north of the fell to Hawes and the east.

The dramatic Artengill Viaduct, which has 11 arches and is 117ft high, was constructed from the locally quarried 'Dent Marble' a type of dark limestone. Worked from the middle of the eighteenth century the decorative marble was sawn in Arten Gill at High Mill which had a 60ft waterwheel and the articles, mainly fireplaces and gravestones, were finished and polished at Stone House. Originally carried by horses these were later transported by the railway, but with the importing of Italian marble the bottom dropped out of the market and although some of the new imports were even sent to Arten Gill to be cut and polished, the quarry and mills were closed by 1900.

Originally an old drove road, the Coal Road or Galloway Gate which runs to Garsdale Head from Dent station was one of the main routes from Scotland. The mounds near its highest point are the remains of old coal pits which provided domestic coal, carried by pack horses in the eighteenth century, and fuelled the many kilns built locally for lime burning.

ROUTE DESCRIPTION

GREAT KNOUTBERRY HILL *(Big Cloudberry Hill)*
Take the bridleway signed 'Stone House & Widdale' and then immediately leave it to make your way up beside the ruined fence. There is a bit of a path through the cloudberry leading south-east directly to the summit which is unmistakable. The OS stone trig point is on the other side of the converging new fence and a high stone pile has been built from the ruins of the wall it replaces. This new fence continues north-east to disappear into the waters

Artengill Viaduct

of Widdale Great Tarn, an attractive and unexpectedly large stretch of water a third of a mile along the ridge.

The views from this rather insignificant top are most extensive, particularly to the west and it is worth the climb for these alone. All the major hills of the Dales are on show with the Three Peaks having pride of place on the south side, to the east is the stepped edge of Drumaldrace and to the west the Howgills, Baugh Fell and Wild Boar Fell.

Following the wall south-east downhill, there is a fair path on the eastern side and after two thirds of a mile the bridleway is met again. Turn right along to a gate and then right again climbing a little to follow the delightful grassy track which contours round the slopes of the fellside high above the Settle to Carlisle Railway line. Even on this lower path you feel on top of the world with a superb view of Dentdale and Artengill Viaduct down to the left. Rounding the corner Dent station appears ahead. A rusty notice declares 'BEWARE OF BULL', but we found only a few timid sheep grazing in the fields above the railway and all too soon you are back on Galloway Gate.

WALK 12.4 PEN-Y-GHENT

SUMMITS	Pen-y-ghent	2277 ft (694m)
	Plover Hill	2231 ft (680m)
	Darnbrook Fell	2047 ft (624m)
	Fountains Fell South Top	2172 ft (662m)
	Fountains Fell	2192 ft (668m)
DISTANCE	15 miles	
ASCENT	2650 feet	
MAPS	OS Landranger sheet 98	
	Outdoor Leisure - Yorkshire Dales, Northern & Central areas & Yorkshire Dales, Western area	
STARTING POINT		
	(98-843715) 5 miles north of Settle on the minor road to Littondale. Roadside parking area.	

Rising steeply above Horton in Ribblesdale, Pen-y-ghent is easily recognisable with its distinctive two tier shape, the layers separated by cliffs. As with Ingleborough away to the west, the geology of the two cliffs is markedly different. The upper which defends the moor-like summit is of millstone grit while the lower in dramatic contrast is the Great Scar limestone and it is on this lower tier that the lovely and quite rare Purple Saxifrage, *Saxifraga*

273

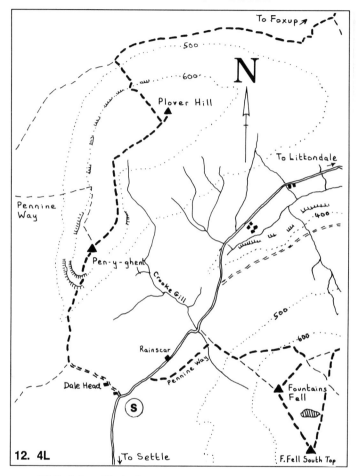

12. 4L

oppositifolia, is found in April.

Pen-y-ghent is crossed by the Pennine Way, which having reached the summit descends again hurridly as if afraid to stay too long on the high ground. It is usually the first of the peaks to be climbed on the Three Peaks Walk which starts from Horton in Ribblesdale and continues over Whernside to Ingleborough. The total distance is about 24 miles with 4500ft of climbing, the

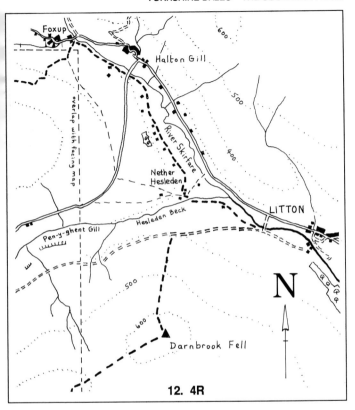

12. 4R

aim being to complete the challenge in less than 12 hours. It's a pity to rush and certainly spending most of the 12 hours over it, as we did, gives time to explore. The walk was first done by two Giggleswick teachers, Canon J R Wynne-Edwards and D R Smith in 1887, who walked to the Hill Inn for tea via Ingleborough, then climbed Whernside and Pen-y-ghent on the way back. Now there is an annual fell race in the spring and a cyclo-cross race in the autumn, both completed in well under 3 hours. All these feet have left their mark on the hills and erosion is a big problem. The Three Peaks Project was established in 1987 to repair the footpaths in, as they say 'an environmentally sensitive way', and also to restore the eroded soil and vegetation. Hopefully when the work is completed the artificial suburban park-like appearance of the paths will mellow and in time blend with the surrounding countryside.

Fountains Fell is named after Fountains Abbey for this fell was one of the many sheepwalks owned by the monks in the thirteenth century. One of the largest of the Cistercian communities in England, they used advanced farming methods and were the founders of Yorkshire's woollen trade. Fountains Fell is distinguished from all the other 2000ft summits by having a coalmine on the highest point. Mined here from 1790 until 1860 the coal was used domestically and also for lead smelting on Malham Moor and much remains of interest. There are many bell-pits, some deep fenced shafts which plunge into black depths and a small square stone building which was a coke oven, the coke being used to smelt zinc from calamine ore. Mid-way between the main and the subsidiary summit lies the attractive Fountains Fell Tarn with its sandy beach and although the mountain is crossed by the Pennine Way this bypasses the tarn and the tops which are usually quite deserted.

ROUTE DESCRIPTION

PEN-Y-GHENT *(Hill of the Winds)*
Take the metalled lane to Dale Head Farm, signposted 'Pen-y-ghent' and go through the gate on the right of the farm, the route of the Pennine Way. Turn right after Churn Milk Hole on the very obvious track and the heavy traffic it takes becomes evident as height is gained with much repair work being carried out on the path. Climbing steeply through the twin cliffs, the path eases to the final peaty slopes and then follows a wall to the summit. Beside the twin ladder stiles, catering for Pennine Way walkers, there is a stone OS trig point and a rough cairn. One of the best viewpoints in Yorkshire, away to the west is Ingleborough and to the east Fountains Fell. Morecambe Bay, the Lake District mountains and the Cross Fell range are all also on show.

PLOVER HILL *(Lapwing Hill)*
The summit wall on Pen-y-ghent runs north all the way to Plover Hill and provides a useful guide. The footpath, which is on its left side, is signposted to the Foxup Road. The crowds disappear now that the Pennine Way has been left and on a sunny April day we were to see only one more walker for the rest of the day. After a mile the wall turns east and in another half mile, at a ladder stile, the high wall has been realigned so the highest point about 100 yards further, and now marked by a small cairn, is on the other side of this wall.

DARNBROOK FELL *(Hidden Brook Fell)*
Waymarked posts lead down northwards over the open moor to the band of limestone where it is quite steep. Meeting the Foxup Road which is a track linking Horton in Ribblesdale to the hamlet of Foxup, turn right along it contouring Plover Hill and descend to Foxup. Turn right and follow the River Skirfare on the south bank on a well signed footpath towards Litton. After crossing the minor road below Halton Gill, where the houses date from the seventeenth century, the path wanders away from the river to Nether Hesleden, a group of cottages dated 1703. Littondale, the home of Charles

Kingsley's 'Water Babies', is reckoned to be botanically speaking the finest dale in Yorkshire. Its many flowers include the Bird's-eye Primrose, Bloody Cranesbill and the rare Mountain Avens. Walking along its paths is no easy option, as the proliferation of ladder stiles gives plenty of excercise for the legs. Take the footpath over Hesleden Beck, signposted Litton, where a very friendly little cat joined us on our last visit and bounced along down the valley while the sheep eyed us suspiciously as they nuzzled their new born lambs. Although the track which climbs the slopes of Darnbrook Fell is only a short way above, it is necessary first to follow the footpath downstream for half a mile to a small gate beyond which the two paths converge.

Doubling back onto the rough track, climb steadily for three quarters of a mile between stone walls to emerge onto open fields. Continue for another couple of hundred yards to where there is again a wall on the left with a gate and a shed beside it. Go through the gate and follow the wall up the hillside climbing steadily over grass until after an ascent of about 650ft, a wall comes in from the right. Crossing through one of the gaps in either wall, follow the joining wall south-east which continues as a fence to the concrete summit trig point standing on a high plinth on the edge of a peaty wilderness. There are good views of Pen-y-ghent and Plover Hill with the twin tops of Fountains Fell ahead.

FOUNTAINS FELL SOUTH TOP

Return along the fence to a small gate then follow the wall heading south-west. Malham Tarn can be seen far away to the left and to the right a silvery line on the horizon down the valley is the sea at Morecambe Bay. After nearly a mile a ladder stile is reached. Below on the left is a baby forest, at present hardly justifying the dark green on the map. Crossing the ladder stile aim just west of south for the summit, passing the outflow of Fountains Fell Tarn with its little beach. The highest point is the unmarked knoll 20 yards from the adjacent wall. There is nothing to distinguish this top which just makes mountain status and the 'Weather Station disused' marked on the map proves a disappointment being merely a few rusty bits of iron and rotted wood. Somehow one hopes for something more. Pen-y-ghent rises dramatically to the left of the main Fountains Fell top with its bump of a summit cairn.

FOUNTAINS FELL *(Fountains Abbey Fell)*

Follow the wall to the col above the tarn and then aim north directly for the summit. The tub shaped cairn gives grand views of Pen-y-ghent with Ingleborough beyond and in clear conditions the Lake District fells on the far horizon. Walking back through the old mine workings to join the Pennine Way, the area is pock marked with depressions which were coal pits, triangular fences enclose deep open shafts, while the base of a furnace has been adapted as a primitive shelter into which one might crawl if hard pressed by the weather. A step stile leads to the old mine road which is followed down to a cross wall. Go over the left of two ladder stiles on the original line of the Pennine Way. Most followers of the Way now go down to the road and the path over the moor is indistinct at first and later vanishes completely, but it is softer underfoot than tarmac. Keep up the slope until Rainscar Farm is passed and then descend to the wall corner and ladder stile and across the field to the road.

Pen-y-ghent

WALK 12.5 DODD FELL HILL AND DRUMALDRACE

SUMMITS	Dodd Fell Hill	2192 ft (668m)
	Drumaldrace	2014 ft (614m)

DISTANCE	11½ miles

ASCENT	1600 feet

MAPS	OS Landranger sheet 98
	Outdoor Leisure - Yorkshire Dales, Northern & Central areas & Yorkshire Dales, Western area

STARTING POINT	(98-877898) Hawes National Park Information Centre, car park and toilets.

South of the market town of Hawes, crammed at peak season with cars and tourists mingling uneasily with local people trying to do their shopping, rise two high moorland summits, both quiet and peaceful surrounded by a far horizon of Pennine hills. One of the great markets of Wensleydale, Hawes was granted a market charter in 1700. The tradition of cheesemaking, with which Wensleydale has long been associated, started with the monks of Jervaulx Abbey who used the milk from their sheep and after the coming of the railway in 1878 a cheese factory was opened in the town. The railway departed a quarter of a century ago and the station buildings now house the Upper Dales Folk Museum, with the 200 year old rope-making works close by.

It is perhaps not surprising that Dodd Fell Hill is so seldom visited despite the thousands of walkers that pass every year within a quarter of a mile of its summit. Although the detour is short and the ascent not particularly great, there is little to encourage Pennine Way walkers to leave the easy track descending gently to Hawes and tackle the rough rise to Dodd Fell Hill. However it is hills like this that are responsible for turning walkers into peak baggers. Temptation whispers that a few extra minutes added to the walk and one more peak will be in the bag. To find two such peaks on a pleasant circular walk from one of Yorkshire's attractive towns is riches indeed.

ROUTE DESCRIPTION

DODD FELL HILL *(Round Fell Hill)*
Turn right out of the car park and take the left branch of the one way traffic system through the town as far as the church. Go up the steps and follow the path beside the church through a squeezer stile where a paved footpath crosses the fields by Gayle Beck to emerge on the road. Almost opposite

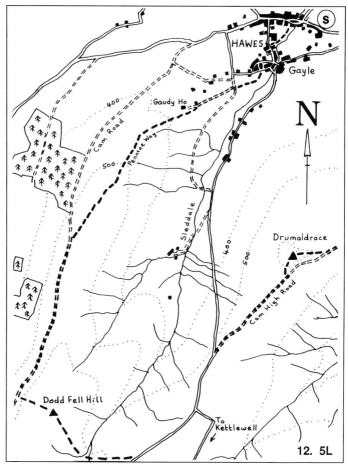

12. 5L

there is a Pennine Way sign, but ignore this as it misses all the best bits of the village and walk left up into Gayle. At the top of the road, don't cross the bridge, but turn up the cobbled alleyway beside the river in front of some cottages. Continue on the minor road beyond and as the houses end, turn left up a few steps and through a kissing gate where a footpath leads across the field to a fingerpost and the Pennine Way is rejoined. Continue across the next field and out onto a lane where you turn right and then immediately left on a stony

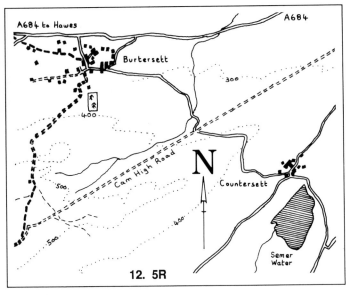

12. 5R

track to Gaudy House.

Reaching the farm gate, follow the Pennine Way sign through the left hand gate and the clear path progresses steadily uphill over grass. As Pennine Way walkers almost invariably head north, you will be swimming against the tide for nearly four miles. To the right is Widdale with Great Knoutberry Hill beyond. After a couple of miles the Cam Road comes in from the right and Dodd Fell Hill rises ahead. Careful navigation will minimise the distance to be travelled over the rough and pathless moor; the easiest way is to continue on the track for over a mile and leave it to make a beeline for the top just when it starts to dip down, but there is no obvious landmark at which to turn off. The top is flat and apart from the OS trig point, featureless. South is Pen-y-ghent, south-west Ingleborough and west Whernside, while the rest of the horizon is of more distant hills.

DRUMALDRACE

A little more rough walking is now necessary. Descend due south-east to round the head of Sleddale, avoiding too much loss of height, and thread a way through peaty hummocks out to the limestone where there is a fine stone man perched on a boulder. Easy grass now leads out to the unfenced road. This is the Cam High Road connecting Lancaster with the Roman fort of Virosidum at Bainbridge on Brough Hill which was occupied by a garrison of 500 men from AD 80 until the end of the Roman occupation. Later used as

281

a drove road, the Roman road was turnpiked in 1751, but in 1795 the route was altered to go via Hawes and Widdale. The road is followed past a signposted turn to Kettlewell and then half a mile beyond, just as the tarmac road is about to start the descent to Hawes, continue through a gate in the same direction onto the rough track rising towards Drumaldrace. When after a mile of easy uphill between limestone walls, the left wall turns away, take to the slopes up which a faint path leads to the flat top. There is a cairn and fine distant views of Baugh Fell, Swarth Fell and Wild Boar Fell with the Howgills beyond away to the north-west. Ingleborough has almost disappeared behind Dodd Fell Hill.

Return to the Cam High Road and continue until the left wall re-appears, then go left at the wall corner through a gate onto the unsigned right of way. Gradually the path becomes more distinct, descending the hillside to join a track coming in from the left. Continue downhill on this clear track which brings you to Burtersett. Turn right and then left into the village and go up the footpath beside the chapel. The paved way beyond is typical of this part of Yorkshire. The gritstone slabs, provided by local quarries, were laid by the farmers in a vain attempt to keep quarrymen to the straight and narrow when crossing the fields on their way to and from work. The path leads across the field through narrow stiles, which have small gates with unusual hinges, and forks right by a barn to emerge on a minor road. Go straight across and soon the main road into Hawes is joined a little short of the car park.

Stile near Hawes

WALK 12.6 GREAT WHERNSIDE AND BUCKDEN PIKE

SUMMITS	Great Whernside	2310 ft (704m)
	Buckden Pike	2303 ft (702m)
DISTANCE	14½ miles	
ASCENT	2300 feet	
MAPS	OS Landranger sheet 98	
	Outdoor Leisure - Yorkshire Dales, Northern & Central areas	
STARTING POINT	(98-968723) Kettlewell in Wharfedale.	
	Car park and toilets	

On the eastern fringe of the Yorkshire Dales National Park and forming the skyline of Wharfedale above the village of Kettlewell, is Great Whernside. Like its namesake Whernside eighteen miles to the west, the name comes from cwern or millstone for the summit crags are of rough millstone grit. Beneath the surface though lies limestone which swallows the water draining from the high moorland into fissures, caves and potholes. The long level summit ridge stretches north until it turns away east above the steep narrow road of Park Rash Pass. This pass, which has a gradient of 1 in 4, is an old road which led from Scotland through the Dales. At the summit of the pass, Tor Dike on Great Hunters Sleets was a fortified ditch built by the Brigantes under the leadership of Venutius around AD 70 to repel the Romans.

Further north the mountain moorland continues high above Wharfedale with its meandering river to Buckden Pike, while in the valley are the attractive villages of Kettlewell, Starbotton and Buckden. Kettlewell, which means Cetel's Spring, was an important local centre sited on the Roman road from Ilkley to Bainbridge and in 1320 it was granted a market charter. The village, whose oldest houses date from the sixteenth century, stands aside from the main road and is one of the most attractive in Wharfedale. In the beginning of the nineteenth century as lead mining prospered many mines were dug on the moors above the village, new cottages were built and the population reached twice its present number. Nowadays Kettlewell, which is a conservation area, has three pubs, a good outdoor pursuits shop and a handful of tea rooms and gift shops.

Buckden, the highest village in Wharfedale, was the headquarters of the medieval hunting forest of Langstrothdale Chase. This was a royal hunting forest around the head of Wharfedale in Norman times and wild deer survived in the area until the eighteenth century. The Roman road from Kettlewell passes over the natural terrace of Buckden Rake to the Kidstones Pass. The

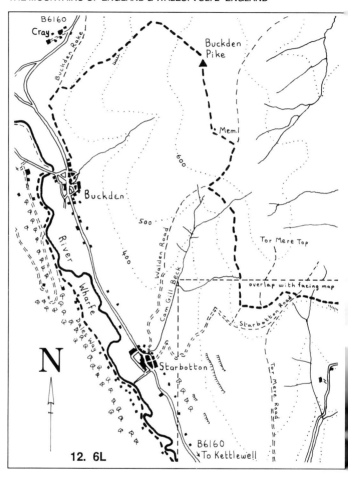

12. 6L

village has a predominance of holiday cottages while the Buck Inn, the village store, post office and tea room, plus an art gallery and information centre cate for the needs of tourists.

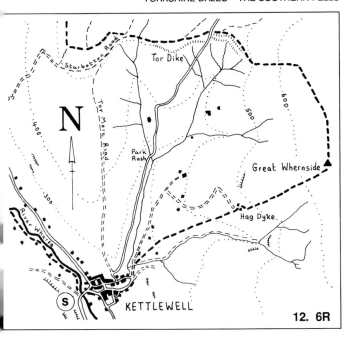

ROUTE DESCRIPTION

GREAT WHERNSIDE *(Big Millstone Hill Slope)*
Walk east through Kettlewell taking the lane to the right of Cam Gill Beck
which divides the village. When the houses have been left behind, the track
forks to cross the beck. Take the path beside the gill and then the old green
track which leads uphill signed Hag Dike. The two signposts barely 50 yards
apart indicate this is the shortest quarter mile anywhere. After climbing
steeply at first, the path hugs the valley edge with extensive downward views.
In a mile Hag Dike, which has belonged to the scouts since 1947, is reached.
Circle round the front of the buildings to a stile at the left end and then climb
to a motley collection of cairns on the skyline. A path continues just north of
east for another mile, first over a flattish, boggy section and then climbs to the
summit through chunky boulders littering the steep grassy slopes. The OS
concrete trig column shelters beside a large jumbled cairn on deeply fissured
tilted stone blocks. There are fine views to the west towards Pen-y-ghent,
Whernside and Ingleborough.

BUCKDEN PIKE *(Deer Valley Peak)*
Walk north along the ridge for a mile to the wall corner above the source of the River Nidd, and then follow the wall westwards downhill, soon crossing it at a ladder stile. Below is the Iron Age fortification ditch of Tor Dike. Crossing the Park Rash Pass a grassy track continues beside the wall contouring round to the Starbotton Road. When after 1½ miles of following signs for Starbotton the track becomes enclosed, immediately turn sharp right. After 100ft of ascent the track bends north past old mine workings bypassing Tor Mere Top. After another 1½ miles turn right to join the Walden Road, an old track from Starbotton which climbs to the ridge. At a small gate follow the ridge wall northwards past the cross, which was erected to five Polish RAF airmen who died here in 1942. The survivor crawled to safety by following the footprints of a fox in the snow, which led down into the valley, and a bronze fox's head is incorporated into the memorial. The wall continues to the flat grassy summit of Buckden Pike where a ladder stile crosses to the concrete OS trig point and cairn. The panorama is extensive with the Howgills to the left of Swarth Fell. To the north-west are Great Shunner Fell, Lovely Seat and Rogan's Seat and in the far distance is the Cross Fell range.

The bridleway to Buckden has been re-aligned to follow the wall down before joining its original route south-west to Buckden Rake, where a natural limestone shelf, the course of the Roman road, descends left to the village. Cross the River Wharfe by the road bridge and take the Dales Way for the 4 miles back to Kettlewell. At Starbotton a private chain, stepping stones and a footbridge all give access to the village and pub.

The summit of Great Whernside

WALK 12.7 YOCKENTHWAITE MOOR

SUMMITS	Yockenthwaite Moor	2110 ft (643m)
NOTE	Grouse moor	
DISTANCE	5½ miles	
ASCENT	1350 feet	
MAPS	OS Landranger sheet 98	
	Outdoor Leisure - Yorkshire Dales, Northern & Central areas	
STARTING POINT	(98-927782) Hubberholme village, 1 mile north-west of Buckden. Roadside parking.	

Staunchly defended on all sides by unappetising, black, squelchy peat bogs, Yockenthwaite Moor is rarely visited, and then usually only once. For other than peak baggers it has little to offer. It holds the award for the boggiest hill in Yorkshire and if the OS trig point did not stand on a little island of grass, it would surely have sunk without trace years ago. But Yockenthwaite Moor, because of its very remoteness and the added difficulty of attaining its highest places is a challenge, and climbing it, even on a dull, misty, grey day is a lot better than being at work.

Our first assault was from Gilbert Lane at the summit of the Kidstones Pass. It is not recommended. The going is rough, very rough, and wet. We arrived black to the knees and vowing never again. Although repeating the route during a long drought we had a much easier approach over dry springy peat, the tiny village of Hubberholme makes a much better starting point. The ascent beside Strans Gill with its little falls and pools is very pleasant, and the amount of soggy bog to be traversed at the top is cut to a minimum.

Hubberholme church dates from the twelfth century. It has a rood loft and was originally used as a forest chapel. The pews, choir stalls and chairs are modern, being made by Robert Thompson of Kilburn near Thirsk in 1934 and his trade mark, a mouse, can be found on his work. The ancient custom of land-letting takes place here in January when a field behind the George Inn is auctioned. The proceeds go to the parish poor and the whole transaction has to take place during the burning of a candle.

The adjacent ridge of Birks Fell at one time ranked as a mountain with a height of 2001ft, indeed the current OS Landranger sheet still gives the top as 610m. However most of the heights shown on the 1:50 000 scale maps are metricated versions of the Imperial heights on the old One Inch series and therefore the new height of only 608m on the 1:25 000 scale map is more

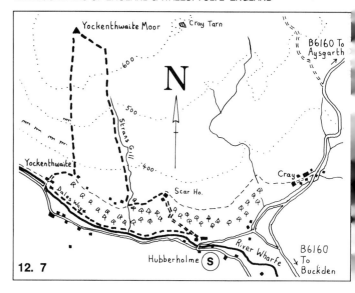

12. 7

accurate. Just to be sure we tramped over Birks Fell on a freezing New Year's Eve to check the tops and then, with a twinge of regret, removed Birks Fell from our list. Nearly 2 miles to the west, the 609m Sugar Loaf is now the highest point on the ridge.

ROUTE DESCRIPTION

YOCKENTHWAITE MOOR *(The Moor of Eogan's Clearing)*
Take the track by the church, signed 'Yockenthwaite', which winds steeply uphill to the seventeenth century Scar House. Turn left behind the buildings and follow the path for a quarter of a mile to a little wood and footbridge. At the top of the field, a gate leads to the open hillside where the wall beside Strans Gill sets off unerringly towards the summit plateau. In just over a mile the wall stops abruptly amid peat hags. Two cairns ahead mark the boundary ditch, and on a clear day, aiming north-west, the concrete OS trig pillar soon comes into view. After a quarter of a mile of bog hopping, a welcome oasis of grass is reached and terra firma which is fortuitously the highest point. Though the foreground is dull, the surrounding hills of Dodd Fell, Fountains Fell, Pen-y-ghent and Ingleborough can be seen.

Heading south the peat is less wet and after passing a small stone hut, grassy slopes are reached which drop steeply over old workings, shake holes and limestone outcrops. Aim for the corner of the intake wall and then follow it down to a barn where a stony track leads to the hamlet of Yockenthwaite, an old Norse settlement with a Bronze Age stone circle, where the houses date from the seventeenth century. The Dales Way then provides an easy return in 1½ miles to Hubberholme church following the north bank of the River Wharfe.

Wain Stones, Bleaklow

CHAPTER 13 THE PEAK DISTRICT AND DARTMOOR

TOP	NAME	HEIGHT	GRID REF	WALK No.
1	Bleaklow Head	633m	110-092959 SK	13.1
2	Higher Shelf Stones	621m	110-089948 SK	13.1
3	Kinder Scout	636m	110-085875 SK	13.2
4	Yes Tor	619m	191-581902 SX	13.3
5	High Willhays	621m	191-580893 SX	13.3

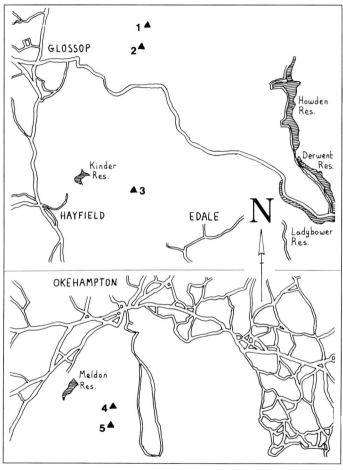

13 THE PEAK DISTRICT AND DARTMOOR

WALK 13.1 BLEAKLOW

SUMMITS	Bleaklow Head	2077 ft (633m)
	Higher Shelf Stones	2037 ft (621m)

NOTE   Moors in the Peak District may be closed for grouse
            shooting for a few days from 12 August to 10 December.
            Dates are displayed locally.
            There is no shooting on Sundays

DISTANCE   9 miles

ASCENT   1500 feet

MAPS   OS Landranger sheet 110
            Outdoor Leisure - The Peak District, Dark Peak area

STARTING
POINT   (110-045948) Old Glossop, 1 mile north-east of Glossop
            town centre. Parking by the road side. If time is short the
            two tops can be quickly visited from the summit of the A57,
            the Snake Road, by following the Pennine Way to the Wain
            Stones then returning via Higher Shelf Stones.

In spring with the larks singing high in a brilliantly clear sky above the subtle reds, browns, purples and yellows of the moor, or in winter under a covering of snow, the peat iron hard beneath ones feet and long blue shadows cast by the low sun, Bleaklow is magnificent. Even when after weeks of rain one ploughs knee deep through clinging black ooze with little to see but the grey mist, there is still satisfaction in the wildness and the wet, but love it or loathe it, Bleaklow cannot be ignored.

Between the flanking cities of Manchester and Sheffield, Bleaklow is within an hour's drive for several million people, yet this wild upland moor is well named, a wilderness of black peat, bog and weirdly eroded gritstone. To the north is the trough of the A628, the Woodhead Pass, with its chain of five reservoirs supplying Manchester. When built in the mid nineteenth century this was the largest stretch of man made water in the world and the two railway tunnels constructed about the same time were the longest anywhere. Southwards the plateau is incised by lovely Alport Dale and the Derwent Valley whose waters are impounded in Sheffield's reservoirs of Derwent and Ladybower. From the foot of Ladybower the A57 climbs to the Snake Pass, the first road to be blocked every year by snow heralding the onset of winter. The Snake Pass takes its name from the Snake Inn which was built in 1821. Originally called Lady Clough House the name was soon changed as a

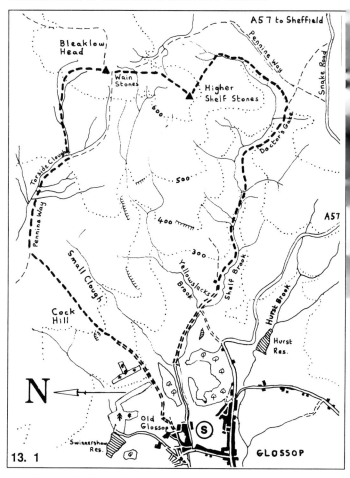

13. 1

compliment to the Duke of Devonshire, whose coat of arms features a snake.

The walk back to Glossop is down Doctor's Gate which was named after Dr John Talbot a rector of Glossop, who lived from 1494 to 1550. The illegitimate son of the Earl of Shrewsbury, he probably used this road to visit his father who had a castle in Sheffield. The gate or way, which was used by packhorses until the new turnpike was built in 1821, followed the line of the old Roman Road which linked the fort of Navio at Hope with Melandra at Glossop. The upper section at its intersection with the Pennine Way is the best preserved with upright paving slabs set between kerbstones, though the paving was probably done by seventeenth century quarrymen rather than being of Roman origin.

ROUTE DESCRIPTION

BLEAKLOW HEAD *(Dark Coloured Hill Summit)*
From the bus turning-circle at the end of the factory, follow the road uphill and round the corner to join Charles Lane. The lane leads up to a stile and a footpath to Open Country and the old trackway, with its high stone walls, climbs steeply to the Boundary of Open Country. Roofing and paving slabs from the quarry on Cock Hill were transported this way to Glossop. The nearly vanished track then leads to the disused quarry, which closed at the end of the nineteenth century. With a choice of stiles, continue through the tumbled rocks climbing to the trig point on Cock Hill which gives good views of Glossop sprawling in the valley below. Heading north-east half a mile of easy walking over the moor brings you to the ruins of a shooting hut, with a converging line of grouse butts a guide in bad visibility. It is an excellent view point and the two summits, both silhouetted on the skyline, still look quite a distance away. Continuing north-east past another ruin, follow a faint path to join the deserted Pennine Way and turn right along the rim of Torside Clough. Most walkers who started from Edale will still be battling with the bogs of Kinder Scout, not reaching here until early evening. The heathery clough is a dramatic contrast to the featureless moors and the stream is followed for a mile to a left fork marked as John Track Well. Crossing the stream head east up Wildboar Grain for a further mile with the path gradually swinging round to the right, then suddenly, just when you think you will never arrive, a very large pile of stones is reached which marks the spot generally accepted as the summit. Strictly speaking the unmarked knoll to the east, which has a sprinkling of cloudberry, is marginally higher, while the OS mark their spot height over towards the Wain Stones, but there is nothing much to choose between them. To the north is the winking mast on Black Hill across the hidden trough of the Woodhead Pass and with a foreground of stones, silver sand and peat, the moor stretches away into the distance.

HIGHER SHELF STONES *(High Hill with Stones)*
The ease with which the next summit is reached depends very much on the conditions. When frozen hard or very dry it is an easy stroll, but during a wet spell navigating through the groughs can take a long time with frequent detours in a vain attempt to avoid the morass. Head south-west to the nearby Wain Stones, known from its resemblance to two heads as 'The Kiss', and then follow the marker posts of the Pennine Way south across the peat hags to Hern Stones. Here the Pennine Way diverges left, but continue south-west

to pass the sad remains of a Super Fortress aircraft which crashed in 1948 into a grough just below the summit, killing the crew of 14. The concrete OS trig point stands on the brink of White Clough and the views more than compensate for their absence on Bleaklow Head. To the west lies Glossop, to the north-east are Bleaklow Stones and Grinah Stones with the Howden and Derwent Moors beyond, while to the south-east the distinctive bump of Win Hill is seen to the left of the Kinder plateau. The nearby rocks are carved with initials, some of the graffiti dating from the early nineteenth century.

To avoid the Pennine Way with its afternoon traffic, descend south-east towards an obvious straight ditch and then follow Crooked Clough where a little path makes its way along the valley rim to join Doctor's Gate. This good path then descends to join Shelf Brook for the final easy walk back to Glossop.

Flying Fortress engine

WALK 13.2   KINDER SCOUT

SUMMITS	Kinder Scout	2087 ft (636m)

NOTE   Moors in the Peak District may be closed for grouse
          shooting for a few days from 12 August to 10 December.
          Dates are displayed locally.
          There is no shooting on Sundays.

DISTANCE   8 miles

ASCENT   1300 feet

MAPS   OS Landranger sheet 110
           Outdoor Leisure - The Peak District, Dark Peak area

STARTING
POINT   (110-107847) Barber Booth, 1 mile west of Edale.
           Free car park just beyond the railway bridge.

Kinder Scout, the highest of the three mountain summits in the Peak District, is an extensive upland plateau of bilberry, cotton grass, crowberry and peat. Above all peat; vast mountains of the stuff, cut into by a thousand wriggling streams that slowly and reluctantly drain the spongelike mass. There is no peak, the word comes from paec, Old English for a hill, and the highest point is the centre of the plateau defended by ten foot deep groughs, the natural drainage channels. As you attempt to climb out of these traps the sides crumble throwing you down again into their depths. Make no mistake, it is a struggle crossing Kinder, but it exerts an attraction born of wide open skies, rough grey, brown and black rock, the gutteral call of the grouse, the feathery white whisps of the cotton grass, the pink flush of new bilberry leaves and the warm wet smell of the ground.

Every weekend walkers converge upon the area, thronging Edale like an alpine village, but despite its popularity as the start of the 250 mile Pennine Way, Edale retains much of its charm. Fred Heardman, Bill the Bogtrotter to his friends for his many tough walks and runs in the Peak, was at one time the landlord of both the Nags Head and the Church (now Rambler) Inn. He was both a rural district councillor and a member of the Peak branch of the CPRE and through his efforts the valley was saved from industrialisation.

The gritstone edge of the plateau is the chief delight with cliffs of rough stone and strangely sculpted rocks like the Wool Packs, worn by wind and weather into fantastic shapes. The Downfall, fed by the Kinder River, is often only a trickle in summer, but in winter it can freeze to a magnificent wall of ice, while after rain when a westerly wind is blowing, the water fails to fall at all and

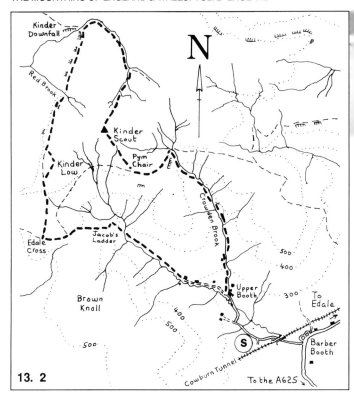

13. 2

is blown vertically into the air, arching back over the edge.

A large portion of the area belongs to the National Trust who are restoring the paths and woodland and together with the Botany Department of Sheffield University, attempting to re-vegetate the eroded plateau by concentrating on the use of cotton grass which is now the dominant species. Once reserved for grouse shooting by the privileged few, the irresistable demands of walkers for access to these moors culminated in the celebrated mass trespass of 1932. Gradually restrictions were eased and with the formation of the Peak District National Park in 1951, agreements were reached with the landowners which now guarantee free access to much of the high moorland.

ROUTE DESCRIPTION

KINDER SCOUT *(Water Over the Edge)*
From the car park, where the grass covered mounds known as The Tips are
the spoil from the 2 mile long Cowburn tunnel completed in 1893, walk up the
tarmac lane to the tiny hamlet of Upper Booth. Turn right on the footpath
beside the lovely Crowden Brook and after a pleasant walk through the fields,
cross a footbridge to the Boundary of Open Country. The path hops from side
to side of the stream before climbing steeply left to below Crowden Tower, the
stream bed providing an interesting alternative scramble for the final ascent.
When the Kinder plateau is reached turn left and follow the edge path through
the Wool Packs, an incredible assortment of strange and beautifully shaped
rocks. The most northerly isolated rock is Pym Chair, named after John Pym,
a non-comformist minister who preached here in the seventeenth century. A
mere 500 yards north-west, across the peat, is point 636 and on a fine day the
stout wooden posts set in the midst of the cairn can be clearly seen.

Despite it being our nearest 2000ft mountain we can recall very few visits
to Kinder's highest point and even that has recently been moved. Although
the OS have in fact now supplied three identical spot heights all within a few
yards of each other, the cairn with the posts marks the position accepted as

Edale

the summit, while one to the east is the place recognised prior to the current survey. But whichever point is chosen, both as a viewpoint and as a place of interest the summit of Kinder is a disappointment. Surrounded by black eroding peat, most of Kinder's best is around the edge. To the south-east in the distance is the Mam Tor ridge, and to the north the mast on Black Hill, but there is at least the advantage of solitude as few walkers bother to visit the spot.

If the weather is bad, or the peat too soggy for comfortable progress, head north-west to join the edge path above Red Brook on the far side of the plateau, but to visit Kinder Downfall via the real delights of the peat groughs, walk just east of north to join the head waters of the Kinder River. This is about the easiest bit of bog trotting on the plateau as all the groughs lead eventually into the main channel making navigation simple as the river winds its way towards the 100ft Kinder Downfall.

At the Downfall turn left and follow the edge path with the tiny Mermaid's Pool above Kinder Reservoir in the valley below. Keep well uphill and after about a mile and a half strike left to Kinder Low. This OS trig point on top of a massive gritstone boulder would make a far more satisfactory summit than the true one. Passing to the right of both Edale Rocks and Swine's Back a faint path leads to the medieval Edale Cross which marks the junction of four forest wards. This is much earlier than the date 1810 and John Gee's initials

Edale Cross

which refer only to the date of restoration. Turn left and follow the ancient trackway to the steep section known as Jacob's Ladder. Renovated in 1987, the steps were originally made as a short cut in the eighteenth century by Jacob Marshall who lived at Edale Head House whose ruined walls stand beside the zigzag packhorse route. After the packhorse bridge and ford it is a further half mile to the National Trust information shelter at Lee Farm, then an easy return down the lane to Upper Booth.

WALK 13.3 DARTMOOR

SUMMITS	Yes Tor	2031 ft (619m)
	High Willhays	2037 ft (621m)
CAUTION	Most of the walk lies within the Okehampton military live firing range. Check firing times locally or by telephoning Okehampton Police Station. At the time of writing there is no firing at weekends, Bank Holidays or during the main summer holiday period.	
DISTANCE	8 miles	
ASCENT	1150 feet	
MAPS	OS Landranger sheet 191	
	Outdoor Leisure - Dartmoor	
STARTING POINT	(191-562918) Meldon Reservoir, 3 miles south-west of Okehampton. Car park and toilets.	

The high wild windswept moor of Northern Dartmoor, entirely devoid of roads or habitation, is one of the largest areas of wilderness in England. The park extends to 365 square miles, one for each day of the year, but while the land is high with most of the northern part and a great deal of the generally lower southern part in excess of 1500ft, it is an area where peak baggers rest their ambitions. There are but two summits over 2000ft and these are right on the edge.

Carefully timing our visit to coincide with the end of the long hot summer of 1989 and after months of drought with stand pipes in Devon streets in anticipation of worse to come, we sloshed through several inches of water pouring down Yes Tor. The drought had broken with gale force winds and torrential rain, but after a wild night conditions had eased, the rain had stopped

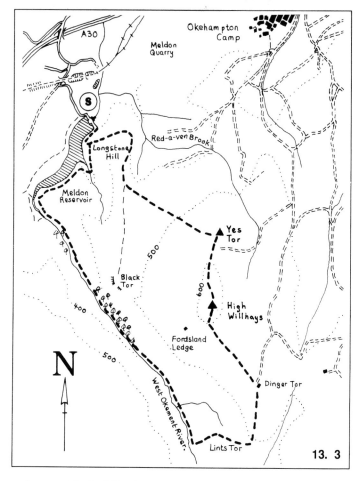

13. 3

and we squelched uphill under a grey sky past the red and white striped poles that mark the limits of the artillery range. A pair of red grouse sprang up from the heather; today firing was suspended for both grouse and man.

Military training has taken place on Dartmoor since 1870, a camp being established in 1873 and now over 50 square miles are set aside for this purpose. Oakhampton Camp is large and Royal Marines, regulars and

302

territorials are all trained there. Red flags are flown to indicate when there is live firing and entry into the danger area is forbidden, though dry training using blanks can take place at any time. During live firing, the observation posts high on the moor are manned by local farmers employed by the military to clear stock from the area and to ensure the public don't stray onto the range. As the work is done on horseback this explains the stables next to many of the huts.

For many centuries there have been ponies on Dartmoor. At one time they were used locally by farmers and miners, then around 1900, Shetland ponies were introduced to produce by cross breeding smaller, but still sturdy ponies to work down the coal mines. The numbers have now declined from as many as 25,000 ponies to less than 5000. They are no longer of any commercial use and sadly are mainly sold for meat. Galloway cattle and Scottish Blackface sheep also roam these moors.

Okehampton is a small market town just outside the National Park which has been recently bypassed by the busy main road. No longer snarled with traffic, it has a National Park Information Centre, the museum of Dartmoor Life and the ruined Okehampton Castle, which dates from the eleventh century and is open to the public.

The famous Ten Tors event in May starts from Okehampton Camp when over 2000 young people take part in a gruelling walk, covering as much as 55 miles and involving a night camping on the moor. 400 teams of 6 compete in this closely supervised event which is organised by the army and first took place in 1959.

"Have you come for the carnival?" were the welcoming words of our host. Okehampton had chosen the weekend of our visit for their annual celebrations. After an early evening meal so that we, and eleven telephone engineers from Okehampton Camp who were our fellow guests, shouldn't miss any of the fun, we strolled down the road to watch the procession. "It usually rains" confided the lady next to us, but it didn't. On a damp and chilly October evening half Okehampton were in the procession and the other half were watching. Hours of work and miles of crêpe paper had gone into producing the tableaux. A 1920s party followed 'Wind in the Willows' with a cute little mole in a furry suit, while the 'Young Farmer's Club' appeared to be having a drunken orgy on the top of pile of straw bales. Drum majorettes, brass bands and Scottish Pipers from Plymouth joined the floats which were pulled by gleaming tractors, a reflection of the rural nature of the community, Carnival Queens and Rose Queens from Chagford to Lydford sat sedately smiling from bowers in the back of estate cars. A lovely end to a grand day.

ROUTE DESCRIPTION

YES TOR

From the reservoir which supplies Tavistock and Bideford cross the dam, where on the far side there is an oddly positioned trig point, and turn right taking the bridleway which zigzags uphill and round the end of Longstone Hill.

There are good views to the left of the Meldon viaduct, now a scheduled ancient monument, and the quarry opened in 1895 to provide ballast for the railways as it still does. When the path flattens out heading south for Black Tor, fork left to round the boggy head of the stream on the left and then climb south-east to the flagpole, up the slopes of grass and heather to the stones which defend Yes Tor.

The summit tor rises gradually from the moor on its north and west sides, but on the east the eroded granite is exposed in a steep wall. On the top of the rocks the concrete trig point is dwarfed by a tall steel mast on which a red flag flies when the range is active. At the foot of the wall is a military observation post, a scruffy hut with an iron stove, while on the north side of the rocks is a stable. A tarmac road for military vehicles, now somewhat overgrown, goes nearly to the summit from Okehampton Camp.

HIGH WILLHAYS *(High Stream Enclosure)*
A broad stony path leads south over the moor for about half a mile to the higher of Dartmoor's two mountain tops. A grassy mound and less impressive than its twin, its highest point is at the southern end marked by a cairn on the granite slabs, while just beyond is a more obvious, but lower, rocky tor. To the west on Fordsland Ledge is another stable and observation post, again with an iron stove, but if they really are vital to the military, it is a pity that these huts have to be so prominent and such eyesores of corrugated iron and breeze blocks. From here it is nearly ten miles across wild and rough moorland to Princetown in the centre of Dartmoor. Great Links Tor is outlined to the south-west against the sky and the views over the moors to the south are extensive.

A rapid return can be made descending now to the West Okement River, but it seems a shame to go back so soon. A path goes south-east over the moor to Dinger Tor where there is another scruffy hut, and continues south towards Kneeset Nose. Half a mile beyond Dinger Tor swing right to Lints Tor, which sits atop a small hill, and cross it to meet the upper reaches of the beautiful and deserted valley of the West Okement River, a haunt of the Dartmoor ponies. Follow the river downstream on a bit of a path passing through Black Tor Copse, an ancient stunted oak woodland which grows among a tumble of mossy granite boulders with Black Tor on the skyline high above. This wood, the highest on the moor, has been a nature reserve since 1961. A little further downstream the rapidly growing river squeezes down a narrow gorge fringed with more oak woodland and soon the reservoir is reached. Keeping outside the perimeter fence, follow the eastern edge of the reservoir back to the dam.

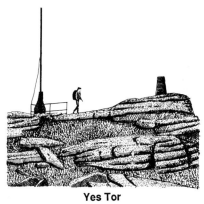

Yes Tor

DELETED TOPS

Enthusiastic peak-baggers may be interested in why some 2000ft tops didn't make it into our list. The following table therefore gives the reason for each exclusion. In some cases it has been possible to prove the matter by reference to the latest OS 1:10 000 maps, either because no separate contour ring is present (and hence the maximum difference between top and col is less than 10m), or because spot heights are given for both top and col which show a difference of less than15m. Where no spot height was available and where even with on the spot inspection we were in any doubt, we have carried out surveys using a method recommended to us by the Ordnance Survey.

NAME OF TOP	SHEET REF		SEPARATION	REASON
Hangingstone Hill	80-895193	NT	5m	top 743 col 738
Auchope Cairn	80-891198	NT	9m	top 726 col 717
Cairn Hill	80-903195	NT	10m	top 777 col 767
Nags Head	86-793409	NY	10m	top 678 col 668
Knoutberry Hill	86-803421	NY	10m	surveyed
Stangend Rigg	87-841436	NY	10m	top 634 col 624
Middle Scoat Fell	89-157115	NY	<10m	no ring contour
Great Scoat Fell	89-154111	NY	<10m	no ring contour
Slight Side	89-210050	NY	14m	top 762 col 748
Blunt Top	89-224078	NY	<11m	top 901 one ring
Ullock Pike	89-244287	NY	14m	surveyed
Gunson Knott	89-250050	NY	14m	surveyed
Sergeant Man	89-286089	NY	12m	surveyed
Great Sca Fell	89-291339	NY	13m	top 651 col 638
Miller Moss	90-303338	NY	at 609m too low	
Knowe Crags	90-312270	NY	14m	surveyed
Calfhow Pike	90-331211	NY	9m	top 660 col 651
High Crag	90-343137	NY	<14m	top 884 one ring
Tar Crags Top	90-340310	NY	14m	top 665 col 651
The Knott	90-437127	NY	13m	top 739 col 726
Mardale Ill Bell	90-448101	NY	10m	top 760 col 750

NAME OF TOP	SHEET REF		SEPARATION	REASON
Adam Seat	90-471091	NY	9m	top 666 col 657
Goat Scar	90-473069	NY	10m	top 626 col 616
Bullman Hills	91-705371	NY	14m	surveyed (see 9.1)
Long Fell	91-770198	NY	14m	surveyed
White Mossy Hill	91-829053	NY	8m	surveyed
Long Crag	91-843252	NY	7m	top 686 col 679
Black Hill	91-906334	NY	<15m	top 645 1 ring
Outberry Plain	91-938330	NY	<10m	no ring contour
Brown Pike	96-261966	SD	12m	surveyed
Swarth Fell Pike	98-761958	SD	12m	top 651 col 639
Birks Fell	98-916764	SD		at 608m too low (see 12.7)
Tor Mere Top	98-970765	SD	10m	surveyed

ALPHABETICAL INDEX OF TOPS

Name of Top	Height metres	Sheet-grid ref.	Walk number	Date of ascent
Allen Crags	785m	89-237085 NY	5.4	
Archy Styrigg	695m	91-802004 NY	11.5	
Atkinson Pike	845m	90-324283 NY	1.1	
Backstone Edge	699m	91-726277 NY	9.3	
Bannerdale Crags	683m	90-335290 NY	1.1	
Base Brown	646m	89-225115 NY	3.1	
Baugh Fell	678m	98-741916 SD	11.2	
Bellbeaver Rigg	620m	91-763351 NY	9.6	
Bink Moss	619m	91-875243 NY	9.5	
Birkhouse Moor	718m	90-363160 NY	6.1	
Birks	622m	90-380144 NY	6.1	
Black Crag	828m	89-166116 NY	3.2	
Black Fell	664m	86-648444 NY	9.8	
Black Sails	745m	89-283008 NY	5.5	
Bleaklow Head	633m	110-092959 SK	13.1	
Blencathra	868m	90-323277 NY	1.1	
Bloodybush Edge	610m	80-902143 NT	8.2	
Bowfell	902m	89-245064 NY	5.2	
Bowfell North Top	866m	89-245070 NY	5.2	
Bowscale Fell	702m	90-333305 NY	1.1	
Bram Rigg Top	672m	98-668965 SD	11.1	
Brandreth	715m	89-215119 NY	3.1	
Branstree	713m	90-478100 NY	7.4	
Branstree North East Top	673m	90-488103 NY	7.4	
Brim Fell	796m	96-271985 SD	5.5	
Broad Crag	934m	89-219075 NY	5.1	
Buckden Pike	702m	98-961788 SD	12.6	

Name of Top	Height metres	Sheet-grid ref.	Walk number	Date of ascent
Bullman Hills	610m	91-706373 NY	9.1	
Burnhope Seat	746m	91-788375 NY	10.1	
Bush Howe	623m	97-659981 SD	11.1	
Calders	674m	98-671960 SD	11.1	
Calf (The)	676m	98-667971 SD	11.1	
Carl Side	746m	90-255281 NY	1.2	
Carrock Fell	660m	90-342336 NY	1.3	
Catstye Cam	890m	90-348158 NY	6.2	
Causey Pike	637m	90-219208 NY	2.3	
Caw Fell	690m	89-132109 NY	3.4	
Chapelfell Top	703m	91-876346 NY	10.4	
Cheviot (The)	815m	75-909205 NT	8.1	
Clough Head	726m	90-334225 NY	6.4	
Codale Head	730m	89-289091 NY	4.1	
Cold Fell	621m	86-606556 NY	9.7	
Cold Pike	701m	89-263036 NY	5.3	
Cold Pike Far West Top	670m	89-256037 NY	5.3	
Cold Pike West Top	683m	89-259036 NY	5.3	
Combe Door Top	676m	89-253109 NY	5.4	
Combe Head	735m	89-250109 NY	5.4	
Comb Fell	652m	80-924187 NT	8.1	
Coniston Old Man	803m	96-272978 SD	5.5	
Crag Hill	839m	90-193204 NY	2.3	
Crinkle Crags	859m	89-249049 NY	5.3	
Crinkle Crags South Top	834m	89-250046 NY	5.3	
Cross Fell	893m	91-687343 NY	9.1	
Cushat Law	615m	80-928137 NT	8.2	

Name of Top	Height metres	Sheet-grid ref.	Walk number	Date of ascent
Dale Head	753m	89-223153 NY	2.1	
Darnbrook Fell	624m	98-885728 SD	12.4	
Dead Stones	710m	91-794399 NY	10.1	
Dodd (Buttermere)	641m	89-164158 NY	3.5	
Dodd Fell Hill	668m	98-841846 SD	12.5	
Dodd (The) (Nenthead)	614m	87-791458 NY	10.2	
Dollywagon Pike	858m	90-346131 NY	6.1	
Dove Crag	792m	90-374105 NY	6.3	
Dovenest Top	632m	89-256114 NY	5.4	
Dow Crag	778m	96-262978 SD	5.5	
Drumaldrace	614m	98-874867 SD	12.5	
Esk Pike	885m	89-237075 NY	5.2	
Fairfield	873m	90-359118 NY	6.3	
Fell Head	640m	97-650982 SD	11.1	
Fendrith Hill	696m	91-877333 NY	10.4	
Fiend's Fell	634m	86-643406 NY	9.2	
Fleetwith Pike	648m	89-206142 NY	3.1	
Flinty Fell	614m	87-771423 NY	10.3	
Fountains Fell	668m	98-864716 SD	12.4	
Fountains Fell South Top	662m	98-869708 SD	12.4	
Froswick	720m	90-435085 NY	7.1	
Gategill Fell Top	851m	90-318274 NY	1.1	
Glaramara	783m	89-246105 NY	5.4	
Gragareth	627m	98-688793 SD	12.2	
Grasmoor	852m	89-175203 NY	2.2	
Gray Crag (Hartsop)	699m	90-428117 NY	7.3	
Great Borne	616m	89-124164 NY	3.6	
Great Calva	690m	90-291312 NY	1.3	

Name of Top	Height metres	Sheet-grid ref.	Walk number	Date of ascent
Great Carrs	785m	89-270009 NY	5.5	
Great Coum	687m	98-701836 SD	12.2	
Great Dodd	857m	90-342206 NY	6.4	
Great Dun Fell	848m	91-710322 NY	9.1	
Great End	910m	89-227084 NY	5.1	
Great Gable	899m	89-211103 NY	3.1	
Great Knott	696m	89-260043 NY	5.3	
Great Knoutberry Hill	672m	98-789872 SD	12.3	
Great Lingy Hill	616m	90-310340 NY	1.3	
Great Rigg	766m	90-356104 NY	6.3	
Great Shunner Fell	716m	98-849973 SD	11.6	
Great Stony Hill	708m	91-824359 NY	10.1	
Great Whernside	704m	98-002739 SE	12.6	
Green Gable	801m	89-215107 NY	3.1	
Green Hill	628m	98-702820 SD	12.2	
Green Side	795m	90-353188 NY	6.4	
Grey Crag (Sleddale)	638m	90-497072 NY	7.4	
Grey Friar	770m	89-260004 NY	5.5	
Grey Knotts	697m	89-217126 NY	3.1	
Grey Nag	656m	86-665476 NY	9.8	
Grisedale Pike	791m	90-198225 NY	2.3	
Hare Stones	627m	90-315344 NY	1.3	
Harrison Stickle	736m	89-282074 NY	4.1	
Harrop Pike	637m	90-501078 NY	7.4	
Hart Crag	822m	90-368113 NY	6.3	
Harter Fell (Duddon valley)	653m	96-219997 SD	5.6	
Harter Fell (Kentmere)	778m	90-460093 NY	7.1	
Hart Side	756m	90-359197 NY	6.4	
Hartsop Dodd	618m	90-411119 NY	7.3	

Name of Top	Height metres	Sheet-grid ref.	Walk number	Date of ascent
Harwood Common	718m	91-795363 NY	10.1	
Haycock	797m	89-145107 NY	3.4	
Hedgehope Hill	714m	80-944198 NT	8.1	
Helvellyn	950m	90-342151 NY	6.1	
Helvellyn Lower Man	925m	90-337155 NY	6.2	
Heron Pike	612m	90-356083 NY	6.3	
Heron Pike North Top	621m	90-357087 NY	6.3	
Higher Shelf Stones	621m	110-089948 SK	13.1	
High Crag	744m	89-180140 NY	3.5	
High House Tarn Top	684m	89-240092 NY	5.4	
High Pike	658m	90-319350 NY	1.3	
High Raise (Langdale)	762m	89-281095 NY	4.1	
High Raise (High Street)	802m	90-448135 NY	7.2	
High Seat	709m	91-802012 NY	11.5	
High Spy	653m	89-234162 NY	2.1	
High Spy North Top	634m	89-236171 NY	2.1	
High Stile	807m	89-170148 NY	3.5	
High Street	828m	90-441110 NY	7.1	
High Willhays	621m	191-580893 SX	13.3	
Hindscarth	727m	89-216165 NY	2.1	
Hobcarton Crag	739m	90-194220 NY	2.3	
Hobcarton End	634m	90-195235 NY	2.3	
Hopegill Head	770m	89-186221 NY	2.2	
Hugh Seat	689m	98-809991 SD	11.5	
Ill Bell	757m	90-436077 NY	7.1	
Ill Crag	935m	89-223073 NY	5.1	
Ingleborough	723m	98-741746 SD	12.1	
Iron Crag	640m	89-123119 NY	3.4	

Name of Top	Height metres	Sheet-grid ref.	Walk number	Date of ascent
Kentmere Pike	730m	90-466078 NY	7.1	
Kidsty Pike	780m	90-447126 NY	7.2	
Killhope Law	673m	87-819448 NY	10.2	
Kinder Scout	636m	110-085875 SK	13.2	
Kirk Fell	802m	89-195105 NY	3.1	
Kirk Fell East Top	787m	89-199107 NY	3.1	
Knock Fell	794m	91-722303 NY	9.3	
Knott	710m	90-296330 NY	1.3	
Knoutberry Haw	676m	98-731919 SD	11.2	
Ladyside Pike	703m	89-185228 NY	2.2	
Lingmell	800m	89-209082 NY	5.1	
Little Calva	642m	90-282315 NY	1.3	
Little Dun Fell	842m	91-704330 NY	9.1	
Little Fell (Mallerstang)	667m	98-808971 SD	11.5	
Little Fell (Mickle Fell)	748m	91-781223 NY	9.4	
Little Gowder Crag	733m	89-140110 NY	3.4	
Little Hart Crag	637m	90-387100 NY	6.3	
Little Stand	740m	89-250034 NY	5.3	
Loadpot Hill	671m	90-457181 NY	7.2	
Loft Crag	670m	89-277071 NY	4.1	
Long Man Hill	658m	91-724373 NY	9.1	
Long Side	734m	90-249284 NY	1.2	
Lonscale Fell	715m	90-285271 NY	1.2	
Looking Stead (Pillar)	627m	89-186118 NY	3.2	
Looking Steads (Glaramara)	775m	89-246102 NY	5.4	
Lovely Seat	675m	98-879951 SD	11.6	
Low Saddle	656m	89-288133 NY	4.2	

Name of Top	Height metres	Sheet-grid ref.	Walk number	Date of ascent
Meldon Hill	767m	91-772291 NY	9.3	
Melmerby Fell	709m	91-652380 NY	9.2	
Mickle Fell	788m	91-804243 NY	9.4	
Middleboot Knotts	703m	89-214081 NY	5.1	
Middlehope Moor	612m	87-862432 NY	10.2	
Murton Fell	675m	91-754246 NY	9.4	
Nethermost Pike	891m	90-344142 NY	6.1	
Nine Standards Rigg	662m	91-825061 NY	11.4	
Pavey Ark	700m	89-285079 NY	4.1	
Pen-y-ghent	694m	98-838734 SD	12.4	
Pike of Blisco	705m	89-271042 NY	5.3	
Pike of Stickle	709m	89-274074 NY	4.1	
Pillar	892m	89-171121 NY	3.2	
Pillar Rock	780m	89-174124 NY	3.3	
Place Fell	657m	90-406170 NY	7.2	
Plover Hill	680m	98-849752 SD	12.4	
Raise	883m	90-343174 NY	6.2	
Rampsgill Head	792m	90-443128 NY	7.2	
Randygill Top	625m	91-687001 NY	11.1	
Red Beck Top	721m	89-243097 NY	5.4	
Red Pike (Buttermere)	755m	89-160155 NY	3.5	
Red Pike (Wasdale)	826m	89-165106 NY	3.2	
Red Screes	776m	90-396088 NY	6.3	
Rest Dodd	696m	90-433137 NY	7.2	
Robinson	737m	89-202169 NY	2.1	
Rogan's Seat	672m	91-919031 NY	11.3	
Rossett Pike	651m	89-249076 NY	5.2	
Rosthwaite Fell	612m	89-256118 NY	5.4	

Name of Top	Height metres	Sheet-grid ref.	Walk number	Date of ascent
Rough Crag	628m	90-454112 NY	7.1	
Round Hill	686m	91-744361 NY	9.1	
Round How	741m	89-219081 NY	5.1	
Sail	773m	90-198203 NY	2.3	
Sale How	666m	90-276286 NY	1.2	
Sand Hill	756m	89-187219 NY	2.2	
Sca Fell	964m	89-207065 NY	5.1	
Scafell Pike	978m	89-215072 NY	5.1	
Scar Crags	672m	90-208206 NY	2.3	
Scoat Fell	841m	89-160114 NY	3.2	
Seatallan	693m	89-140084 NY	3.4	
Seathwaite Fell	632m	89-227097 NY	5.4	
Seathwaite Fell South Top	631m	89-228094 NY	5.4	
Seat Sandal	736m	90-344115 NY	6.1	
Selside Pike	655m	90-490112 NY	7.4	
Sheffield Pike	675m	90-369182 NY	6.2	
Shelter Crags	815m	89-250053 NY	5.3	
Shelter Crags North Top	775m	89-249057 NY	5.3	
Simon Fell	650m	98-755752 SD	12.1	
Skiddaw	931m	90-260291 NY	1.2	
Skiddaw Little Man	865m	90-267278 NY	1.2	
Starling Dodd	633m	89-142158 NY	3.6	
Steeple	819m	89-157117 NY	3.2	
Stony Cove Pike	763m	90-418100 NY	7.3	
Striding Edge	860m	90-351149 NY	6.1	
St Sunday Crag	841m	90-369134 NY	6.1	
Stybarrow Dodd	843m	90-343189 NY	6.4	
Swarth Fell	681m	98-756967 SD	11.2	
Swirl How	802m	89-273005 NY	5.5	
Symonds Knott	959m	89-208068 NY	5.1	

Name of Top	Height metres	Sheet-grid ref.	Walk number	Date of ascent
Tarn Crag	664m	90-488078 NY	7.4	
Thornthwaite Crag	784m	90-432100 NY	7.3	
Three Pikes	651m	91-834343 NY	10.1	
Thunacar Knott	723m	89-279080 NY	4.1	
Tom Smith's Stone Top	637m	86-655467 NY	9.8	
Ullscarf	726m	89-292122 NY	4.2	
Viewing Hill	649m	91-789332 NY	9.6	
Walna Scar	621m	96-258963 SD	5.5	
Wandope	772m	89-188197 NY	2.2	
Water Crag	668m	91-929046 NY	11.3	
Westernhope Moor	675m	91-923326 NY	10.4	
Wether Hill	670m	90-456167 NY	7.2	
Wetherlam	763m	89-288011 NY	5.5	
Whernside	736m	98-738814 SD	12.2	
Whiteless Pike	660m	89-180190 NY	2.2	
White Maiden	610m	96-254957 SD	5.5	
White Side (Helvellyn)	863m	90-338167 NY	6.2	
Whiteside (Crummock)	707m	89-170219 NY	2.2	
Whiteside East Top	719m	89-175221 NY	2.2	
Wild Boar Fell	708m	98-758988 SD	11.2	
Windy Gyle	619m	80-855152 NT	8.2	
Yarlside	639m	98-686985 SD	11.1	
Yes Tor	619m	191-581902 SX	13.3	
Yewbarrow	628m	89-173085 NY	3.2	
Yewbarrow North Top	616m	89-176092 NY	3.2	
Yockenthwaite Moor	643m	98-909811 SD	12.7	
Yoke	706m	90-438067 NY	7.1	

CICERONE GUIDES

Cicerone publish a wide range of reliable guides to walking and climbing in Europe

FRANCE
TOUR OF MONT BLANC
CHAMONIX MONT BLANC - A Walking Guide
TOUR OF THE OISANS: GR54
WALKING THE FRENCH ALPS: GR5
THE CORSICAN HIGH LEVEL ROUTE: GR20
THE WAY OF ST JAMES: GR65
THE PYRENEAN TRAIL: GR10
TOUR OF THE QUEYRAS
ROCK CLIMBS IN THE VERDON

FRANCE / SPAIN
WALKS AND CLIMBS IN THE PYRENEES
ROCK CLIMBS IN THE PYRENEES

SPAIN
WALKS & CLIMBS IN THE PICOS DE EUROPA
WALKING IN MALLORCA
BIRDWATCHING IN MALLORCA
COSTA BLANCA CLIMBS

FRANCE / SWITZERLAND
THE JURA - Walking the High Route and
  Winter Ski Traverses

SWITZERLAND
WALKS IN THE ENGADINE
THE VALAIS - A Walking Guide
THE ALPINE PASS ROUTE

GERMANY / AUSTRIA
THE KALKALPEN TRAVERSE
KLETTERSTEIG - Scrambles
WALKING IN THE BLACK FOREST
MOUNTAIN WALKING IN AUSTRIA
WALKING IN THE SALZKAMMERGUT
KING LUDWIG WAY

ITALY
ALTA VIA - High Level Walkis in the Dolomites
VIA FERRATA - Scrambles in the Dolomites
ITALIAN ROCK - Selected Rock Climbs in
  Northern Italy
CLASSIC CLIMBS IN THE DOLOMITES

OTHER AREAS
THE MOUNTAINS OF GREECE - A Walker's
  Guide
CRETE: Off the beaten track
Treks & Climbs in the mountains of RHUM &
PETRA, JORDAN
THE ATLAS MOUNTAINS

GENERAL OUTDOOR BOOKS
LANDSCAPE PHOTOGRAPHY
FIRST AID FOR HILLWALKERS
MOUNTAIN WEATHER
MOUNTAINEERING LITERATURE
SKI THE NORDIC WAY
THE ADVENTURE ALTERNATIVE

CANOEING
SNOWDONIA WILD WATER, SEA & SURF
WILDWATER CANOEING
A CANOEIST'S GUIDE TO NORTHERN
  ENGLAND (East)

CARTOON BOOKS
ON FOOT & FINGER
ON MORE FEET & FINGERS
LAUGHS ALONG THE PENNINE WAY

*Also a full range of guidebooks
to walking, scrambling, ice-climbing,
rock climbing, and other adventurous
pursuits in Britain and abroad*

CICERONE

*Other guides are constantly being added to the Cicerone List.
Available from bookshops, outdoor equipment shops or direct (send for price list)
from CICERONE, 2 POLICE SQUARE, MILNTHORPE, CUMBRIA, LA7 7PY*

CICERONE GUIDES

Cicerone publish a wide range of reliable guides to walking and climbing in
Britain - and other general interest books

LAKE DISTRICT - General Books
LAKELAND VILLAGES
WORDSWORTH'S DUDDON REVISITED
THE REGATTA MEN
REFLECTIONS ON THE LAKES
OUR CUMBRIA
PETTIE
THE HIGH FELLS OF LAKELAND
CONISTON COPPER A History
LAKELAND - A taste to remember (Recipes)
THE LOST RESORT?
CHRONICLES OF MILNTHORPE
LOST LANCASHIRE

LAKE DISTRICT - Guide Books
CASTLES IN CUMBRIA
WESTMORLAND HERITAGE WALK
IN SEARCH OF WESTMORLAND
CONISTON COPPER MINES
SCRAMBLES IN THE LAKE DISTRICT
MORE SCRAMBLES IN THE LAKE DISTRICT
WINTER CLIMBS IN THE LAKE DISTRICT
WALKS IN SILVERDALE/ARNSIDE
BIRDS OF MORECAMBE BAY
THE EDEN WAY

NORTHERN ENGLAND (outside the Lakes
THE YORKSHIRE DALES A walker's guide
WALKING IN THE SOUTH PENNINES
LAUGHS ALONG THE PENNINE WAY
WALKS IN THE YORKSHIRE DALES (2 VOL)
WALKS TO YORKSHIRE WATERFALLS
NORTH YORK MOORS Walks
THE CLEVELAND WAY & MISSING LINK
DOUGLAS VALLEY WAY
THE RIBBLE WAY
WALKING NORTHERN RAILWAYS EAST
WALKING NORTHERN RAILWAYS WEST
HERITAGE TRAILS IN NW ENGLAND
BIRDWATCHING ON MERSEYSIDE
THE LANCASTER CANAL
FIELD EXCURSIONS IN NW ENGLAND
ROCK CLIMBS LANCASHIRE & NW
THE ISLE OF MAN COASTAL PATH

DERBYSHIRE & EAST MIDLANDS
WHITE PEAK WALKS - 2 Vols
HIGH PEAK WALKS
WHITE PEAK WAY
KINDER LOG
THE VIKING WAY
THE DEVIL'S MILL (Novel)
WHISTLING CLOUGH (Novel)
WALES & WEST MIDLANDS
THE RIDGES OF SNOWDONIA
HILLWALKING IN SNOWDONIA
ASCENT OF SNOWDON
WELSH WINTER CLIMBS
SNOWDONIA WHITE WATER SEA & SURF
SCRAMBLES IN SNOWDONIA
ROCK CLIMBS IN WEST MIDLANDS
THE SHROPSHIRE HILLS A Walker's Guide

SOUTH & SOUTH WEST ENGLAND
WALKS IN KENT
THE WEALDWAY & VANGUARD WAY
SOUTH DOWNS WAY & DOWNS LINK
COTSWOLD WAY
WALKING ON DARTMOOR
SOUTH WEST WAY - 2 Vol

SCOTLAND
SCRAMBLES IN LOCHABER
SCRAMBLES IN SKYE
THE ISLAND OF RHUM
CAIRNGORMS WINTER CLIMBS
WINTER CLIMBS BEN NEVIS & GLENCOE
SCOTTISH RAILWAY WALKS
TORRIDON A Walker's Guide
SKI TOURING IN SCOTLAND

THE MOUNTAINS OF ENGLAND & WALES
VOL 1 WALES
VOL 2 ENGLAND

*Also a full range of guidebooks
to walking, scrambling, ice-climbing,
rock climbing, and other adventurous
pursuits in Europe*

*Other guides are constantly being added to the Cicerone List.
Available from bookshops, outdoor equipment shops or direct (send for price list)
from CICERONE, 2 POLICE SQUARE, MILNTHORPE, CUMBRIA, LA7 7PY*